The Clementine Homilies

A Classic of the Early Christian Church

By Pope Clement I

Homilies I to V are translated by Rev. Thomas Smith

Homilies VI to XII are translated by Peter Peterson

Homilies XIII to XX are translated by James Donaldson

Published by Pantianos Classics

ISBN-13: 978-1-78987-645-1

First published in 1870

Contents

Introductory Notice v

Epistle of Peter to James 6

Epistle of Clement to James 9

Clementine Homilies 17

Homily I 17

Homily II 27

Homily III 44

Homily IV 67

Homily V 75

Homily VI 84

Homily VII 94

Homily VIII 98

Homily IX 106

Homily X 114

Homily XI 123

Homily XII 135

Homily XIII 148

Homily XIV 157

Homily XV 163

Homily XVI 169

Homily XVII 179

Homily XVIII 190

Homily XIX 201

Homily XX 216

Introductory Notice

We have already given an account of the *Clementines* in the Introductory Notice to the *Recognitions*. All that remains for us to do here, is to notice the principal editions of the *Homilies*. The first edition was published by Cotelerius in his collection of the *Apostolic Fathers,* from a manuscript in the Royal Library at Paris, the only manuscript of the work then known to exist. He derived assistance from an epitome of the work which he found in the same library. The text of Cotelerius was revised by Clericus in his edition of Cotelerius, but more carefully by Schwegler, Stuttgart 1847. The Paris MS. breaks off in the middle of the fourteenth chapter of the nineteenth book.

In 1853 (Göttingen) Dressel published a new recension of the *Homilies,* having found a complete manuscript of the twenty Homilies in the Ottobonian Library in Pome. In 1859 (Leipzig) he published an edition of two Epitomes of the Homilies, — the one previously edited by Turnebus and Cotelerius being given more fully, and the other appearing for the first time. To these Epitomes were appended notes by Frederic Wieseler on the Homilies. The last edition of the *Clementines* is by Paul de Lagarde (Leipzig, 1865), which has no new sources, is pretentious but far from accurate.

Epistle of Peter to James

Peter to James, the lord and bishop of the holy church, under the Father of all, through Jesus Christ, wishes peace always.

Chap. I. — *Doctrine of reserve*

Knowing, my brother, your eager desire after that which is for the advantage of us all, I beg and beseech you not to communicate to any one of the Gentiles the books of mv preachings which I sent to you, nor to any one of our own tribe before trial; but if any one has been proved and found worthy, then to commit them to him, after the manner in which Moses delivered [his books] to the Seventy who succeeded to his chair. Wherefore also the fruit of that caution appears even till now. For his countrymen keep the same rule of monarchy and polity everywhere, being unable in any way to think otherwise, or to be led out of the way of the much-indicating Scriptures. For, according to the rule delivered to them, they endeavour to correct the discordances of the Scriptures, if any one, haply not knowing the traditions, is confounded at the various utterances of the prophets. Wherefore they charge no one to teach, unless he has first learned how the Scriptures must be used. And thus they have amongst them one God, one law, one hope.

Chap. II. — *Misrepresentation of Peter's doctrine*

In order, therefore, that the like may also happen to those among us as to these Seventy, give the books of my preachings to our brethren, with the like mystery of initiation, that they may indoctrinate those who wish to take part in teaching; for if it be not so done, our word of truth will be rent into many opinions. And this I know, not as being a prophet, but as already seeing the beginning of this very evil. For some from among the Gentiles have rejected my legal preaching, attaching themselves to certain lawless and trifling preaching of the man who is my enemy. And these things some have attempted while I am still alive, to transform my words by certain various interpretations, in order to the dissolution of the law; as though I also myself were of such a mind, but did not freely proclaim it, which God forbid! For such a thing were to act in opposition to the law of God which was spoken by Moses, and was borne witness to by our Lord in respect of its eternal continuance; for thus He spoke: "The heavens and the earth shall pass away, but one jot or one tittle shall in no wise pass from the law." [1] And this He has said, that all things might come to pass. But these men, professing, I know not how, to know my mind, undertake to explain my words, which they have heard of me, more intelligently than I who spoke them, telling their catechumens that this is my meaning, which indeed I never thought of. But if, while I am still alive, they dare thus to misrepresent me, how much more will those who shall come after me dare to do so!

Chap. III. — *Initiation*

Therefore, that no such thing may happen, for this end I have prayed and besought you not to communicate the books of my preaching which I have sent you to any one, whether of our own nation or of another nation, before trial; but if any one, having been tested, has been found worthy, then to hand them over to him, according to the initiation of Moses, by which he delivered [his books] to the Seventy who succeeded to his chair; in order that thus they may keep the faith, and everywhere deliver the rule of truth, explaining all things after our tradition; lest being themselves dragged down by ignorance, being drawn into error by conjectures after their mind, they bring others into the like pit of destruction. Now the things that seemed good to me, I have fairly pointed out to you; and what seems good to you, do you, my lord, becomingly perform. Farewell.

Chap. IV. — *An adjuration concerning the receivers of the book*

1. Therefore James, having read the epistle, sent for the elders; and having read it to them, said: "Our Peter has strictly and becomingly charged us concerning the establishing of the truth, that we should not communicate the books of his preachings, which have been sent to us, to any one at random, but to one who is good and religious, and who wishes to teach, and who is circumcised, and faithful. And these are not all to be committed to him at once; that, if he be found injudicious in the first, the others may not be entrusted to him. Wherefore let him be proved not less than six years. And then according to the initiation of Moses, he [that is to deliver the books] should bring him to a river or a fountain, which is living water, where the regeneration of the righteous takes place, and should make him, not swear — for that is not lawful — but to stand by the water and adjure, as we ourselves, when we were regenerated, were made to do for the sake of not sinning.

2. "And let him say: 'I take to witness heaven, earth, water, in which all things are comprehended, and in addition to all these, that air also which pervades all things, and without which I cannot breathe, that I shall always be obedient to him who gives me the books of the preachings; and those same books which he may give me, I shall not communicate to any one in any way, either by writing them, or giving them in writing, or giving them to a writer, either myself or by another, or through any other initiation, or trick, or method, or by keeping them carelessly, or placing them before [any one], or granting him permission [to see them], or in any way or manner whatsoever communicating them to another; unless I shall ascertain one to be worthy, as I myself have been judged, or even more so, and that after a probation of not less than six years; but to one who is religious and good, chosen to teach, as I have received them, so I will commit them, doing these things also according to the will of my bishop.

3. "'But otherwise, though he were my son or my brother, or my friend, or otherwise in any way pertaining to me by kindred, if he be unworthy, that I will not vouchsafe the favour to him, as is not meet; and I shall neither be terrified by plot nor mollified by gifts. But if even it should ever seem to me that the books of the preachings given to me are not true, I shall not so communicate them, but shall give them back. And when I go abroad, I shall carry them with me, whatever of them I happen to possess. But if I be not minded to carry them about with me, I shall not suffer them to be in my house, but shall deposit them with my bishop, having the same faith, and setting out from the same persons [as myself]. [2] But if it befall me to be sick, and in expectation of death, and if I be childless, I shall act in the same manner. But if I die having a son who is not worthy, or not yet capable, I shall act in the same manner. For I shall deposit them with my bishop, in order that if my son, when he grows up, be worthy of the trust, he may give them to him as his father's bequest, according to the terms of this engagement.

4. "And that I shall thus do, I again call to witness heaven, earth, water, in which all things are enveloped, and in addition to all these, the all-pervading air, without which I cannot breathe, that I shall always be obedient to him who giveth me these books of the preachings, and shall observe in all things as I have engaged, or even something more. To me, therefore, keeping this covenant, there shall be a part with the holy ones; but to me doing anything contrary to what I have covenanted, may the universe be hostile to me, and the all-pervading ether, and the God who is over all, to whom none is superior, than whom none is greater. But if even I should come to the acknowledgment of another God, I now swear by him also, be he or be he not, that I shall not do otherwise. And in addition to all these things, if I shall lie, I shall be accursed living and dying, and shall be punished with everlasting punishment.'

"And after this, let him partake of bread and salt with him who commits them to him."

Chap. V. — *The adjuration accepted*

James having thus spoken, the elders were in an agony of terror. Therefore James, perceiving that they were greatly afraid, said: "Hear me, brethren and fellow-servants. If we should give the books to all indiscriminately, and they should be corrupted by any daring men, or be perverted by interpretations, as you have heard that some have already done, it will remain even for those who really seek the truth, always to wander in error. Wherefore it is better that they should be with us, and that we should communicate them with all the fore-mentioned care to those who wish to live piously, and to save others. But if any one, after taking this adjuration, shall act otherwise, he shall with good reason incur eternal punishment. For why should not he who is the cause of the destruction of others not be destroyed himself?" The elders, therefore, being pleased with the sentiments of James, exclaimed, "Blessed be He who, as foreseeing all things, has graciously appointed thee as our bishop;" and when they had said this, we all rose up, and prayed to the Father and God of all, to whom be glory for ever. Amen.

[1] Mark XIII. 31; Matt. V. 18.
[2] Unless the reading be corrupt here, I suppose the reference must be to episcopal succession.

Epistle of Clement to James

Clement to James, the lord, [1] and the bishop of bishops, who rules Jerusalem, the holy church of the Hebrews, and the churches everywhere excellently founded by the providence of God, with the elders and deacons, and the rest of the brethren, peace be always.

Chap. I. — *Peter's martyrdom*

Be it known to you, my lord, that Simon, who, for the sake of the true faith, and the most sure foundation of his doctrine, was set apart to be the foundation of the church, and for this end was by Jesus Himself, with His truthful mouth, named Peter, the first-fruits of our Lord, the first of the apostles; to whom first the Father revealed the Son; whom the Christ, with good reason, blessed; the called, and elect, and associate at table and in the journeyings [of Christ]; the excellent and approved disciple, who, as being fittest of all, was commanded to enlighten the darker part of the world, namely the West, and was enabled to accomplish it, — and to what extent do I lengthen my discourse, not wishing to indicate what is sad, which yet of necessity, though reluctantly, I must tell you, — he himself, by reason of his immense love towards men, having come as far as Rome, clearly and publicly testifying, in opposition to the wicked one who withstood him, that there is to be a good King over all the world, while saving men by his God-inspired doctrine, himself, by violence, exchanged this present existence for life.

Chap. II. — *Ordination of Clement*

But about that time, when he was about to die, the brethren being assembled together, he suddenly seized my hand, and rose up, and said in presence of the church: "Hear me, brethren and fellow-servants. Since, as I have been taught by the Lord and Teacher Jesus Christ, whose apostle I am, the day of my death is approaching, I lay hands upon this Clement as your bishop; and to him I entrust my chair of discourse, even to him who has journeyed with me from the beginning to the end, and thus has heard all my homilies — who, in a word, having had a share in all my trials, has been found stedfast in the faith; whom I have found, above all others, pious, philanthropic, pure, learned, chaste, good, upright, large-hearted, and striving generously to bear the ingratitude of some of the catechumens. Wherefore I communicate to him the power of binding and loosing, so that with respect to everything which he shall ordain in the earth, it shall be decreed in the heavens. For he shall k bind what ought to be bound, and loose what ought to be loosed, as knowing the rule of the church. Therefore hear him, as knowing that he who grieves the president of the truth, sins against Christ, and offends the Father of all. Wherefore he shall not live; and therefore it becomes him who presides to hold the place of a physician, and not to cherish the rage of an irrational beast."

Chap. III. — *Nolo episcopari*

While he thus spoke, I knelt to him, and entreated him, declining the honour and the authority of the chair. But he answered: "Concerning this matter do not ask me; for it has seemed to me to be good that thus it be, and all the more if you decline it. For this chair has not need of a presumptuous man, ambitious of occupying it, but of one pious in conduct and deeply skilled in the word [of God]. But show me a better [than yourself], who has travelled more with me, and has heard more of my discourses, and has learned better the regulations of the church, and I shall not force you to do well against your will. But it will not be in your power to show me your superior; for you are the choice first-fruits of the multitudes saved through me. However, consider this further, that if you do not undertake the administration of the church, through fear of the danger of sin, you may be sure that you sin more, when you have it in your power to help the godly, who are, as it were, at sea and in danger, and will not do so, providing only for your own interest, and not for the common advantage of all. But that it behoves you altogether to undertake the danger, while I do not cease to ask it of you for the help of all, you well understand. The sooner, therefore, you consent, so much the sooner will you relieve me from anxiety.

Chap. IV. — *The recompense of the reward*

"But I myself also, O Clement, know the griefs and anxieties, and dangers and reproaches, that are appointed you from the uninstructed multitudes; and these you will be able to bear nobly, looking to the great reward of patience bestowed on you by God. But also consider this fairly with me: When has Christ need of your aid? Now, when the wicked one has sworn war against His bride; or in the time to come, when He shall reign victorious, having no need of further help? Is it not evident to any one who has even the least understanding, that it is now? Therefore with all good-will hasten in the time of the present necessity to do battle on the side of this good King, whose character it is to give great rewards after victory. Therefore take the oversight gladly; and all the more in good time, because you have learned from me the administration of the church, for the safety of the brethren who have taken refuge with us.

Chap. V. — *A charge*

"However, I wish, in the presence of all, to remind you, for the sake of all, of the things belonging to the administration. It becomes you, living without reproach, with the greatest earnestness to shake off all the cares of life, being neither a surety, nor an advocate, nor involved in any other secular business. For Christ does not wish to appoint you either a judge or an arbitrator in business, or negotiator of the secular affairs of the present life, lest, being confined to the present cares of men, you should not have leisure by the word of truth to separate the good among men from the bad. But let the disciples perform these offices to one another, and not withdraw [you] from the discourses which are able to save. For as it is wicked for you to undertake secular cares, and to omit the doing of what you have been commanded to do, so it is sin for every layman, if they do not stand by one another even in secular necessities. And if all do not understand to take order that you be without care in respect of the things in which you ought to be, let them learn it from the deacons; that you may have the care of the church always, in order both to your administering it well, and to your holding forth the words of truth.

Chap. VI. — *The duty of a bishop*

"Now, if you were occupied with secular cares, you should deceive both yourself and your hearers. For not being able, on account of occupation, to point out the things that are advantageous, both you should be punished, as not having taught what was profitable, and they, not having learned, should perish by reason of ignorance. Wherefore do you indeed preside over them without occupation, so as to send forth seasonably the words that are able to save them; and so let them listen to you, knowing that whatever the ambassador of the truth shall bind upon earth is bound also in heaven, and what he shall loose is loosed. But you shall bind what ought to be bound, and loose what ought to be loosed. And these, and such like, are the things that relate to you as president.

Chap. VII. — *Duties of presbyters*

"And with respect to the presbyters, take these [instructions]. Above all things, let them join the young betimes in marriage, anticipating the entanglements of youthful lusts. But neither let them neglect the marriage of those who are already old; for lust is vigorous even in some old men. Lest, therefore, fornication find a place among you, and bring upon you a very pestilence, take precaution, and search, lest at any time the fire of adultery be secretly kindled among you. For j| adultery is a very terrible thing, even such that it holds the second place in respect of punishment, the first being assigned to those who are in error, even although they be chaste. Wherefore do you, as elders of the church, exercise the spouse of Christ to chastity (by the spouse I mean the body of the church); for if she be apprehended to be chaste by her royal Bridegroom, she shall obtain the greatest honour; and you, as wedding guests, shall receive great commendation. But if she be caught having sinned, she herself indeed shall be cast out; and you shall suffer punishment, if at any time her sin has been through your negligence.

Chap. VIII. — *"Do good unto all."*

"Wherefore above all things be careful about chastity; for fornication has been marked out as a bitter thing in the estimation of God. But there are many forms of fornication, as also Clement himself will explain to you. The first is adultery, that a man should not enjoy his own wife alone, or a woman not enjoy her own husband alone. If any one be chaste, he is able also to be philanthropic, on account of which he shall obtain eternal mercy. For as adultery is a great evil, so philanthropy is the greatest good. Wherefore love all your brethren with grave and compassionate eyes, performing to orphans the part of parents, to widows that of husbands, affording them sustenance with all kindliness, arranging marriages for those who are in their prime, and for those who are without a profession the means of necessary support through employment; giving work to the artificer, and alms to the incapable.

Chap. IX. — *"Let brotherly love continue."*

"But I know that ye will do these things if you fix love into your minds; and for its entrance there is one only fit means, viz. the common partaking of food. [2] Wherefore see to it that ye be frequently one another's guests, as ye are able, that you may not fail of it. For it is the cause of well-doing, and well-doing of salvation. Therefore all of you present your provisions in common to all your brethren in God, knowing that, giving temporal things, you shall receive eternal things. Much more feed the hungry, and give drink to the thirsty, and clothing to the naked; visit the sick; showing yourselves to those who are in prison, help them as ye are able, and receive strangers into your houses with all alacrity. However, not to speak in detail, philanthropy will teach you to do everything that is good, as misanthropy suggests ill-doing to those who will not be saved.

Chap. X. — *"Whatsoever things are honest."*

"Let the brethren who have causes to be settled not be judged by the secular authorities; but let them by all means be reconciled by the elders of the church, yielding ready obedience to them. Moreover, also, flee avarice, inasmuch as it is able, under pretext of temporal gain, to deprive you of eternal blessings. Carefully keep your balances, your measures, your weights, and the things belonging to your traffic, just. Be faithful with respect to your trusts. Moreover, you will persevere in doing these things, and things similar to these, until the end, if you have in your hearts an ineradicable remembrance of the judgment that is from God. For who would sin, being persuaded that at the end of life there is a judgment appointed of the righteous God, who only now is longsuffering and good, [3] that the good may in future enjoy for ever unspeakable blessings; but the sinners being found as evil, shall obtain an eternity of unspeakable punishment. And, indeed, that these things are so, it would be reasonable to doubt, were it not that the Prophet of the truth has said and sworn that it shall be.

Chap. XI. — *Doubts to be satisfied*

"Wherefore, being disciples of the true Prophet, laying aside double-mindedness, from which comes ill-doing, eagerly undertake well-doing. But if any of you doubt concerning the things which I have said are to be, let him confess it without shame, if he cares for his own soul, and he shall be satisfied by the president. But if he has believed rightly, let his conversation be with confidence, as fleeing from the great fire of condemnation, and entering into the eternal good kingdom of God.

Chap. XII. — *Duties of deacons*

"Moreover let the deacons of the church, going about with intelligence, be as eyes to the bishop, carefully inquiring into the doings of each member of the church, [ascertaining] who is about to sin, in order that, being arrested with admonition by the president, he may haply not accomplish the sin. Let them check the disorderly, that they may not desist from assembling to hear the discourses, so that they may be able to counteract by the word of truth those anxieties that fall upon the heart from every side, by means of worldly casualties and evil communications; for if they long remain fallow, they become fuel for the fire. And let them learn who are suffering under bodily disease, and let them bring them to the notice of the multitude who do not know of them, that they may visit them, and supply their wants according to the judgment of the president. Yea, though they do this without his knowledge, they do nothing amiss. These things, then, and things like to these, let the deacons attend to.

Chap. XIII. — *Duties of catechists*

"Let the catechists instruct, being first instructed; for it is a work relating to the souls of men. For the teacher of the word must accommodate himself to the various judgments of the learners. The catechists must therefore be learned, and unblameable, of much experience, and approved, as you will know that Clement is, who is to be your instructor after me. For it were too much for me now to go into details. However, if ye be of one mind, you shall be able to reach the haven of rest, where is the peaceful city of the great King.

Chap. XIV. — *The vessel of the church*

"For the whole business of the church is like unto a great ship, bearing through a violent storm men who are of many places, and who desire to inhabit the city of the good kingdom. Let, therefore, God be your shipmaster; and let the pilot be likened to Christ, the mate [4] to the bishop, the sailors to the deacons, the midshipmen to the catechists, the multitude of the brethren to the passengers, the world to the sea; the foul winds to temptations, persecutions, and dangers; and all manner of afflictions to the waves; the land winds and their squalls to the discourses of deceivers and false prophets; the promontories and rugged rocks to the judges in high places threatening terrible things; the meetings of two seas, and the wild places, to unreasonable men and those who doubt of the promises of truth. Let hypocrites be regarded as like to pirates. Moreover, account the strong whirlpool, and the Tartarean Charybdis, and murderous wrecks, and deadly founderings, to be nought but sins. In order, therefore, that, sailing with a fair wind, you may safely reach the haven of the hoped-for city, pray so as to be heard. But prayers become audible by good deeds.

Chap. XV. — *Incidents of the voyage*

"Let therefore the passengers remain quiet, sitting in their own places, lest by disorder they occasion rolling or careening. Let the midshipmen give heed to the fare. Let the deacons neglect nothing with which they are entrusted; let the presbyters, like sailors, studiously arrange what is needful for each one. Let the bishop, as the mate, wakefully ponder the words of the pilot alone. Let Christ, even the Saviour, be loved as the pilot, and alone believed in the matters of which He speaks; and let all pray to God for a prosperous voyage. Let those sailing expect every tribulation, as travelling over a great and troubled sea, the world: sometimes, indeed, disheartened, persecuted, dispersed, hungry, thirsty, naked, hemmed in; and, again, sometimes united, congregated, at rest; but also sea-sick, giddy, vomiting, that is, confessing sins, like disease-producing bile, — I mean the sins proceeding from bitterness, and the evils accumulated from disorderly lusts, by the confession of which, as by vomiting, you are relieved of your disease, attaining healthful safety by means of carefulness.

Chap. XVI. — *The bishop's labours and reward*

"But know all of you that the bishop labours more than you all; because each of you suffers his own affliction, but he his own and that of every one. Wherefore, O Clement, preside as a helper to every one according to your ability, being careful of the cares of all. Whence I know that in your undertaking the administration, I do not confer, but receive, a favour. But take courage and bear it generously, as knowing that God will recompense you when you enter the haven of rest, the greatest of blessings, a reward that cannot be taken from you, in proportion as you have undertaken more labour for the safety of all. So that, if many of the brethren should hate you on account of your lofty righteousness, their hatred shall nothing hurt you, but the love of the righteous God shall greatly benefit you. Therefore endeavour to shake off the praise that arises from injustice, and to attain the profitable praise that is from Christ on account of righteous administration."

Chap. XVII. — *The people's duties*

Having said this, and more than this, he looked again upon the multitude, and said: "And you also, my beloved brethren and fellow-servants, be subject to the president of the truth in all things, knowing this, that he who grieves him has not received Christ, with whose chair he has been entrusted; and he who has not received Christ shall be regarded as having despised the Father; wherefore he shall be cast out of the good kingdom. On this account, endeavour to come to all the assemblies, lest as deserters you incur the charge of sin through the disheartening of your captain. Wherefore all of you think before all else of the things that relate to him, knowing this, that the wicked one, being the more hostile on account of every one of you, wars against him alone. Do you therefore strive to live in affection towards him, and in kindliness towards one another, and to obey him, in order that both he may be comforted and you may be saved.

Chap. XVIII. — *"As a heathen man and a publican."*

"But some things also you ought of yourselves to consider, on account of his not being able to speak openly by reason of the plots. Such as: if he be hostile to any one, do not wait for his speaking; and do not take part with that man, but prudently follow the bishop's will, being enemies to those to whom he is an enemy, and not conversing with those with whom he does not converse, in order that every one, desiring to have you all as his friends, may be reconciled to him and be saved, listening to his discourse. But if any one remain a friend of those to whom he is an enemy, and speak to those with whom he does not converse, he also himself is one of those who would waste the church. For, being with you in body, but not with you in judgment, he is against you; and is much worse than the open enemies from without, since with seeming friendship he disperses those who are within."

Chap. XIX. — *Installation of Clement*

Having thus spoken, he laid his hands upon me in the presence of all, and compelled me to sit in his own chair. And when I was seated, he immediately said to me: "I entreat you, in the presence of all the brethren here, that whensoever I depart from this life, as depart I must, you send to James the brother of the Lord a brief account of your reasonings from your boyhood, and how from the beginning until now you have journeyed with me, hearing the discourses preached by me in every city, and [seeing] my deeds. And then at the end you will not fail to inform him of the manner of my death, as I said before. For that event will not grieve him very much, when he knows that I piously went through what it behoved me to suffer. And he will get the greatest comfort when he learns, that not an unlearned man, or one ignorant of life-giving words, or not knowing the rule of the church, shall be entrusted with the chair of the teacher after me. For the discourse of a deceiver destroys the souls of the multitudes who hear."

Chap. XX. — *Clement's obedience*

Whence I, my lord James, having promised as I was ordered, have not failed to write in books by chapters the greater part of his discourses in every city, which have been already written to you, and sent by himself, as for a token; and thus I despatched them to you, inscribing them *Clement's Epitome of the Popular Sermons of Peter*. However, I shall begin to set them forth, as I was ordered.

[1] More probably "the Lord's brother." So it must have been in the text from which Rufinus translated.
[2] Literally, "of salt."
[3] The common reading would give "who alone is now long-suffering;" but the change of a letter gives the reading which we have adopted.
[4] It is impossible to translate these terms very accurately. I suppose the πρωρεύς was rather the "bow-oarsman" in the galley.

Clementine Homilies

Homily I

Chap. I. — *Boyish questionings*

I, Clement, being a Roman citizen, even from my earliest youth was able to live chastely, my mind from my boyhood drawing away the lust that was in me to dejection and distress. For I had a habit of reasoning — how originating I know not — making frequent cogitations concerning death: When I die, shall I neither exist, nor shall any one ever have any remembrance of me, while boundless time bears all things of all men into forgetfulness? and shall I then be without being, or acquaintance with those who are; neither knowing nor being known, neither having been nor being? And has the world ever been made? and was there anything before it was made? For if it has been always, it shall also continue to be; but if it has been made, it shall also be dissolved. And after its dissolution, shall there ever be anything again, unless, perhaps, silence and forgetfulness? Or perhaps something shall be which it is not possible now to conceive.

Chap. II. — *Good out of evil*

As I pondered without ceasing these and such like questions — I know not whence arising — I had such bitter grief, that, becoming pale, I wasted away; and, what was most terrible, if at any time I wished to drive away this meditation as unprofitable, my suffering became all the more severe; and I grieved over this, not knowing that I had a fair inmate, even my thought, which was to be to me the cause of a blessed immortality, as I afterwards knew by experience, and gave thanks to God, the Lord of all. For it was by this thought, which at first afflicted me, that I was compelled to come to the search and the finding of things; and then I pitied those whom at first, through ignorance, I ventured to call blessed.

Chap. III. — *Perplexity*

From my boyhood, then, being [involved] in such reasonings, in order to learn something definite, I used to resort to the schools of the philosophers. But nought else did I see than the setting up and knocking down of doctrines, and strifes, and seeking for victory, and the arts of syllogisms, and the skill of assumptions; and sometimes one [opinion] prevailed, — as, for example, that the soul is immortal, and sometimes that it is mortal. If, therefore, at any time the doctrine prevailed that it is immortal, I was glad; and when the doctrine prevailed that it is mortal, I was grieved. And again, I was the more disheartened because I could not establish either doctrine to my satisfaction. However, I perceived that the opinions on subjects under discussion are taken as true or false, according to their defenders, and do not appear as they really are. Perceiving, therefore, now that the acceptance does not depend on the real nature of the subjects discussed, but that opinions are proved to be true or false according to ability of those who defend them, I was still more than ever at a loss in regard of things. Wherefore I groaned from the depth of my soul. For neither was I able to establish anything, nor could I shake off the consideration of such things, though, as I said before, I wished it. For although I frequently charged myself to be at peace, in some way or other thoughts on these subjects, accompanied with a feeling of pleasure, would come into my mind.

Chap. IV. — *More perplexity*

And again, living in doubt, I said to myself, Why do I labour in vain, when the matter is clear, that if I lose existence when I die, it is not fitting that I should distress myself now while I do exist? Wherefore I shall reserve my grief till that [day], when, ceasing to exist, I shall not be affected with grief. But if I am to exist, what does it profit me now to distress myself gratuitously? And immediately after this another reasoning assailed me; for I said. Shall I not have something worse to suffer then than that which distresses me now, if I have not lived piously; and shall I not be delivered over, according to the doctrines of some philosophers, to Pyriphlegethon and Tartarus, like Sisyphus, or Tityus, or Ixion, or Tantalus, and be punished for ever in Hades? But again I replied, saying: But there are no such things as these. Yet again I taid: But if there be? Therefore, said I, since the matter is uncertain, the safer plan is for me rather to live piously. But how shall I be able, for the sake of righteousness, to subdue bodily pleasures, looking, as I do, to an uncertain hope? But I am neither fully persuaded what is that righteous thing that is pleasing to God, nor do I know whether the soul is immortal or mortal. Neither can I find any well-established doctrine, nor can I abstain from such debatings.

Chap. V. — *A resolution*

What, then, am I to do, unless this? I shall go into Egypt, and I shall become friendly with the hierophants of the shrines, and with the prophets; and I shall seek and find a magician, and persuade him with large bribes to effect the calling up of a soul, which is called necromancy, as if I were going to inquire of it concerning some business. And the inquiry shall be for the purpose of learning whether the soul is immortal. But the answer of the soul that it is immortal shall not give me the knowledge from its speaking or my hearing, but only from its being seen; so that, seeing it with my very eyes, I may have a self-sufficient and fit assurance, from the very fact of its appearing, that it exists; and never again shall the uncertain words of hearing be able to overturn the things which the eyes have made their own. However, I submitted this very plan to a certain companion who was a philosopher; and he counselled me not to venture upon it, and that on many accounts. . "For if," said he, "the soul shall not listen to the magician, you will live with an evil conscience, as having acted against the laws which forbid the doing of these things. But if it shall listen to him, then, besides your living with an evil conscience, I think that matters of piety will not be promoted to you on account of your making this attempt. For they say that the Deity is angry with those who disturb souls after their release from the body." [1] And I, when I heard this, became indeed more backward to -undertake such a thing, but I did not abandon my original plan; but I was distressed, as being hindered in the execution of it.

Chap. VI. — *Tidings from Judea*

And, not to discuss such matters to you in a long speech, while I was occupied with such reasonings and doings, a certain report, taking its rise in the spring-time, in the reign of Tiberius Caesar, gradually grew everywhere, and ran through the world as truly the good tidings of God, being unable to stifle the counsel of God in silence. Therefore it everywhere became greater and louder, saying that a certain One in Judea, beginning in the spring season, was preaching to the Jews the kingdom of the invisible God, and saying that whoever of them would reform his manner of living should enjoy it. And in order that He might be believed that He uttered these things full of the Godhead, He wrought many wonderful miracles and signs by His mere command, as having received power from God. For He made the deaf to hear, the blind to see, the lame to walk, raised up the bowed down, drove away every disease, put to flight every demon; and even scabbed lepers, by only looking on Him from a distance, were sent away cured by Him; and the dead, being brought to Him, were raised; and there was nothing which He could not do. And as time advanced, so much the greater, through the arrival of more persons, and the stronger grew — I say not now the report, but — the truth of the thing; for now at length there were meetings in various places for consultation and inquiry as to who He might be that had appeared, and what was His purpose.

Chap. VII. — *The gospel in Rome*

And then in the same year, in the autumn season, a certain one, standing in a public place, cried and said, "Men of Rome, hearken. The Son of God is come in Judea, proclaiming eternal life to all who will, if they shall live according to the counsel of the Father, who hath sent Him. Wherefore change your manner of life from the worse to the better, from things temporal to things eternal; for know ye that there is one God, who is in heaven, whose world ye unrighteously dwell in before His righteous eyes. But if ye be changed, and live according to His counsel, then, being born into the other world, and becoming eternal, ye shall enjoy His unspeakable good things. But if ye be unbelieving, your souls, after the dissolution of the body, shall be thrown into the place of fire, where, being punished eternally, they shall repent of their unprofitable deeds. For every one, the term of repentance is the present life." I therefore, when I heard these things, was grieved, because no one among so great multitudes, hearing such an announcement, said: I shall go into Judea, that I may know if this man who tells us these things speaks the truth, that the Son of God has come into Judea, for the sake of a good and eternal hope, revealing the will of the Father who sent Him. For it is no small matter which they say that He preaches: for He asserts that the souls of some, being [themselves] immortal, shall enjoy eternal good things; and that those of others, being thrown into unquenchable fire, shall be punished for ever.

Chap. VIII. — *Departure from Home*

While I spoke thus concerning others, I also lectured myself, saying. Why do I blame others, being myself guilty of the very same crime of heedlessness? But I shall hasten into Judea, having first arranged my affairs. And when I had thus made up my mind, there occurred a long time of delay, my worldly affairs being difficult to arrange. Therefore, meditating further on the nature of life, that by involving [2] men in hope it lays snares for those who are making haste, yea, and how much time I had been robbed of while tossed by hopes, and that we men die while thus occupied, I left all my affairs as they were, and sped to Portus; [3] and coming to the harbour, and being taken on board a ship, I was borne by adverse winds to Alexandria instead of Judea; and being detained there by stress of weather, I consorted with the philosophers, and told them about the rumour and the sayings of him who had appeared in Rome. And they answered that indeed they knew nothing of him who had appeared in Rome; but concerning Him who was born in Judea, and who was said by the report to be the Son of God, they had heard from many who had come from thence, and had learned respecting all the wonderful things that He did with a word.

Chap. IX. — *Preaching of Barnabas*

And when I said that I wished I could meet with some one of those who had seen Him, they immediately brought me to one, saying, "There is one here who not only is acquainted with Him, but is also of that country, a Hebrew, by name Barnabas, who says that he himself is one of His disciples; and hereabouts he resides, and readily announces to those who will the terms of His promise." Then I went with them; and when I came, I stood listening to his words with the crowd that stood round him; and I perceived that he was speaking truth not with dialectic art, but was setting forth simply and without preparation what he had heard and seen the manifested Son of God do and say. And even from the crowd who stood around him he produced many witnesses of the miracles and discourses which he narrated.

Chap. X. — *Cavils of the philosophers*

But while the multitudes were favourably disposed towards the things that he so artlessly spoke, the philosophers, impelled by their worldly learning, set upon laughing at him and making sport of him, upbraiding and reproaching him with excessive presumption, making use of the great armoury of syllogisms. But he set aside their babbling, and did not enter into their subtle questioning, but without embarrassment went on with what he was saying. And then one of them asked, Wherefore it was that a gnat, although it be so small, and has six feet, has wings also; while an elephant, the largest of beasts, is wingless, and has but four feet? But he, after the question had been put, resuming his discourse, which had been interrupted, as though he had answered the question, resumed his original discourse, only making use of this preface after each interruption: "We have a commission only to tell you the words and the wondrous doings of Him who sent us; and instead of logical demonstration, we present to you many witnesses from amongst yourselves who stand by, whose faces I remember, as living images. These sufficient testimonies it is left to your choice to submit to, or to disbelieve. [4] But I shall not cease to declare unto you what is for your profit; for to be silent were to me a loss, and to disbelieve is ruin to you. But indeed I could give answers to your frivolous questions, if you asked them through love of truth. But the reason of the different structure of the gnat and the elephant it is not fitting to tell to those who are ignorant of the God of all."

Chap. XI. — *Clement's zeal*

When he said this, they all, as in concert, set up a shout of laughter, trying to silence him and put him out, as a barbarous madman. But I, seeing this, and seized, I know not how, with enthusiasm, could no longer keep silence with righteous indignation, but boldly cried out, saying, "Well has God ordained that His counsel should be incapable of being received by you, foreseeing you to be unworthy, as appears manifestly to such of those who are now present as have minds capable of judging. For whereas now heralds of His counsel have been sent forth, not making a show of grammatical art, but setting forth His will in simple and inartificial words, so that whosoever hear can understand what is spoken, and not with any invidious feeling, as though unwilling to offer it to all; you come here, and besides your not understanding what is for your advantage, to your own injury you laugh at the truth, which, to your condemnation, consorts with the barbarians, and which you will not entertain when it visits you, by reason of your wickedness and the plainness of its words, lest you be convicted of being merely lovers of words, and not lovers of truth and lovers of wisdom. How long will you be learning to speak, who have not the power of speech? [5] For many sayings of yours are not worth one word. What, then, will your Grecian multitude say, being of one mind, if, as he says, there shall be a judgment? "Why, O God, didst Thou not proclaim to us Thy counsel?" Shall you not, if you be thought worthy of an answer at all, be told this?" I, knowing before the foundation of the world all characters that were to be, acted towards each one by anticipation according to his deserts without making it known; [6] but wishing to give full assurance to those who have fled to me that this is so, and to explain why from the beginning, and in the first ages, I did not suffer my counsel to be publicly proclaimed; I now, in the end of the world, [7] have sent heralds to proclaim my will, and they are insulted and flouted by those who will not be benefited, and who wilfully reject my friendship. Oh, great wrong! The preachers are exposed to danger even to the loss of life, [8] and that by the men who are called to salvation.

Chap. XII. — *Clement's rebuke of the people*

"And this wrongful treatment of my heralds would have been against all from the beginning, if from the beginning the unworthy had been called to salvation. For that which is now done wrongfully by these men serves to the vindication of my righteous foreknowledge, that it was well that I did not choose from the beginning to expose uselessly to public contempt the word which is worthy of honour; but determined to suppress it, as being honourable, not indeed from those who were worthy from the beginning — for to them also I imparted it — but from those, and such as those, unworthy, as you see them to be, — those who hate me, and who will not love themselves. And now, give over laughing at this man, and hear me with respect to his announcement, or let any one of the hearers who pleases answer. And do not bark like vicious dogs, deafening with disorderly clamour the ears of those who would be saved, ye unrighteous and God-haters, and perverting the saving method to unbelief. How shall you be able to obtain pardon, who scorn him who is sent to speak to you of the Godhead of God? And this you do towards a man whom you ought to have received on account of his good-will towards you, even if he did not speak truth."

Chap. XIII. — *Clement instructed by Barnabas*

While I spake these words, and others to the same effect, there arose a great excitement among the crowd; and some, as pitying Barnabas, sympathized with me; but others, being senseless, terribly gnashed their teeth against me. But, as the evening had already come, I took Barnabas by the hand, and by force conducted him, against his will, to my lodging, and constrained him to remain there, lest some one might lay hands on him. And having spent several days, and instructed me briefly in the true doctrine, as well as he could in a few days, he said that he should hasten into Judea for the observance of the festival, and also because he wished for the future to consort with those of his own nation.

Chap. XIV. — *Departure of Barnabas*

But it plainly appeared to me that he was disconcerted. For when I said to him, "Only set forth to me the words which you have heard of the Man who has appeared, and I will adorn them with my speech, and preach the counsel of God; and if you do so, within a few days I will sail with you, for I greatly desire to go to the land of Judea, and perhaps I shall dwell with you all my life;" — when he heard this, he answered: "If you wish to inquire into our affairs, and to learn what is for your advantage, sail with me at once. But if you will not, I shall now give you directions to my house, and that of those whom you wish [to meet], that when you choose to come you may find us. For I shall set out to-morrow for my home." And when I saw that he could not be prevailed upon, I went with him as far as the harbour; and having learned of him the directions which he had promised to give me for finding the dwellings, I said to him, "Were it not that to-morrow I am to recover a debt that is due to me, I should straightway set sail with you. But I shall soon overtake you." And having said this, and having given him in charge to those who commanded the ship, I returned grieving, remembering him as an excellent and dear friend.

Chap. XV. — *Introduction to Peter*

But having spent [some] days, and not having been able to recover the whole debt, for the sake of speed I neglected the balance, as being a hindrance, and myself also set sail for Judea, and in fifteen days arrived at Caesarea Stratonis. And when I had landed, and was seeking for a lodging, I learned that one named Peter, who was the most esteemed disciple of the Man who had appeared in Judea, and had done signs and wonders, was going to have a verbal controversy next day with Simon, a Samaritan of Gitthi. When I heard this, I begged to be shown his lodging; and as soon as I learned it, I stood before the door. And those who were in the house, seeing me, discussed the question who I was, and whence I had come. And, behold, Barnabas came out; and as soon as he saw me he embraced me, rejoicing greatly, and weeping. And he took me by the hand, and conducted me to where Peter was, saying to me, "This is Peter, of whom I told you as being the greatest in the wisdom of God, and I have spoken to him of you continually. Therefore enter freely, [9] for I have told him your excellent qualities, without falsehood; and, at the same time, have disclosed to him your intention, so that he himself also is desirous to see you. Therefore I offer him a great gift when by my hands I present you to him." Thus saying, he presented me, and said, "This, O Peter, is Clement."

Chap. XVI. — *Peter's salutation*

Then the blessed man, springing forward as soon as he heard my name, kissed me; and making me sit down, straightway said, "You acted nobly in entertaining Barnabas, a herald of the truth, to the honour of the living God, being magnanimously not ashamed, nor fearing the resentment of the rude multitude. Blessed shall yon be. For as you thus with all honour entertained the ambassador of the truth, so also truth herself shall constitute you, who are a stranger, a citizen of her own city. And thus you shall greatly rejoice, because you have now lent a small favour; I mean the kindness of good words. You shall be heir of blessings which are both eternal and cannot possibly be taken from you. And do not trouble yourself to detail to me your manner of life; for the veracious Barnabas has detailed to us everything relating to you, making favourable mention of you almost every day. And in order that I may tell to you briefly, as to a genuine friend, what is in hand, travel with us, unless anything hinders you, partaking of the words of truth which I am going to speak from city to city, as far as Rome itself. And if you wish [to say] anything, speak on."

Chap. XVII. — *Questions propounded*

Then I set forth my purpose from the beginning, and how I had spent myself upon difficult questions, and all the things that I disclosed to you at the outset, so that I need not write the same things again. Then I said, "I hold myself in readiness to journey with you; for this, I know not how, I gladly wish. However, I wish first to be convinced concerning the truth, that I may know whether the soul is mortal or immortal; and whether, if it is eternal, it is to be judged concerning the things which it hath done here. Also, whether there is anything that is righteous and well-pleasing to God; and whether the world was made, and for what end it was made; and whether it shall be dissolved; and if it shall be dissolved, whether it shall be made better, or shall not be at all." And not to mention them in detail, I said that I wished to learn these things, and things consequent upon these. And to this he answered: "I shall shortly convey to you, O Clement, the knowledge of the things that are; and even now listen."

Chap. XVIII. — *Causes of ignorance*

"The will of God has been [kept] in obscurity in many ways. In the first place, there is evil instruction, wicked association, terrible society, unseemly discourses, wrongful prejudice. Thereby is error, then fearlessness, unbelief, fornication, covetousness, vainglory; and ten thousand other such evils, filling the world as a quantity of smoke fills a house, have obscured the sight of the men inhabiting the world, and have not suffered them to look up and become acquainted with God the Creator from the delineation [of Himself which He has given], and to know what is pleasing to Him. Wherefore it behoves the lovers of truth, crying out inwardly from their breasts, to call for aid, with truth-loving reason, that some one living within the house [10] which is filled with smoke may approach and open the door, so that the light of the sun which is without may be admitted into the house, and the smoke of the fire which is within may be driven out.

Chap. XIX. — *The true Prophet*

"Now the Man who is the helper I call the true Prophet; and He alone is able to enlighten the souls of men, so that with our own eyes we may be able to see the way of eternal salvation. But otherwise it is impossible, as you also know, since you said a little while ago that every doctrine is set up and pulled down, and the same is thought true or false, according to the power of him who advocates it; so that doctrines do not appear as they are, but take the appearance of being or not being truth or falsehood from those who advocate them. On this account the whole business of religion needed a true prophet, that he might tell us things that are, as they are, and how we must believe concerning all things. So that it is first necessary to test the prophet by every prophetic sign, and having ascertained that he is true, thereafter to believe him in everything, and not to sit in judgment upon his several sayings, but to receive them as certain, being accepted indeed by seeming faith, yet by sure judgment. For by our initial proof, and by strict inquiry on every side, all things are received with right reason. Wherefore before all things it is necessary to seek after the true Prophet, because without Him it is impossible that any certainty can come to men."

Chap. XX. — *Peter's satisfaction with Clement*

And, at the same time, he satisfied me by expounding to me who He is, and how He is found, and holding Him forth to me as truly to be found, showing that the truth is more manifest to the ear by the discourse of the prophet than things that are seen with the eye; so that I was astonished, and wondered that no one sees those things which are sought after by all, though they lie before him. However, having written this discourse concerning the Prophet by his order, he caused the volume to be despatched to you from Caesarea Stratonis, saying that he had a charge from you to send you his discourses and his acts year by year. [11] Thus, on the very first day, beginning only concerning the prophet of the truth, he confirmed me in every respect; and then he spoke thus, "Henceforth give heed to the discussions that take place between me and those on the other side; and even if I come off at a disadvantage, I am not afraid of your ever doubting of the truth that has been delivered to you, knowing well that I seem to be beaten, but not the doctrine that has been delivered to us by the Prophet. However, I hope not to come off in our inquiries at a disadvantage with men who have understanding — I mean lovers of truth, who are able to know what discourses are specious, artificial, and pleasant, and what are unartificial and simple, trusting only to the truth [that is conveyed] through them."

Chap. XXI. — *Unalterable conviction*

"When he had thus spoken, I answered: "Now do I thank God; for as I wished to be convinced, so He has vouchsafed to me. However, so far as concerns me, be you so far without anxiety that I shall never doubt; so much so, that if you yourself should ever wish to remove me from the prophetic doctrine, you should not be able, so well do I know what I have received. And do not think that it is a great thing that I promise you that I shall never doubt; for neither I myself, nor any man who has heard your discourse concerning the Prophet, can ever doubt of the true doctrine, having first heard and understood what is the truth of the prophetic announcement. Wherefore have confidence in the God-willed dogma; for every art of wickedness has been conquered. For against prophecy, neither arts of discourses, nor tricks of sophisms, nor syllogisms, nor any other contrivance, can prevail anything; that is, if he who has heard the true Prophet really is desirous of truth, and does not give heed to aught else under pretext of truth. So that, my lord Peter, be not disconcerted, as though you had presented the greatest good to a senseless person; for you have presented it to one sensible of the favour, and who cannot be seduced from the truth that has been committed to him. For I know that it is one of those things which one wishes to receive quickly, and not to attain slowly. Therefore I know that I should not despise, on account of the quickness [with which I have got it], what has been committed to me, what is incomparable, and what alone is safe."

Chap. XXII. — *Thanksgiving*

When I had thus spoken, Peter said: "I give thanks to God, both for your salvation and for my satisfaction. For I am truly pleased to know that you apprehend what is the greatness of prophecy. Since, then, as you say, if I myself should ever wish — which God forbid — to transfer you to another doctrine, I shall not be able to persuade you, begin from to-morrow to attend upon me in the discussions with the adversaries. And to-morrow I have one with Simon Magus." And having spoken thus, and he himself having partaken of food in private, he ordered me also to partake; and having blessed the food, and having given thanks after being satisfied, and having given me an account of this matter, he went on to say: "May God grant you in all things to be made like unto me, and having been baptized, to partake of the same table with me." And having thus spoken, he enjoined me to go to rest; for now indeed my bodily nature demanded sleep.

[1] This rendering is from the text in the corresponding passage of the *Epitome de gestis S. Petri*.

[2] For ἐχπλοχῶν "Wieseler proposes ἐχχλέπτων, "that deceiving by hopes it lays snares," etc.

[3] Portus, the port of Rome. One MS. reads πόντον, "the sea."

[4] We have here adopted a conjectural reading of Davis. The common text is thus translated: "whose faces I remember, and who as being living images are satisfactory testimonies. These it is left," etc.

[5] The Vatican MS. and Epit. have "the power of speaking well."

[6] Lit., "I met each one beforehand secretly." The Latin has, "unicuique praevius occurri."

[7] The Greek is βίον, "life."

[8] The Paris MS. reads φθίνου, "envy," instead of φόνου, "murder."
[9] The text is corrupt. Dressel's reading is adopted in the text, being based on Rufinus's translation. Some conjecture, "as you will know of your own accord."
[10] A conjectural reading, "being without the house," seems preferable.

[11] The text is probably corrupt or defective. As it stands, grammatically Peter writes the discourse and sends it, and yet "by his order" must also apply to Peter. The Recognitions make Clement write the book and send it. The passage is deemed important, and is accordingly discussed in Schliemann, p. 83; Hilgenfeld, p. 37; and Uhlhorn, p. 101.

Homily II

Chap. I. — *Peter's attendants*

Therefore the next day, I Clement, awaking from sleep before dawn, and learning that Peter was astir, and was conversing with his attendants concerning the worship of God (there were sixteen of them, and I have thought good to set forth their names, as I subsequently learned them, that you may also know who they were. The first of them was Zaccheus, who was once a publican, and Sophonias his brother; Joseph and his foster-brother Michaias; also Thomas and Eliezer the twins; also Aeneas and Lazarus the priests; besides also Elisaeus, and Benjamin the son of Saphrus; as also Rubilus and Zacharias the builders; and Ananias and Haggaeus the Jamminians; and Nicetas and Aquila the friends), — accordingly I went in and saluted him, and at his request sat down.

Chap. II. — *A sound mind in a sound body*

And he, breaking off the discourse in which he was engaged, assured me, by way of apology, why he had not awakened me that I might hear his discourses, assigning as the reason the discomfort of my voyage. As he wished this to be dispelled, [1] he had suffered me to sleep. "For," said he, "whenever the soul is distracted concerning some bodily want, it does not properly approach the instructions that are presented to it. On this account I am not willing to converse, either with those who are greatly grieving through some calamity, or are immoderately angry, or are turned to the frenzy of love, or are suffering under bodily exhaustion, or are distressed with the cares of life, or are harassed with any other sufferings, whose soul, as I said, being downcast, and sympathizing with the suffering body, occupies also its own intelligence therewith.

Chap. III. — *Forewarned is forearmed*

"And let it not be said, Is it not, then, proper to present comforts and admonitions to those who are in any bad case? To this I answer, that if, indeed, any one is able, let him present them; but if not, let him bide his time. For I know [2] that all things have their proper season. Wherefore it is proper to ply men with words which strengthen the soul in anticipation of evil; so that, if at any time any evil comes upon them, the mind, being forearmed with the right argument, may be able to bear up under that which befalls it: for then the mind knows in the crisis of the struggle to have recourse to him who succoured it by good counsel.

Chap. IV. — *A request*

"However, I have learned, O Clement, how that in Alexandria Barnabas perfectly expounded to you the word respecting prophecy. Was it not so?" I answered, "Yes, and exceeding well." Then Peter: "Therefore it is not necessary now to occupy with the instructions which you know, the time which may serve us for other instructions which you do not know." Then said I: "You have rightly said,

Peter. But vouchsafe this to me, who purpose always to attend upon you, continuously to expound to me, a delighted hearer, the doctrine of the Prophet. For, apart from Him, as I learned from Barnabas, it is impossible to learn the truth."

Chap. V. — *Excellence of the knowledge of the true Prophet*

And Peter, being greatly pleased with this, answered: "Already hath the rectifying process taken its end, as regards you, knowing as you do the greatness of the infallible prophecy, without which it is impossible for any one to receive that which is supremely profitable. For of many and diverse blessings which are in the things which are or which may be, the most blessed of all — whether it be eternal life, or perpetual health, or a perfect understanding, or light, or joy, or immortality, or whatever else there is or that can be supremely good in the nature of things — cannot be possessed without first knowing things as they are; and this knowledge cannot be otherwise obtained than by first becoming acquainted with the Prophet of the truth.

Chap. VI. — *The true Prophet*

"Now the Prophet of the truth is He who always knows all things — things past as they were, things present as they are, things future as they shall be; sinless, merciful, alone entrusted with the declaration of the truth. Read, and you shall find that those [were deceived] [3] who thought that they had found the truth of themselves. For this is peculiar to the Prophet, to declare the truth, even as it is peculiar to the sun to bring the day. Wherefore, as many as have even desired to know the truth, but have not had the good fortune to learn it from Him, have not found it, but have died seeking it. For how can he find the truth who seeks it from his own ignorance? And even if he find it, he does not know it, and passes it by as if it were not. Nor yet shall he be able to obtain possession of the truth from another, who, in like manner, promises to him knowledge from ignorance; excepting only the knowledge of morality and things of that sort, which can be known through reason, which affords to every one the knowledge that he ought not to wrong another, through his not wishing [himself] to be wronged.

Chap. VII. — *Unaided quest of truth profitless*

"All therefore who ever sought the truth, trusting to themselves to be able to find it, fell into a snare. This is what both the philosophers of the Greeks, and the more intelligent of the barbarians, have suffered. For, applying themselves to things visible, they have given decisions by conjecture on things not apparent, thinking that that was truth which at any time presented itself to them [as such]. For, like persons who know the truth, they, still seeking the truth, reject some of the suppositions that are presented to them, and lay hold of others, as if they knew, while they do not know, what things are true and what are false. And they dogmatize concerning truth, even those who are seeking after truth, not knowing that he who seeks truth cannot learn it from his own wandering. For not even, as I said, can he recognise her when she stands by him, since he is unacquainted with her.

Chap. VIII. — *Test of truth*

"And it is by no means that which is true, but that which is pleasing, which persuades every one who seeks to learn from himself. Since, therefore, one thing is pleasing to one, and another to another, one thing prevails over one as truth, and another thing over another. But the truth is that which is approved by the Prophet, not that which is pleasant to each individual. For that which is one would be many, if the pleasing were the true; which is impossible. Wherefore also the Grecian philologers — rather than philosophers [4] — going about matters by conjectures, have dogmatized much and diversely, thinking that the apt sequence of hypotheses is truth, not knowing that when they have assigned to themselves false beginnings, their conclusion has corresponded with the beginning.

Chap. IX. — *"The weak things of the world."*

"Whence a man ought to pass by all else, and commit himself to the Prophet of the truth alone. And we are all able to judge of Him, whether he is a prophet, even although we be wholly unlearned, and novices in sophisms, and unskilled In geometry, and uninitiated in music. For God, as caring for all, has made the discovery concerning Himself easier to all, in order that neither the barbarians might be powerless, nor the Greeks unable to find Him. Therefore the discovery concerning Him is easy; and thus it is:

Chap. X. — *Test of the prophet*

"If he is a Prophet, and is able to know how the world was made, and the things that are in it, and the things that shall be to the end, if He has foretold us anything, and we have ascertained that it has been perfectly accomplished, we easily believe that the things shall be which [He says] are to be, from the things that have been already; we believe Him, I say, as not only knowing, but foreknowing. To whom then, however limited an understanding he may have, does it not appear, that it behoves us, with respect to the things that are pleasing to God, to believe beyond all others Him who beyond all men knows, even though He has not learned? Wherefore, if any one should be unwilling to concede the power of knowing the truth to such an one — I mean to Him who has foreknowledge through the divinity of the Spirit that is in Him — conceding the power of knowing to any one else, is he not void of understanding, in conceding to him who is no prophet, that power of knowing which he would not concede to the Prophet?

Chap. XI. — *Ignorance, knowledge, foreknowledge*

"Wherefore, before all things, we must test the Prophet with all judgment by means of the prophetic promise; and having ascertained Him to be the Prophet, we must undoubtingly follow the other words of His teaching; and having confidence concerning things hoped for, we must conduct ourselves according to the first judgment, knowing that He who tells us these things has not a nature to lie. Wherefore, if any of the things that are afterwards spoken by Him do not appear to us to be well spoken, we must know that it is not that it has been spoken amiss, but that it is that we have not conceived it aright. For ignorance does not rightly judge knowledge, and so neither is knowledge competent truly to judge foreknowledge; but foreknowledge affords knowledge to the ignorant.

Chap. XII. — *Doctrine of the true Prophet*

"Hence, O beloved Clement, if you would know the things pertaining to God, you have to learn them from Him alone, because He alone knows the truth. For if any one else knows anything, he has received it from Him or from His disciples. And this is His doctrine and true proclamation, that there is one God, whose work the world is; who being altogether righteous, shall certainly at some time render to every one according to his deeds.

Chap. XIII. — *Future rewards and punishments*

"For there is every necessity, that he who says that God is by His nature righteous, should believe also that the souls of men are immortal: for where would be His justice, when some, having lived piously, have been evil-treated, and sometimes violently cut off, while others who have been wholly impious, and have indulged in luxurious living, have died the common death of men? Since therefore, without all contradiction, God who is good is also just. He shall not otherwise be known to be just, unless the soul after its separation from the body be immortal, so that the wicked man, being in hell, [5] as having here received his good things, may there be punished for his sins;

and the good man, who has been punished here for his sins, may then, as in the bosom of the righteous, be constituted an heir of good things. Since therefore God is righteous, it is fully evident to us that there is a judgment, and that souls are immortal.

Chap. XIV. — *Righteousness and unrighteousness*

"But if any one, according to the opinion of this Simon the Samaritan, will not admit that God is just, to whom then can any one ascribe justice, or the possibility of it? For if the Root of all have it not, there is every necessity to think that it must be impossible to find it in human nature, which is, as it were, the fruit. And if it is to be found in man, how much more in God! But if righteousness can be found nowhere, neither in God nor in man, then neither can unrighteousness. But there is such a thing as righteousness, for unrighteousness takes its name from the existence of righteousness; for it is called unrighteousness, when righteousness is compared with it, and it is found to be opposite to it.

Chap. XV. — *Pairs*

"Hence therefore God, teaching men with respect to the truth of existing things, being Himself one, has distinguished all principles into pairs and opposites, [6] Himself being one and sole God from the beginning, having made heaven and earth, day and night, light and fire, sun and moon, life and death. But man alone amongst these He made self-controlling, having a fitness to be either righteous or unrighteous. To him also he hath varied the figures of combinations, placing before him small things first, and great ones afterwards, such as the world and eternity. But the world that now is, is temporary; that which shall be, is eternal. First is ignorance, then knowledge. So also has He arranged the leaders of prophecy. For, since the present world is female, as a mother bringing forth the souls of her children, but the world to come is male, as a father receiving his children [from their mother], therefore in this world there come a succession of prophets, as being sons of the world to come, and having knowledge of men. And if pious men had understood this mystery, they would never have gone astray, but even now they should have known that Simon, who now enthralls all men, is a fellow-worker of error and deceit. Now, the doctrine of the prophetic rule is as follows.

Chap. XVI. — *Man's ways opposite to God's*

"As in the beginning God, who is one, like a right hand and a left, made the heavens first and then the earth, so also He constituted all the combinations in order; but upon men He no more does this, but varies all the combinations. For whereas from Him the greater things come first, and the inferior second, we find the opposite in men — the first worse, and the second superior. Therefore from Adam, who was made after the image of God, there sprang first the unrighteous Cain, and then the righteous Abel. Again, from him who amongst you is called Deucalion, [7] two forms of spirits were sent forth, the impure namely, and the pure, first the black raven, and then the white dove. From Abraham also, the patriarchs of our nation, two firsts [8] sprang - Ishmael first, then Isaac, who was blessed of God. And from Isaac himself, in like manner, there were again two — Esau the profane, and Jacob the pious. So. first in birth, as the first born in the world, was the high priest [Aaron], then the lawgiver [Moses].

Chap. XVII. — *First the worse, then the better*

"In like manner, the combination with respect to Elias, which behoved to have come, has been willingly put off to another time, having determined to enjoy it conveniently hereafter. [9] Wherefore, also, he who was among those born of woman came first; then he who was among the sons of men came second. It were possible, following this order, to perceive to what series Simon belongs, who came before me to the Gentiles, and to which I belong who have come after him, and have come in upon him as light upon darkness, as knowledge upon ignorance, as healing upon disease. And thus, as the true Prophet has told us, a false prophet must first come from some deceiver; and then, in like manner, after the removal of the holy place, the true gospel must be secretly sent abroad for the rectification of the heresies that shall be. After this, also, towards the end, Antichrist must first come, and then our Jesus must be revealed to be indeed the Christ; and after this, the eternal light having sprung up, all the things of darkness must disappear.

Chap. XVIII. — *Mistake about Simon Magus*

"Since, then, as I said, some men do not know the rule of combination, thence they do not know who is my precursor Simon. For if he were known, he would not be believed; but now, not being known, he is improperly believed; and though his deeds are those of a hater, he is loved; and though an enemy, he is received as a friend; and though he be death, he is desired as a saviour; and though fire, he is esteemed as light; and though a deceiver, he is believed as a speaker of truth."

Then I Clement, when I heard this, said, "Who then, I pray you, is this who is such a deceiver? I should like to be informed." Then said Peter: "If you wish to learn, it is in your power to know it from those from whom I also got accurate information on all points respecting him.

Chap. XIX. — *Justa, a proselyte*

"There is amongst us one Justa, a Syro-Phoenician, by race a Canaanite, whose daughter was oppressed with a grievous disease. And she came to our Lord, crying out, and entreating that He would heal her daughter. But He, being asked also by us, said, 'It is not lawful to heal the Gentiles, who are like to dogs on account of their using various [10] meats and practices, while the table in the kingdom has been given to the sons of Israel.' But she, hearing this, and begging to partake like a dog of the crumbs that fall from this table, having changed what she was, [11] by living like the sons of the kingdom, she obtained healing for her daughter, as she asked. For she being a Gentile, and remaining in the same course of life. He would not have healed had she remained a Gentile, on account of its not being lawful to heal her as a Gentile. [12]

Chap. XX. — *Divorced for the faith*

"She, therefore, having taken up a manner of life according to the law, was, with the daughter who had been healed, driven out from her home by her husband, whose sentiments were opposed to ours. But she, being faithful to her engagements, and being in affluent circumstances, remained a widow herself, but gave her daughter in marriage to a certain man who was attached to the true faith, and who was poor. And, abstaining from marriage for the sake of her daughter, she bought two boys and educated them, and had them in place of sons. And they being educated from their boyhood with Simon Magus, have learned all things concerning him. For such was their friendship, that they were associated with him in all things in which he wished to unite with them.

Chap. XXI. — *Justas adopted sons, associates with Simon*

"These men having fallen in with Zaccheus, who sojourned here, and having received the word of truth from him, and having repented of their former innovations, and immediately denouncing Simon as being privy with him in all things, as soon as I came to sojourn here, they came to me with their foster-mother, being presented to me by him [Zaccheus], and ever since they continue with me, enjoying instructions in the truth." When Peter had said this, he sent for them, and charged them that they should accurately relate to me all things concerning Simon. And they, having called God to witness that in nothing they would falsify, proceeded with the relation.

Chap. XXII. — *Doctrines of Simon*

First Aquila began to speak in this wise: "Listen, O dearest brother, that you may know accurately everything about this man, whose he is, and what, and whence; and what the things are which he does, and how and why he does them. This Simon is the son of Antonius and Rachel, a Samaritan by race, of the village of Gitthae, which is six schoeni distant from the city. He having disciplined himself greatly in Alexandria, [13] and being very powerful in magic, and being ambitious, wishes to be accounted a certain supreme power, greater even than the God who created the world. And sometimes intimating that he is Christ, he styles himself the Standing One. And this epithet he employs, as intimating that he shall always stand, and as not having any cause of corruption so that his body should fall. And he neither says that the God who created the world is the Supreme, nor does he believe that the dead will be raised. He rejects Jerusalem, and substitutes Mount Gerizzim for it. Instead of our Christ, he proclaims himself. The things of the law he explains by his own presumption; and he says, indeed, that there is to be a judgment, but he does not expect it. For if he were persuaded that he shall be judged by God, he would not dare be impious towards God Himself. Whence some not knowing that, using religion as a cloak, he spoils the things of the truth, and faithfully believing the hope and the judgment which in some way he says are to be, are ruined.

Chap. XXIII. — *Simon a disciple of the Baptist*

"But that he came to deal with the doctrines of religion happened on this wise. There was one John, a day-baptist, [14] who was also, according to the method of combination, the forerunner of our Lord Jesus; and as the Lord had twelve apostles, bearing the number of the twelve months of the sun, so also he [John] had thirty chief men, fulfilling the monthly reckoning of the moon, in which number was a certain woman called Helena, that not even this might be without a dispensational significance. For a woman, being half a man, made up the imperfect number of the triacontad; as also in the case of the moon, whose revolution does not make the complete course of the month. But of these thirty, the first and the most esteemed by John was Simon; and the reason of his not being chief after the death of John was as follows: —

Chap. XXIV. — *Electioneering stratagems*

"He being absent in Egypt for the practice of magic, and John being killed, Dositheus desiring the leadership, falsely gave out that Simon was dead, and succeeded to the seat. But Simon, returning not long after, and strenuously holding by the place as his own, when he met with Dositheus did not demand the place, knowing that a man who has attained power beyond his expectations cannot be removed from it. Wherefore with pretended friendship he gives himself for a while to the second place, under Dositheus. But taking his place after a few days among the thirty fellow-disciples, he began to malign Dositheus as not delivering the instructions correctly. And this he said that he did, not through unwillingness to deliver them correctly, but through ignorance. And on one occasion, Dositheus, perceiving that this artful accusation of Simon was dissipating the opinion of him with respect to many, so that they did not think that he was the standing one, came in a rage to the usual place of meeting, and finding Simon, struck him with a staff. But it seemed to pass through the body of Simon as if he had been smoke. Thereupon Dositheus, being confounded, said to him, 'If you are the standing one, I also will worship you.' Then Simon said that he was; and Dositheus, knowing that he himself was not the standing one, fell down and worshipped; and associating himself with the twenty-nine chiefs, he raised Simon to his own place of repute; and thus, not many days after, Dositheus himself, while he (Simon) stood, fell down and died.

Chap. XXV. — *Simon's deceit*

"But Simon is going about in company with Helena, and even till now, as you see, is stirring up the people. And he says that he has brought down this Helena from the highest heavens to the world; being queen, as the all-bearing being, and wisdom, for whose sake, says he, the Greeks and barbarians fought, having before their eyes but an image of truth; [15] for she, who really is the truth, was then with the chiefest god. Moreover, by cunningly explaining certain things of this sort, made up from Grecian myths, he deceives many; especially as he performs many signal marvels, so that if we did not know that he does these things by magic, we ourselves should also have been deceived. But whereas we were his fellow-labourers at the first, so long as he did such things without doing wrong to the interests of religion; now that he has madly begun to attempt to deceive those who are religious, we have withdrawn from him.

Chap. XXVI. — *His wickedness*

"For he even began to commit murder, as himself disclosed to us, as a friend to friends, that, having separated the soul of a child from its own body by horrid incantations, as his assistant for the exhibition of anything that he pleased, and having drawn the likeness of the boy, he has it set up in the inner room where he sleeps, saying that he once formed the boy of air, by divine arts, and having painted his likeness, he gave him back again to the air. And he explains that he did the deed thus. He says that the first soul of man, being turned into the nature of heat, drew to itself, and sucked in the surrounding air, after the fashion of a gourd; [16] and then that he changed it into water, when it was within the form of the spirit; and he said that he changed into the nature of blood the air that was in it, which could not be poured out on account of the consistency of the spirit, and that he made the blood solidified into flesh; then, the flesh being thus consolidated, that he exhibited a man not [made] from earth, but from air. And thus, having persuaded himself that he was able to make a new [sort of] man, he said that he reversed the changes, and again restored him to the air. And when he told this to others, he was believed; but by us who were present at his ceremonies he was religiously disbelieved. Wherefore we denounced his impieties, and withdrew from him."

Chap. XXVII. — *His promises*

When Aquila had thus spoken, his brother Nicetas said: "It is necessary, O Clement our brother, for me to mention what has been left out by Aquila. For, in the first place, God is witness that we assisted him in no impious work, but that we looked on while he wrought; and as loner as he did harmless things, and exhibited them, we were also pleased. But when, in order to deceive the godly, he said that he did, by means of godhead, the things that were done by magic, we no longer endured him, though he made us many promises, especially that our statues should be thought worthy of [a place in] the temple, [17] and that we should be thought to be gods, and should be worshipped by the multitude, and should be honoured by kings, and should be thought worthy of public honours, and enriched with boundless wealth.

Chap. XXVIII. — *Fruitless counsel*

"These things, and things reckoned greater than these, he promised us, on condition only that we should associate with him, and keep silence as to the wickedness of his undertaking, so that the scheme of his deceit might succeed. But still we would not consent, but even counselled him to desist from such madness, saying to him: 'We, O Simon, remembering our friendship towards you from our childhood, and out of affection for you, give you good counsel. Desist from this attempt. You cannot be a God. Fear Him who is really God. Know that you are a man, and that the time of your life is short; and though you should get great riches, or even become a king, few things accrue to the short time of your life for enjoyment, and things wickedly gotten soon flee away, and procure everlasting punishment for the adventurer. Wherefore we counsel you to fear God, by whom the soul of every one must be judged for the deeds that he hath done here.'

Chap. XXIX. — *Immortality of the soul*

"When he heard this he laughed; and when we asked him why he laughed at us for giving him good counsel, he answered: 'I laugh at your foolish supposition, because you believe that the soul of man is immortal.' Then I said: 'We do not wonder, O Simon, at your attempting to deceive us, but we are confounded at the way in which you deceive even yourself. Tell me, O Simon, even if no one else has been fully convinced that the soul is immortal, at all events you and we [ought to be so]: you as having separated one from a human body, and conversed with it, and laid your commands upon it; and we as having been present, and heard your commands, and clearly witnessed [the performance of] what was ordered.' Then said Simon: 'I know what you mean; but you know nothing of the matters concerning which you reason.' Then said Nicetas: 'If you know, speak; but if you do not know, do not suppose that we can be deceived by your saying that you know, and that we do not. For we are not so childish, that you can sow in us a shrewd suspicion that we should think that you know some unutterable things, and so that you should take and hold us in subjection, by holding us in restraint through means of desire.'

Chap. XXX. — *An argument*

"Then Simon said: 'I am aware that you know that I separated a soul from a human body; but I know that you are ignorant that it is not the soul of the dead person that ministers to me, for it does not exist; but a certain demon works, pretending to be the soul.' Then said Nicetas: 'Many incredible things we have heard in our lifetime, but aught more senseless than this speech we do not expect ever to hear. For if a demon pretends to be the soul of the dead person, what is the use of the soul at all, that it should be separated from the body? Were not we ourselves present, and heard you conjuring the soul from the body? And how comes it that, when one is conjured, another who is not conjured obeys, as if it were frightened? And you yourself, when at any time we have asked you why the conferences sometimes cease, did not you say that the soul, having fulfilled the time upon earth which it was to have passed in the body, goes to Hades? And you added, that the souls of those who commit suicide are not easily permitted to come, because, having gone home into Hades, they are guarded.'"

Chap. XXXI. — *A dilemma*

Nicetas having thus spoken, Aquila himself in turn said: "This only should I wish to learn of you, Simon, whether it is the soul or whether it is a demon that is conjured: what is it afraid of, that it does not despise the conjuration?" Then Simon said: "It knows that it should suffer punishment if it were disobedient." Then said Aquila: "Therefore, if the soul comes when conjured, there is also a judgment. If, therefore, souls are immortal, assuredly there is also a judgment. As you say, then, that those which are conjured on wicked business are punished if they disobey, how are you not afraid to compel them, when those that are compelled are punished for disobedience? For it is not wonderful that you do not already suffer for your doings, seeing the judgment has not yet come, when you are to suffer the penalty of those deeds which you have compelled others to do, and when that which has been done under compulsion shall be pardoned, as having been out of respect for the oath which led to the evil action." [18] And he hearing this was enraged, and threatened death to us if we did not keep silence as to his doings.

Chap. XXXII. — *Simon's prodigies*

Aquila having thus spoken, I Clement inquired: "What, then, are the prodigies that he works?" And they told me that he makes statues walk, and that he rolls himself on the fire, and is not burnt; and sometimes he flies; and he makes loaves of stones; he becomes a serpent: lie transforms himself into a goat; he becomes two-faced; he changes himself into gold; he opens lockfast gates; he melts iron; at banquets he produces images of all manner of forms. In his house he makes dishes be seen as borne of themselves to wait upon him, no bearers being seen. I wondered when I heard them speak thus; but many bore witness that they had been present, and had seen such things.

Chap. XXXIII. — *Doctrine of pairs*

Those things having been thus spoken, the excellent Peter himself also proceeded to speak: "You must perceive, brethren, the truth of the rule of conjunction, from which he who departs not cannot be misled. For since, as we have said, we see all things in pairs and contraries, and as the night is first, and then the day; and first ignorance, then knowledge; first disease, then healing, so the things of error come first into our life, then truth supervenes, as the physician upon the disease. Therefore straightway, when our God-loved nation was about to be ransomed from the oppression of the Egyptians, first diseases were produced by means of the rod turned into a serpent, which was given to Aaron, and then remedies were superinduced by the prayers of Moses. And now" also, when the Gentiles are about to be ransomed from the superstition with respect to idols, wickedness, which reigns over them, has by anticipation sent forth her ally like another serpent, even this Simon whom you see, who works wonders to astonish and deceive, not signs of healing to convert and save. Wherefore it behoves you also from the miracles that are done to judge the doers, what is the character of the performer, and what that of the deed. If he do unprofitable miracles, he is the agent of wickedness; but if he do profitable things, he is a leader of goodness.

Chap. XXXIV. — *Useless and plulanthropic miracles*

"Those, then, are useless signs, which you say that Simon did. But I say that the making statues walk, and rolling himself on burning coals, and becoming a dragon, and being changed into a goat, and flying in the air, and all such things, not being for the healing of man, are of a nature to deceive many. But the miracles of compassionate truth are philanthropic, such as you have heard that the Lord did, and that I after Him accomplish by my prayers; at which most of you have been present, some being freed from all kinds of diseases, and some from demons, some having their hands restored, and some their feet, some recovering their eyesight, and some their hearing, and whatever else a man can do, being of a philanthropic spirit."

Chap. XXXV. — *Discussion postponed*

When Peter had thus spoken, towards dawn Zaccheus entered and saluted us, and said to Peter: "Simon puts off the inquiry till to-morrow; for to-day is his Sabbath, which occurs at intervals of eleven days." To him Peter answered: "Say to Simon, Whenever thou wishest; and know thou that we are always in readiness to meet thee, by divine providence, when thou desirest." And Zaccheus hearing this, went out to return the answer.

Chap. XXXVI. — *All for the best*

But he (Peter) saw me disheartened, and asked the reason; and being told that it proceeded from no cause but the postponement of the inquiry, he said: "He who has apprehended that the world is regulated by the good providence of God, O beloved Clement, is not vexed by things howsoever occurring, considering that things take their course advantageously under the providence of the Ruler. Whence, knowing that He is just, and living with a good conscience, he knows how by right reason to shake off from his soul any annoyance that befalls him, because, when complete, it must come to some unknown good. Now then, let not Simon the magician's postponement of the inquiry grieve you; for perhaps it has happened from the providence of God for your profit. Wherefore I shall not scruple to speak to you as being my special friend.

Chap. XXXVII. — *Spies in the enemy's camp*

"Some of our people attend feignedly upon Simon as companions, as if they were persuaded by his most atheistic error, in order that they may learn his purpose and disclose it to us, so that we may be able to encounter this terrible man on favourable terms. And now I have learned from them what arguments he is going to employ in the discussion. And knowing this, I give thanks to God on the one hand, and I congratulate you on the other, on the postponement of the discussion; for you, being instructed by me before the discussion, of the arguments that are to be used by him for the destruction of the ignorant, will be able to listen without danger of falling.

Chap. XXXVIII. — *Corruption of the law*

"For the Scriptures have had joined to them many falsehoods against God on this account. The prophet Moses having by the order of God delivered the law, with the explanations, to certain chosen men, some seventy in number, in order that they also might instruct such of the people as chose, after a little the written law had added to it certain falsehoods contrary to the law of God, [19] who made the heaven and the earth, and all things in them; the wicked one having dared to work this for some righteous purpose. And this took place in reason and judgment, that those might be convicted who should dare to listen to the things written against God, and those who, through love towards Him, should not only disbelieve the things spoken against Him, but should not even endure to hear them at all, even if they should happen to be true, judging it much safer to incur danger with respect to religious faith, than to live with an evil conscience on account of blasphemous words.

Chap. XXXIX. — *Tactics*

"Simon, therefore, as I learn, intends to come into public, and to speak of those chapters against God that are added to the Scriptures, for the sake of temptation, that he may seduce as many wretched ones as he can from the love of God. For we do not wish to say in public that these chapters are added to the Bible, since we should thereby perplex the unlearned multitudes, and so accomplish the purpose of this wicked Simon. For they not having yet the power of discerning, would flee from us as impious; or, as if not only the blasphemous chapters were false, they would even withdraw from the word. Wherefore we are under a necessity of assenting to the false chapters, and putting questions in return to him concerning them, to draw him into a strait, and to give in private an explanation of the chapters that are spoken against

God to the well-disposed after a trial of their faith; and of this there is but one way, and that a brief one. It is this.

Chap. XL. — *Preliminary instruction*

"Everything that is spoken or written against God is false. But that we say this truly, not only for the sake of reputation, but for the sake of truth, I shall convince you when my discourse has proceeded a little further. Whence you, my most beloved Clement, ought not to be sorry at Simon's having interposed a day between this and the discussion. For to-day, before the discussion, you shall be instructed concerning the chapters added to the Scriptures; and then in the discussion concerning the only one and good God, the Maker also of the world, you ought not to be distracted. But in the discussion you will even wonder how impious men, overlooking the multitudes of things that are spoken in the Scriptures for God, and looking at those that are spoken against Him, gladly bring these forward; and thus the hearers, by reason of ignorance, believing the things against God, become outcasts from His kingdom. Wherefore you, by advantage of the postponement, learning the mystery of the Scriptures, and gaining the [means of] not sinning against God, will incomparably rejoice."

Chap. XLI. — *Asking for information, not contradiction*

Then I Clement, hearing this, said: "Truly I rejoice, and I give thanks to God, who in all things doeth well. However, he knows that I shall be able to think nothing other than that all things are for God. Wherefore do not suppose that I ask questions, as doubting the words concerning God, [20] or those that are to be spoken, but rather that I may learn, and so be able myself to instruct another who is ingenuously willing to learn. Wherefore tell me what are the falsehoods added to the Scriptures, and how it comes that they are really false." Then Peter answered: "Even although you had not asked me, I should have gone on in order, and afforded you the exposition of these matters, as I promised. Learn, then, how the Scriptures misrepresent Him in many respects, that you may know when you happen upon them.

Chap. XLII. — *Rigid notions of God essential to holiness*

"But what I am going to tell you will be sufficient by way of example. But I do not think, my dear Clement, that any one who possesses ever so little love to God and ingenuousness, will be able to take in, or even to hear, the things that are spoken against Him. For how is it that he can have a monarchic [21] soul, and be holy, who supposes that there are many gods, and not one only? But even if there be but one, who will cherish zeal to be holy, that finds Him in many defects, since he will hope that the Beginning of all things, by reason of the defects of his own nature, will not visit the crimes of others?

Chap. XLIII. — *A priori argument on the divine attributes*

"Wherefore, far be it from us to believe that the Lord of all, who made the heaven and the earth, and all things that are in them, shares His government with others, or that He lies. For if He lies, then who speaks truth? Or that He makes experiments as in ignorance; for then who foreknows? And if He deliberates, and changes His purpose, who is perfect in understanding and permanent in design? If He envies, who is above rivalry? If He hardens hearts, who makes wise? If He makes blind and deaf, who has given sight and hearing? If He commits pilfering, who administers justice? If He mocks, who is sincere? If He is weak, who is omnipotent? If He is unjust, who is just? If He makes evil things, who shall make good things? If He does evil, who shall do good?

Chap. XLIV. — *The same continued*

"But if He desires the fruitful hill, [22] whose then are all things? If He is false, who then is true? If He dwells in a tabernacle, who is without bounds? If He is fond of fat, and sacrifices, and offerings, and drink-offerings, who then is without need, and who is holy, and pure, and perfect? If He is pleased with candles and candlesticks, who then placed the luminaries in heaven? If He dwells in shadow, and darkness, and storm, and smoke, who is the light that lightens the universe? If He comes with trumpets, and shoutings, and darts, and arrows, who is the looked-for tranquillity of all? If He loves war, who then wishes peace? If He makes evil things, who makes good things? If He is without affection, who is a lover of men? If He is not faithful to His promises, who shall be trusted? If He loves the wicked, and adulterers, and murderers, who shall be a just judge? If He changes His mind, who is stedfast? If He chooses evil men, who then takes the part of the good?

Chap. XLV. — *How God is to he thought of*

"Wherefore, Clement, my son, beware of thinking otherwise of God, than that He is the only God, and Lord, and Father, good and righteous, the Creator, long-suffering, merciful, the sustainer, the benefactor, ordaining love of men, counseling purity, immortal and making immortal, incomparable, dwelling in the souls of the good, that cannot be contained and yet is contained, [23] who has fixed the great world as a centre in space, who has spread out the heavens and solidified the earth, who has stored up the water, who has disposed the stars in the sky, who has made the fountains flow in the earth, has produced fruits, has raised up mountains, hath set bounds to the sea, has ordered winds and blasts, who by the spirit of counsel has kept safely the body comprehended in a boundless sea.

Chap. XLVI. — *Judgment to come*

"This is our Judge, to whom it behoves us to look, and to regulate our own souls, thinking all things in His favour, speaking well of Him, persuaded that by His long-suffering He brings to light the obstinacy of all, and is alone good. And He, at the end of all, shall sit as a just Judge upon every one of those who have attempted what they ought not."

Chap. XLVII. — *A pertinent question*

When I Clement heard this, I said, "Truly this is godliness; truly this is piety." And again I said: "I would learn, therefore, why the Bible has written anything of this sort? For I remember that you said that it was for the conviction of those who should dare to believe anything that was spoken against God. But since you permit us, we venture to ask, at your command: If any one, most beloved Peter, should choose to say to us, 'The Scriptures are true, although to you the things spoken against God seem to be false, how should we answer him?"

Chap. XLVIII. — *A particular case*

Then Peter answered: "You speak well in your inquiry; for it will be for your safety. Therefore listen: Since there are many things that are spoken by the Scriptures against God, as time presses on account of the evening, ask with respect to any one matter that you please, and I will explain it, showing that it is false, not only because it is spoken against God, but because it is really false." Then I answered: "I wish to learn how, when the Scriptures say that God is ignorant, you can show that He knows?"

Chap. XLIX. — *Reductio ad absurdum*

Then Peter answered: "You have presented us with a matter that can easily be answered. However, listen, how God is ignorant of nothing, but even foreknows. But first answer me what I ask of you. He who wrote the Bible, and told how the world was made, and said that God does not foreknow, was he a man or not?" Then I said: "He was a man." Then Peter answered: "How, then, was it possible for him, being a man, to know assuredly how the world was made, and that God does not foreknow?"

Chap. L. — *A satisfactory answer*

Then I, already perceiving the explanation, smiled, and said that he was a prophet. And Peter said; "If, then, he was a prophet, being a man, he was ignorant of nothing, by reason of his having received foreknowledge from God; how then, should He, who gave to man the gift of foreknowledge, being God, Himself be ignorant?" And I said: "You have spoken rightly." Then Peter said: "Come with me one step further. It being acknowledged by us that God foreknows all things, there is every necessity that the scriptures are false which say that He is ignorant, and those are true which say that He knows." Then said I: "It must needs be so."

Chap. LI. — *Weigh in the balance*

Then Peter said: "If, therefore, some of the Scriptures are true and some false, with good reason said our Master, 'Be ye good money-changers,' [24] inasmuch as in the Scriptures there are some true sayings and some spurious. And to those who err by reason of the false scriptures He fitly showed the cause of their error, saying, 'Ye do therefore err, not knowing the true things of the Scriptures; [25] for this reason ye are ignorant also of the power of God.'" Then said I: "[You have spoken] very excellently."

Chap. LII. — *Sins of the saints denied*

Then Peter answered: "Assuredly, with good reason, I neither believe anything against God, nor against the just men recorded in the law, taking for granted that they are impious imaginations. For, as I am persuaded, neither was Adam a transgressor, who was fashioned by the hands of God; nor was Noah drunken, who was found righteous above all the world; [26] nor did Abraham live with three wives at once, who, on account of his sobriety, was thought worthy of a numerous posterity; nor did Jacob associate with four — of whom two were sisters — who was the father of the twelve tribes, and who intimated the coming of the presence of our Master; nor was Moses a murderer, nor did he learn to judge from an idolatrous priest — he who set forth the law of God to all the world, and for his right judgment has been testified to as a faithful steward.

Chap. LIII. — *Close of the conference*

"But of these and such like things I shall afford you an explanation in due time. But for the rest, since, as you see, the evening has come upon us, let what has been said be enough for to-day. But whenever you wish, and about whatever you wish, ask boldly of us, and we shall gladly explain it at once." Thus having spoken, he rose up. And then, having partaken of food, we turned to sleep, for the night had come upon us.

[1] Literally, "to be boiled out of me."
[2] Eccles. iii. 1.
[3] "Were deceived" is not in the text, but the sense demands that some such expression should be supplied.
[4] φιλόλογοι, οὐ φιλόσοφοι, "lovers of words, not lovers of wisdom."
[5] Lit. Hades.
[6] Literally, "twofoldly and oppositely."
[7] Noah.
[8] For "first" Wieseler conjectures "different," — two different persons.
[9] In this sentence the text is probably corrupted. The general meaning seems to be, that he does not enter fully at present into the subject of Elias, or John the Baptist, the greatest of those born of woman, coming first, and Christ, the greatest among the sons of men, coming after, but that he will return to the subject on a fitting occasion.
[10] For διαφόροις Duncker proposes ἀδιαφόροις, "meats without distinction."

[11] That is, having ceased to be a Gentile, by abstaining from forbidden foods.
[12] There are several various readings in this sentence, and none of them can be strictly construed; but the general sense is obvious.
[13] The Vatican MS. adds, "which is in Egypt [or, on the Nile], in Greek culture."
[14] A day-baptist is taken to mean "one who baptizes every day."
[15] We have here an allusion to the tradition that it was only an image of Helen that was taken to Troy, and not the real Helen herself.
[16] Which was used by the ancients as cupping-glasses are now used.
[17] The Vatican MS. and Epitome read, "that a shrine and statues should be erected in honour of us."
[18] The Latin translates: "as having preferred the oath to the evil action."
[19] The Vatican MS. reads: "against the only God."
[20] The text has ὑπό, "by," which has been altered into ὑπέρ. Davis would read σου, "by you."
[21] Cotelerius doubts whether this expression means a soul ruling over his body, or a soul disposed to favour monarchical rule. The former explanation seems to us the more probable.
[22] Wieseler considers this corrupt, and amends: "if He desires more."
[23] The Latin has here, "imperceptus et perceptus;" but Wieseler points out that χωρούμενος has reference to God's dwelling in the souls of the good, and thus He is contained by them.
[24] This is quoted three times in the Homilies as a saying of our Lord, viz. here and in Homily III. chap. L., and Homily XVIII. chap. XX. It is probably taken from one of the apocryphal Gospels. In Homily XVIII. chap. XX. the meaning is shown to be, that as it is the part of a moneychanger to distinguish spurious coins from genuine, co it is the part of a Christian to distinguish false statements from true.
[25] A corruption of the texts, Matt. XXII. 29, Mark XII. 24.
[26] Gen. VII. 1.

Homily III

Chap. I. — *the morning of the discussion*

Two days, therefore, having elapsed, and while the third was dawning, I Clement, and the rest of our companions, being roused about the second cockcrowing, in order to the discussion with Simon, found the lamp still alight, and Peter kneeling in prayer. Therefore, having finished his supplication, and turning round, and seeing us in readiness to hear, he said:

Chap. II. — *Simon's design*

"I wish you to know that those who, according to our arrangement, associate with Simon that they may learn his intentions, and submit them to us, so that we may be able to cope with his variety of wickedness, these men have sent to me, and informed me that Simon to-day is, as he arranged, prepared to come before all, and show from the Scriptures that He who made the heaven and the earth, and all things in them, is not the Supreme God, but that there is another, unknown and supreme, as being in an unspeakable manner God of gods; and that He sent two gods, one of whom is he who made the world, and the other he who gave the law. And these things he contrives to say, that he may dissipate the right faith of those who would worship the one and only God who made heaven and earth.

Chap. III. — *His object*

"When I heard this, how was I not disheartened! Wherefore I wished you also, my brethren, who associate with me, to know that I am beyond measure grieved in my soul, seeing the wicked one awake for the temptation of men, and men wholly indifferent about their own salvation. For to those from amongst the Gentiles who were about being persuaded respecting the earthly images that they are no gods, he has contrived to bring in opinions of many other gods, in order that, if they cease from the polytheo-mania, they may be deceived to speak otherwise, and even worse [than they now do], against the sole government of God, so that they may not yet value the truths connected with that monarchy, and may never be able to obtain mercy. And for the sake of this attempt Simon comes to do battle with us, armed with the false chapters of the Scriptures. And what is more dreadful, he is not afraid to dogmatize thus against the true God from the prophets whom he does not [in fact] believe.

Chap. IV. — *Snares laid for the Gentiles*

"And with us, indeed, who have had handed down from our forefathers the worship of the God who made all things, and also the mystery of the books which are able to deceive, he will not prevail; but with those from amongst the Gentiles who have the polytheistic fancy bred in them, and who know not the falsehoods of the Scriptures, he will prevail much. And not only he; but if any other shall recount to those from among the Gentiles any vain, dreamlike, richly set out story against God, he will be believed, because from their childhood their minds are accustomed to take in things spoken against God. And few there shall be of them, as a few out of a multitude, who through ingenuousness shall not be willing so much as to hear an evil word against the God who made all things. And to these alone from amongst the Gentiles it shall be vouchsafed to be saved. Let not any one of you, therefore, altogether complain of Simon, or of any one else; for nothing happens unjustly, since even the falsehoods of Scripture are with good reason presented for a test."

Chap. V. — *Use of errors*

Then I Clement, hearing this, said: "How say you, my lord, that even the falsehoods of the Scriptures are set forth happily for the proof of men?" And he answered: "The falsehoods of the Scriptures have been permitted to be written for a certain righteous reason, at the demand of evil. And when I say happily, I mean this: In the account of God, the wicked one, not loving God less than the good one, is exceeded by the good in this one thing only, that he, not pardoning those who are impious on account of ignorance, through love towards that which is profound, desires the destruction of the impious; but the good one desires to present them with a remedy. For the good one desires all to be healed by repentance, but saves those only who know God. But those who know Him not He does not heal: not that He does not wish to do so, but because it is not lawful to afford to those who, through want of judgment, are like to irrational animals, the good things which have been prepared for the children of the kingdom.

Chap. VI. — *Purgatory and hell*

"Such is the nature of the one and only God, who made the world, and who created us, and who has given us all things, that as long as any one is within the limit of piety, and does not blaspheme His Holy Spirit, through His love towards him He brings the soul to Himself by reason of His love towards it. And although it be sinful, it is His nature to save it, after it has been suitably punished for the deeds it hath done. But if any one shall deny Him, or in any other way be guilty of impiety against Him, and then shall repent, he shall be punished indeed for the sins he hath committed against Him, but he shall be saved, because he turned and lived. And perhaps excessive piety and supplication shall even be delivered from punishment, ignorance being admitted as a reason for the pardon of sin after repentance. [1] But those who do not repent shall be destroyed by the punishment of fire, even though in all other things they are most holy. But, as I said, at an appointed time a fifth [2] part, being punished with eternal fire, shall be consumed. For they cannot endure for ever who have been impious against the one God.

Chap. VII. — *What is impiety?*

"But impiety against Him is, in the matter of religion, to die saying there is another God, whether superior or inferior, or in any way saying that there is one besides Him who really is. For He who truly is, is He whose form the body of man bears; for whose sake the heaven and all the stars, though in their essence superior, submit to serve him who is in essence inferior, on account of the form of the Ruler. So much has God blessed man above all, in order that, loving the Benefactor in proportion to the multitude of His benefits, by means of this love he may be saved for the world to come.

Chap. VIII. — *Wiles of the devil*

"Therefore the love of men towards God is sufficient for salvation. And this the wicked one knows; and while we are hastening to sow the love towards Him which makes immortal in the souls of those who from among the Gentiles are ready to believe in the one and only God, this wicked one, having sufficient armour against the ignorant for their destruction, hastens to sow the supposition of many gods, or at least of one greater, in order that men, conceiving and being persuaded of what is not wisdom, may die, as in the crime of adultery, and be cast out from His kingdom.

Chap. IX. — *Uncertainty of the Scriptures*

Worthy, therefore, of rejection is every one who is willing so much as to hear anything against the monarchy of God; but if any one dares to hear anything against God, as trusting in the Scriptures, let him first of all consider with me that if any one, as he pleases, form a dogma agreeable to himself, and then carefully search the Scriptures, he will be able to produce many testimonies from them in favour of the dogma that he has formed. How, then, can confidence be placed in them against God, when what every man wishes is found in them?

Chap. X. — *Simon's intention*

"Therefore Simon, who is going to discuss in public with us to-morrow, is bold against the monarchy of God, wishing to produce many statements from these Scriptures, to the effect that there are many gods, and a certain one who is not He who made this world, but who is superior to Him; and, at the same time, he is going to offer many scriptural proofs. But we also can easily show many passages from them that He who made the world alone is God, and that there is none other besides Him. But if any one shall wish to speak otherwise, he also shall be able to produce proofs from them at his pleasure. For the Scriptures say all manner of things, that no one of those who inquire ungratefully may find the truth, but [simply] what he wishes to find, the truth being reserved for the grateful; now gratitude is to preserve our love to Him who is the cause of our being.

Chap. XI. — *Distinction between prediction and prophecy*

"Whence it must before all things be known, that nowhere can truth be found unless from a prophet of truth. But He is a true Prophet, who always knows all things, and even the thoughts of all men, who is without sin, as being convinced respecting the judgment of God. Wherefore we ought not simply to consider respecting His foreknowledge, but whether His foreknowledge can stand, apart from other cause. For physicians predict certain things, having the pulse of the patient as matter submitted to them; and some predict by means of having fowls, and some by having sacrifices, and others by having many various matters submitted to them; yet these are not prophets.

Chap. XII. — *The same*

"But if any one should say that the foreknowledge [shown] by these predictions is like to that foreknowledge which is really implanted, he were much deceived. For he only declares such things as being present, and that if he speaks truth. However, even these things are serviceable to me, for they establish that there is such a thing as foreknowledge. But the foreknowledge of the one true Prophet does not only know things present, but stretches out prophecy without limit as far as the world to come, and needs nothing for its interpretation, not prophesying darkly and ambiguously, so that the things spoken would need another prophet for the interpretation of them; but clearly and simply, as our Master and Prophet, by the inborn and ever-flowing Spirit, always knew all things.

Chap. XIII. — *Prophetic knowledge constant*

"Wherefore He confidently made statements respecting things that are to be — I mean sufferings, places, limits. For, being a faultless Prophet, and looking upon all things with the boundless eye of His soul. He knows hidden things. But if we should hold, as many do, that even the true Prophet, not always, but sometimes, when He has the Spirit, and through it, foreknows, but when He has it not is ignorant, — if we should suppose thus, we should deceive ourselves and mislead others. For such a matter belongs to those who are madly inspired by the spirit of disorder — to those who are drunken beside the altars, and are gorged with fat.

Chap. XIV. — *Prophetic spirit constant*

"For if it were permitted to any one who will profess prophecy to have it believed in the cases in which he was found false, that then he had not the Holy Spirit of foreknowledge, it will be difficult to convict him of being a false prophet; for among the many things that he speaks, a few come to pass, and then he is believed to have the Spirit, although he speaks the first things last, and the last first; speaks of past events as future, and future as already past; and also without sequence; or things borrowed from others and altered, and some that are lessened, unformed, foolish, ambiguous, unseemly, obscure, proclaiming all unconscientiousness.

Chap. XV. — *Christ's prophecies*

"But our Master did not prophesy after this fashion; but, as I have already said, being a prophet by an inborn and ever-flowing Spirit, and knowing all things at all times. He confidently set forth, plainly as I said before, sufferings, places, appointed times, manners, limits. Accordingly, therefore, prophesying concerning the temple, He said: 'See ye these buildings? Verily I say to you. There shall not be left here one stone upon another which shall not be taken away; and this generation shall not pass until the destruction begin. For they shall come, and shall sit here, and shall besiege it, and shall slay your children here.' [3] And in like manner He spoke in plain words the things that were straightway to happen, which we can now see with our eyes, in order that the accomplishment might be among those to whom the word was spoken. For the Prophet of truth utters the word of proof in order to the faith of His hearers.

Chap. XVI. — *Doctrine of conjunction*

"However, there are many proclaimers of error, having one chief, even the chief of wickedness, just as the Prophet of truth, being one, and being also the chief of piety, shall in His own times have as His prophets all who are found pure. But the chief cause of men being deceived is this, their not understanding beforehand the doctrine of conjunction, which I shall not fail to expound to you in private every day, summarily; for it were too long to speak in detail. Be you therefore to me truth-loving judges of the things that are spoken.

Chap. XVII. — *Whether Adam had the Spirit*

"But I shall begin the statement now. God having made all things, if any one will not allow to a man, fashioned by His hands, to have possessed His great and Holy Spirit of foreknowledge, how does not he greatly err who attributes it to another born of a spurious stock! And I do not think that he will obtain pardon, though he be misled by spurious scripture to think dreadful things against the Father of all. For he who insults the image and the things belonging to the eternal King, has the sin reckoned as committed against Him in whose likeness the image was made. But then, says he, the Divine Spirit left him when he sinned. In that case [the Spirit] sinned along with him; and how can he escape peril who says this? But perhaps he received the Spirit after he sinned. Then it is given to the unrighteous; and where is justice? But it was afforded to the just and the unjust. This were most unrighteous of all. Thus every falsehood, though it be aided by ten thousand reasonings, must receive its refutation, though after a long time.

Chap. XVIII. — *Adam not ignorant*

"Be not deceived. Our father was ignorant of nothing; since, indeed, even the law publicly current, though charging him with the crime of ignorance for the sake of the unworthy, sends to him those desirous of knowledge, saying, 'Ask your father, and he will tell you; your elders, and they will declare to you.' [4] This father, these elders ought to be inquired of. But you have not inquired whose is the time of the kingdom, and whose is the seat of prophecy, though He Himself points out Himself, saying, 'The scribes and the Pharisees sit in Moses' seat; all things whatsoever they say to you, hear them.' [5] Hear *them,* He said, as entrusted with the key of the kingdom, which is knowledge, which alone can open the gate of life, through which alone is the entrance to eternal life. But truly, He says, they possess the key, but those wishing to enter they do not suffer to do so.

Chap. XIX. — *Reign of Christ*

"On this account, I say, He Himself, rising from His seat as a father for his children, proclaiming the things which from the beginning were delivered in secret to the worthy, extending mercy even to the Gentiles, and compassionating the souls of all, neglected His own kindred. For He, being thought worthy to be King of the world to come, [fights against] [6] him who, by predestination, has usurped the kingdom that now is. And the thing which exceedingly grieved Him is this, that by those very persons for whom, as for sons, he did battle, He was assailed, on account of their ignorance. And yet He loved even those who hated Him, and wept over the unbelieving, and blessed those who slandered Him, and prayed for those who were in enmity against Him. [7] And not only did He do this as a father, but also taught His disciples to do the like, bearing themselves as towards brethren. [8] This did our Father, this did our Prophet. This is reasonable, that He should be King over His children; that by the affection of a father towards his children, and the engrafted respect of children towards their father, eternal peace might be produced. For when the good man reigneth, there is true joy among those who are ruled over, on account of him who rules.

Chap. XX. — *Christ the only Prophet has appeared in different ages*

"But give heed to my first discourse of the truth. If any one do not allow the man fashioned by the hands of God to have had the Holy Spirit of Christ, how is he not guilty of the greatest impiety in allowing another born of an impure stock to have it? But he would act most piously, if he should not allow to another to have it, but should say that he alone has it, who has changed his forms and his names from the beginning of the world, and so reappeared again and again in the world, until coming upon his own times, and being anointed with mercy for the works of God, he shall enjoy rest for ever. His honour it is to bear rule and lordship over all things, in air, earth, and waters. But in addition to these, himself having made man, he had breath, the indescribable garment of the soul, that he might be able to be immortal.

Chap. XXI. — *The eating of the forbidden fruit denied*

"He himself being the only true prophet, fittingly gave names to each animal, according to the merits of its nature, as having made it. For if he gave a name to any one, that was also the name of that which was made, being given by him who made it. [9] How, then, had he still need to partake of a tree, that he might know what is good and what is evil, if he was commanded not to eat of it? But this senseless men believe, who think that a reasonless beast was more powerful than the God who made these things.

Chap. XXII. — *Male and female*

"But a companion was created along with him, a female nature, much differing from him, as quality from substance, as the moon from the sun, as fire from light. She, as a female ruling the present world as her like, [10] was entrusted to be the first prophetess, announcing prophecy with all amongst those born of woman. [11] But the other, as the son of man, being a male, prophesies better things to the world to come as a male.

Chap. XXIII. — *Two kinds of prophecy*

"Let us then understand that there are two kinds of prophecy: [12] the one male; and let it be defined that the first, being the male, has been ranked after the other in the order of' advent; but the second, being female, has been appointed to come first in the advent of the pairs. This second, therefore, being amongst those born of woman, as the female superintendent of this present world, wishes to be thought masculine. Wherefore, stealing the seeds of the male, and sowing them with her own seeds of the flesh, she brings forth the fruits — that is, words — as wholly her own. And she promises that she will give the present earthly riches as a dowry, wishing to change the slow for the swift, the small for the greater.

Chap. XXIV. — *The prophetess a misleader*

"However, she, not only presuming to say and to hear that there are many gods, but also believing herself to be one, and in hope of being that which she had not a nature to be, and throwing away what she had, and as a female being in her courses at the offering of sacrifices, is stained with blood; and then she pollutes those who touch her. But when she conceives and brings forth temporary kings, she stirs up wars, shedding much blood; and those who desire to learn truth from her, by telling them all things contrary, and presenting many and various services, she keeps them always seeking and finding nothing, even until death. For from the beginning a cause of death lies upon blind men; for she, prophesying deceit, and ambiguities, and obliquities, deceives those who believe her.

Chap. XXV. — *Cain's name and nature*

"Hence the ambiguous name which she gave to her firstborn son, calling him *Cain,* which has a capability of interpretation in two ways; for it is interpreted both *possession* and *envy,* as signifying that in the future he was to envy either a woman, or possessions, or the love of the parents towards her. [13] But if it be none of these, then it will befall him to be called the possession. For she possessed him first, which also was advantageous to him. For he was a murderer and a liar, and with his sins was not willing to be at peace with respect to the government. Moreover, those who came forth by succession from him were the first adulterers. And there were psalteries, and harps, and forgers of instruments of war. Wherefore also the prophecy of his descendants being full of adulterers and of psalteries, secretly by means of pleasures excites to wars.

Chap. XXVI. — *Abel's name and nature*

"But he who amongst the sons of men had prophecy innate to his soul as belonging to it, expressly, as being a male, indicating the hopes of the world to come, called his own son Abel, which without any ambiguity is translated *grief.* For he assigns to his sons to grieve over their deceived brethren. He does not deceive them when he promises them comfort in the world to come. When he says that we must pray to one only God, he neither himself speaks of gods, nor does he believe another who speaks of them. He keeps the good which he has, and increases more and more. He hates sacrifices, bloodshed, and libations; he loves the chaste, the pure, the holy. He quenches the fire of altars, represses wars, teaches pious preachers wisdom, purges sins, sanctions marriage, approves temperance, leads all to chastity, makes men liberal, prescribes justice, seals those of them who are perfect, publishes the word of peace, prophesies explicitly, speaks decidedly, frequently makes mention of the eternal fire of punishment, constantly announces the kingdom of God, indicates heavenly riches, promises unfading glory, shows the remission of sins by works.

Chap. XXVII. — *The prophet and the prophetess*

"And what need is there to say more? The male is wholly truth, the female wholly falsehood. But he who is born of the male and the female, in some things speaks truth, in some falsehood. For the female, surrounding the white seed of the male with her own blood, as with red fire, sustains her own weakness with the extraneous supports of bones, and, pleased with the temporary flower of flesh, and spoiling the strength of the judgment by short pleasures, leads the greater part into fornication, and thus deprives them of the coming excellent Bridegroom. For every person is a bride, whenever, being sown with the true Prophet's whole word of truth, he is enlightened in his understanding.

Chap. XXVIII. — *Spiritual adultery*

"Wherefore, it is fitting to hear the one only Prophet of the truth, knowing that the word that is sown by another bearing the charge of fornication, is, as it were, cast out by the Bridegroom from His kingdom. But to those who know the mystery, death is also produced by spiritual adultery. For whenever the soul is sown by others, then it is forsaken by the Spirit, as guilty of fornication or adultery; and so the living body, the life-giving Spirit being withdrawn, is dissolved into dust, and the rightful punishment of sin is suffered at the time of the judgment by the soul, after the dissolution of the body; even as, among men, she who is caught in adultery is first cast out from the house, and then afterwards is condemned to punishment."

Chap. XXIX. — *The signal given*

While Peter was about to explain fully to us this mystic word, Zaccheus came, saying: "Now indeed, O Peter, is the time for you to go out and engage in the discussion; for a great crowd awaits you, packed together in the court; and in the midst of them stands Simon, like a war-chieftain attended by his spearmen." And Peter, hearing this, ordered me to withdraw for prayer, as not yet having received baptism for salvation, and then said to those who were already perfected: "Let us rise and pray that God, by His unfailing mercies, may help me striving for the salvation of the men whom He has made." And having thus said, and having prayed, he went out into the uncovered portion of the court, which was a large space; and there were many come together for the purpose of seeing him, his pre-eminence having made them more eagerly hasten to hear.

Chap. XXX. — *Apostolic salutation*

Therefore, standing and seeing all the people gazing upon him in profound silence, and Simon the magician standing in the midst, he began to speak thus: "Peace be to all you who are in readiness to give your right hands to the truth of God, which, being His great and incomparable gift in the present world, He who sent us, being an infallible Prophet of that which is supremely profitable, gave us in charge, by way of salutation before our words of instruction, to announce to you, in order that if there be any son of peace among you, peace may take hold of him through our teaching; but if any of you will not receive it, then we, shaking off for a testimony the road-dust of our feet, which we have borne through our toils, and brought to you that you may be saved, will go to the abodes and the cities of others. [14]

Chap. XXXI. — *Faith in God*

"And we tell you truly, it shall be more tolerable in the day of judgment to dwell in the land of Sodom and Gomorrha, than in the place of unbelief. In the first place, because you have not preserved of yourselves what is reasonable; in the second place, because, hearing the things concerning us, you have not come to us; and in the third place, because you have disbelieved us when we have come to you. Wherefore, being concerned for you, we pray of our own accord that our peace may come upon you. If therefore ye will have it, you must readily promise not to do injustice, and generously to bear wrong; which the nature of man would not sustain, unless it first received the knowledge of that which is supremely profitable, which is to know the righteous nature of Him who is over all, that He defends and avenges those who are wronged, and does good for ever to the pious.

Chap. XXXII. — *Invitation*

"Do you, therefore, as thankful servants of God, perceiving of yourselves what is reasonable, take upon you the manner of life that is pleasing to Him, that so, loving Him, and being loved of Him, you may enjoy good for ever. For to Him alone is it most possible to bestow it, who gave being to things that were not, who created the heavens, settled the earth, set bounds to the sea, stored up the things that are in Hades, and filled all places with air.

Chap. XXXIII. — *Works of creation*

"He alone turned into the four contrary elements [15] the one, first, simple substance. Thus combining them, He made of them myriads of compounds, that, being turned into opposite natures, and mingled, they might effect the pleasure of life from the combination of contraries. In like manner, He alone, having created races of angels and spirits by the *fiat* of His will, peopled the heavens; as also He decked the visible firmament with stars, to which also He assigned their paths and arranged their courses. He compacted the earth for the production of fruits. He set bounds to the sea, marking out a dwelling-place on the dry land. [16] He stores up the things in Hades, designating it as the place of souls; and He filled all places with air, that all living creatures might be able to breathe safely in order that they might live.

Chap. XXXIV. — *Extent of creation*

"O the great hand of the wise God, which doeth all in all! For a countless multitude of birds have been made by Him, and those various, differing in all respects from one another; I mean in respect of their colours, beaks, talons, looks, senses, voices, and all else. And how many different species of plants, distinguished by boundless variety of colours, qualities, and scents! And how many animals on the land and in the water, of which it were impossible to tell the figures, forms, habitats, colour, food, senses, natures, multitude! Then also the multitude and height of mountains, the varieties of stones, awful caverns, fountains, rivers, marshes, seas, harbours, islands, forests, and all the inhabited world, and places uninhabited!

Chap. XXXV. — *"These are a part of His ways."*

"And how many things besides are unknown, having eluded the sagacity of men! And of those that are within our comprehension, who of mankind knows the limit? I mean, how the heaven rolls, how the stars are borne in their courses, and what forms they have, and the subsistence of their being, [17] and what are their ethereal paths. And whence the blasts of winds are borne around, and have different energies; whence the fountains ceaselessly spring, and the rivers, being ever flowing, run down into the sea, and neither is that [fountain] emptied whence they come, nor do they fill that [sea] whither they come! How far reaches the unfathomable depth of the boundless Tartarus! Upon what the heaven is upborne which encircles all! How the clouds spring from air, and are absorbed into air! What is the nature of thunder and lightning, snow, hail, mist, ice, storms, showers, hanging clouds! And how He makes plants and animals! And these things, with all accuracy, continually perfected in their countless varieties!

Chap. xxxvi. — *Dominion over the creatures*

"Therefore, if any one shall accurately scan the whole with reason, he shall find that God has made them for the sake of man. For shower? fall for the sake of fruits, that man may partake of them, and that animals maybe fed, that they may be useful to n:ien. And the sun shines, that he may turn the air into four seasons, and that each time may afford its peculiar service to man. And the fountains spring, that drink may be given to men. And, moreover, who is lord over the creatures, so far as is possible? Is it not man, who has received wisdom to till the earth, to sail the sea; to make fishes, birds, and beasts his prey; to investigate the course of the stars, to mine the earth, to sail the sea, to build cities, to define kingdoms, to ordain laws, to execute justice, to know the invisible God, to be cognizant of the names of angels, to drive away demons, to endeavour to cure diseases by medicines, to find charms against poison-darting serpents, to understand antipathies?

Chap. XXXVII. — *"Whom to know is life eternal."*

But if thou art thankful, O man, understanding that God is thy benefactor in all things, thou mayest even be immortal, the things that are made for thee having continuance through thy gratitude. And now thou art able to become incorruptible, if thou acknowledge Him whom thou didst not know, if thou love Him whom thou didst forsake, if thou pray to Him alone who is able to punish or to save thy body and soul. Wherefore, before all things, consider that no one shares His rule, no one has a name in common with Him — that is, is called God. For He alone is both called and is God. Nor is it lawful to think that there is any other, or to call any other by that name. And if any one should dare do so, eternal punishment of soul is his."

Chap. XXXVIII. — *Simon's challenge*

When Peter had thus spoken, Simon, at the outside of the crowd, cried aloud: "Why would you lie, and deceive the unlearned multitude standing around you, persuading them that it is unlawful to think that there are gods, and to call them so, when the books that are current am on 2 the Jews say that there are many gods? And now I wish, in the presence of all, to discuss with you from these books on the necessity of thinking that there are gods; first showing respecting him whom you call God, that he is not the supreme and omnipotent [Being], inasmuch as he is without foreknowledge, imperfect, needy, not good, and underlying many and innumerable grievous passions. Wherefore, when this has been shown from the Scriptures, as I say, it follows that there is another, not written of, foreknowing, perfect, without want, good, removed from all grievous passions. But he whom you call the Creator is subject to the opposite [evils].

Chap. XXXIX. — *Defects ascribed to God*

"Therefore also Adam, being made at first after his likeness, is created blind, and is said not to have knowledge of good or evil, and is found a transgressor, and is driven out of paradise, and is punished with death. In like manner also, he who made him, because he sees not in all places, says with reference to the overthrow of Sodom, 'Come, and let us go down, and see whether they do according to their cry which comes to me; or if not, that I may know.' [18] Thus he shows himself ignorant. And in his saying respecting Adam, 'Let us drive him out, lest he put forth his hand and touch the tree of life, and eat, and live for ever;' [19] in saying lest he is ignorant: and in driving him out lest he should eat and live for ever, he is also envious. And whereas it is written that "God [20] repented that he had made man," this implies both repentance and ignorance. For this reflection is a view by which one, through ignorance, wishes to inquire into the result of the things which he wills, or it is the act of one repenting on account of the event not being according to his expectation. And whereas it is written, 'And the Lord smelled a scent of sweetness,' [21] it is the part of one in need; and his being pleased with the fat of flesh is the part of one who is not good. But his tempting, as it is written, 'And God did tempt Abraham,' [22] is the part of one who is wicked, and who is ignorant of the issue of the experiment."

Chap. XL. — *Peter's answer*

In like manner Simon, by taking many passages from the Scriptures, seemed to show that God is subject to every infirmity. And to this Peter said: "Does he who is evil, and wholly wicked, love to accuse himself in the things in which he sins? Answer me this." Then said Simon: "He does not." Then said Peter: "How, then, can God be evil and wicked, seeing that those evil things which have been commonly written regarding Him, have been added by His own will!" Then said Simon: "It may be that the charge against Him is written by another power, and not according to His choice." Then said Peter: "Let us then, in the first place, inquire into this. If, indeed. He has of His own will accused Himself, as you formerly acknowledged, then He is not wicked; but if it is done by another power, it must be inquired and investigated with all energy who hath subjected to all evils Him who alone is good."

Chap. XLI. — *"Status quaestionis."*

Then said Simon: "You are manifestly avoiding the hearing of the charge from the Scriptures against your God." Then Peter: "You yourself appear to me to be doing this; for he who avoids the order of inquiry, does not wish a true investigation to be made. Hence I, who proceed in an orderly manner, and wish that the writer should first be considered, am manifestly desirous to walk in a straight path." Then Simon: "First confess that if the things written against the Creator are true, he is not above all, since, according to the Scriptures, he is subject to all evil; then afterwards we shall inquire as to the writer." Then said Peter: "That I may not seem to speak against your want of order through unwillingness to enter upon the investigation, [23] I answer you. I say that if the things written against God are true, they do not show that God is wicked." Then said Simon: "How can you maintain that?"

Chap. XLII. — *Was Adam blind?*

Then said Peter: "Because things are written opposite to those sayings which speak evil of him; wherefore neither the one nor the other can be confirmed." Then Simon: "How, then, is the truth to be ascertained, of those Scriptures that say he is evil, or of those that say he is good?" Then Peter: "Whatever sayings of the Scriptures are in harmony with the creation that was made by Him are true, but whatever are contrary to it are false." Then Simon said: "How can you show that the Scriptures contradict themselves?" And Peter said: "You say that Adam was created blind, which was not so; for He would not have pointed out the tree of the knowledge of good and evil to a blind man, and commanded him not to taste of it." Then said Simon: "He meant that his mind was blind." Then Peter: "How could he be blind in respect of his mind, who, before tasting of the tree, in harmony with Him who made him, imposed appropriate names on all the animals?" Then Simon: "If Adam had foreknowledge, how did he not foreknow that the serpent would deceive his wife?" Then Peter: "If Adam had not foreknowledge, how did he give names to the sons of men as they were born with reference to their future doings, calling the first Cain (which is interpreted 'envy'), who through envy killed his brother Abel (which is interpreted 'grief'); for his parents grieved over him, the first slain?

Chap. XLIII. — *God's foreknowledge*

"But if Adam, being the work of God, had foreknowledge, much more the God who created him. And that is false which is written that God reflected, as if using reasoning on account of ignorance; and that the Lord tempted Abraham, that He might know if he would endure it; and that which is written, 'Let us go down, and see if they are doing according to the cry of them which cometh to me; and if not, that I may know.' And, not to extend my discourse too far, whatever sayings ascribe ignorance to Him, or anything else that is evil, being upset by other sayings which affirm the contrary, are proved to be false. But because He does indeed foreknow. He says to Abraham, 'Thou shalt assuredly know that thy seed shall be sojourners in a land that is not their own; and they shall enslave them, and shall evil entreat them, and humble them four hundred years. But the nation to which they shall be in bondage will I judge, and after that they shall come out hither with much property; but thou shalt depart to thy fathers with peace, being nourished in a good old age; and in the fourth generation they shall return hither, for the sins of the Amorites are hitherto not filled up.' [24]

Chap. XLIV. — *God's decrees*

"But what? Does not Moses pre-intimate the sins of the people, and predict their dispersion among the nations? But if He gave foreknowledge to Moses, how can it be that He had it not Himself? But He has it. And if He has it, as we have also shown, it is an extravagant saying that He reflected, and that He repented, and that He went down to see, and whatever else of this sort. Whatsoever things being foreknown before they come to pass as about to befall, take issue by a wise economy, without repentance.

Chap. XLV. — *Sacrifices*

"But that He is not pleased with sacrifices, is shown by this, that those who lusted after flesh were slain as soon as they tasted it, and were consigned to a tomb, so that it was called the grave of lusts. [25] He then who at the first was displeased with the slaughtering of animals, not wishing them to be slain, did not ordain sacrifices as desiring them; nor from the beginning did He require them. For neither are sacrifices accomplished without the slaughter of animals, nor can the first-fruits be presented. But how is it possible for Him to abide in darkness, and smoke, and storm (for this also is written), who created a pure heaven, and created the sun to give light to all, and assigned the invariable order of their revolutions to innumerable stars? Thus, O Simon, the handwriting of God — I mean the heaven — shows the counsels of Him who made it to be pure and stable.

Chap. XLVI. — *Disparagements of God*

"Thus the sayings accusatory of the God who made the heaven are both rendered void by the opposite sayings which are alongside of them, and are refuted by the creation. For they were not written by a prophetic hand. Wherefore also they appear opposite to the hand of God, who made all things." Then said Simon: "How can you show this?"

Chap. XLVII. — *Foreknowledge of Moses*

Then said Peter: "The law of God was given by Moses, without writing, to seventy wise men, to be handed down, that the government might be carried on by succession. But after that Moses was taken up, it was written by some one, but not by Moses. For in the law itself it is written, 'And Moses died; and they buried him near the house of Phogor, [26] and no one knows his sepulchre till this day.' But how could Moses write that Moses died? And whereas in the time after Moses, about 500 years or thereabouts, it is found lying in the temple which was built, and after about 500 years more it is carried away, and being burnt in the time of Nebuchadnezzar it is destroyed; and thus being written after Moses, and often lost, even this shows the foreknowledge of Moses, because he, foreseeing its disappearance, did not write it; but those who wrote it, being convicted of ignorance through their not foreseeing its disappearance, were not prophets."

Chap. XLVIII. — *Test of truth*

Then said Simon: "Since, as you say, we must understand the things concerning God by comparing them with the creation, how is it possible to recognise the other things in the law which are from the tradition of Moses, and are true, and are mixed up with these falsehoods?" Then Peter said: "A certain verse has been recorded without controversy in the written law, according to the providence of God, so as to show clearly which of the things written are true and which are false." Then said Simon: "Which is that? Show it us."

Chap. XLIX. — *The true Prophet*

Then Peter said: "I shall tell you forthwith. It is written in the first book of the law, towards the end: 'A ruler shall not fail from Judah, nor a leader from his thighs, until He come whose it is; and He is the expectation of the nations.' [27] If, therefore, any one can apprehend Him who came after the failure of ruler and leader from Judah, and who was to be expected by the nations, he will be able by this verse to recognise Him as truly having come; [28] and believing His teaching, he will know what of the Scriptures are true and what are false." Then said Simon: "I understand that you speak of your Jesus as Him who was prophesied of by the scripture. Therefore let it be granted that it is so. Tell us, then, how he taught you to discriminate the Scriptures."

Chap. L. — *His teaching concerning the Scriptures*

Then Peter: "As to the mixture of truth with falsehood, I remember that on one occasion He, finding fault with the Sadducees, said, 'Wherefore ye do err, not knowing the true things of the Scriptures; and on this account ye are ignorant of the power of God.' [29] But if He cast up to them that they knew not the true things of the Scriptures, it is manifest that there are false things in them. And also, inasmuch as He said, 'Be ye prudent money-changers,' [30] it is because there are genuine and spurious words. And whereas He said, 'Wherefore do ye not perceive that which is reasonable in the Scriptures?' He makes the understanding of him stronger who voluntarily judges soundly.

Chap. LI. — *His teaching concerning the law*

"And His sending to the scribes and teachers of the existing Scriptures, as to those who knew the true things of the law that then was, is well known. And also that He said, 'I am not come to destroy the law,' [31] and yet that He appeared to be destroying it, is the part of one intimating that the things which He destroyed did not belong to the law. And His saying, 'The heaven and the earth shall pass away, but one jot or one tittle shall not pass from the law,' [32] intimated that the things which pass away before the heaven and the earth do not belong to the law in reality.

Chap. LII. — *Other sayings of Christ*

"Since, then, while the heaven and the earth still stand, sacrifices heave passed away, and kingdoms, and prophecies among those who are born of woman, and such like, as not being ordinances of God; hence therefore He says, 'Every plant which the heavenly Father has not planted shall be rooted up.' [33] Wherefore He, being the true Prophet, said, 'I am the gate of life; [34] he who entereth through me entereth into life,' there being no other teaching able to save. Wherefore also He cried, and said, 'Come unto me, all who labour,' [35] that is, who are seeking the truth, and not finding it; and again, 'My sheep hear my voice;' [36] and elsewhere, 'Seek and find,' [37] since the truth does not lie on the surface.

Chap. LIII. — *Other sayings of Christ*

"But also a witnessing voice was heard from heaven, saying, "This is my beloved Son, in whom I am well pleased; hear Him.' [38] And in addition to this, willing to convict more fully -of error the prophets from whom they asserted that they had learned. He proclaimed that they died desiring the truth, but not having learned it, saying, 'Many prophets and kings desired to see what ye see, and to hear what you hear; and verily I say to you, they neither saw nor heard.' [39] Still further He said, 'I am he concerning whom Moses prophesied, saying, A Prophet shall the Lord our God raise unto you of your brethren, like unto me: Him hear in all things; and whosoever will not hear that Prophet shall die.' [40]

Chap. LIV. — *Other sayings*

"Whence it is impossible without His teaching to attain to saving truth, though one seek it for ever where the thing that is sought is not. But it was, and is, in the word of our Jesus. Accordingly, He, knowing the true things of the law, said to the Sadducees, asking on what account Moses permitted to marry seven, 'Moses gave you commandments according to your hardheartedness; for from the beginning it was not so: for He who created man at first, made him male and female.' [41]

Chap. LV. — *Teaching of Christ*

"But to those who think, as the Scriptures teach, that God swears, He said, 'Let your yea be yea, and nay, nay; for what is more than these is of the evil one.' [42] And to those who say that Abraham and Isaac and Jacob are dead, He said, 'God is not of the dead, but of the living.' [43] And to those who suppose that God tempts, as the Scriptures say. He said, 'The tempter is the wicked one,' [44] who also tempted Himself. To those who suppose that God does not foreknow, He said, 'For your heavenly Father knoweth that ye need all these things before ye ask Him.' [45] And to those who believe, as the Scriptures say, that He does not see all things. He said, 'Pray in secret, and your Father, who seeth secret things, will reward you.' [46]

Chap. LVI. — *Teaching of Christ*

"And to those who think that He is not good, as the Scriptures say. He said, 'From which of you shall his son ask bread, and he will give him a stone; or shall ask a fish, and he will give him a serpent? If ye then, being evil, know to give good gifts to your children, how much more shall your heavenly Father give good things to those who ask Him, and to those who do His will!" [47] But to those who affirmed that He was in the temple. He said, 'Swear not by heaven, for it is God's throne; nor by the earth, for it is the footstool of His feet.' [48] And to those who supposed that God is pleased with sacrifices. He said, 'God wishes mercy, and not sacrifices' [49] — the knowledge of Himself, and not holocausts.

Chap. LVII. — *Teaching of Christ*

"But to those who are persuaded that He is evil, as the Scriptures say, He said, 'Call not me good, for One [only] is good.' [50] And again, 'Be ye good and merciful, as your Father in the heavens, who makes the sun rise on good and evil men, and brings rain upon just and unjust.' [51] But to those who were misled to imagine many gods, as the Scriptures say. He said, 'Hear, O Israel; the Lord your God is one Lord.'" [52]

Chap. LVIII. — *Flight of Simon*

Therefore Simon, perceiving that Peter was driving him to use the Scriptures as Jesus taught, was unwilling that the discussion should go into the doctrine concerning God, even although Peter had changed the discussion into question and answer, as Simon himself asked. However, the discussion occupied three days. And while the fourth was dawning, he set off darkling as far as Tyre of Phoenicia. And not many days after, some of the precursors came and said to Peter: "Simon is doing great miracles in Tyre, and disturbing many of the people there; and by many slanders he has made you to be hated."

Chap. LIX. — *Peter's resolution to follow*

Peter, hearing this, on the following night assembled the multitude of hearers; and as soon as they were come together, he said: "While I am going forth to the nations which say that there are many gods, to teach and to preach that God is one, who made heaven and earth, and all things that are in them, in order that they may love Him and be saved, evil has anticipated me, and by the very law of conjunction has sent Simon before me, in order that these men, if they shall cease to say that there are many gods, disowning those upon earth that are called gods, may think that there are many gods in heaven; so that, not feeling the excellency of the monarchy, they may perish with eternal punishment. And what is most dreadful, since true doctrine has incomparable power, he forestalls me with slanders, and persuades them to this, not even at first to receive me; lest he who is the slanderer be convicted of being himself in reality a devil, and the true doctrine be received and believed. Therefore I must quickly catch him up, lest the false accusation, through gaining time, wholly get hold of all men.

Chap. LX. — *Successor to be appointed*

"Since, therefore, it is necessary to set apart some one instead of me to fill my place, let us all with one consent pray to God, that He would make manifest who amongst us is the best, that, sitting in the chair of Christ, he may piously rule His church. Who, then, shall be set apart? For by the counsel of God that man is set forth as blessed, 'whom his Lord shall appoint over the ministry of his fellow servants, to give them their meat in their season, not thinking and saying in his heart. My Lord delayeth His coming, and who shall not begin to beat his fellow-servants, eating and drinking with harlots and drunkards. And the Lord of that servant shall come in an hour when he doth not look for Him, and in a day when he is not aware, and shall cut him in sunder, and shall assign his unfaithful part with the hypocrites.' [53]

Chap. LXI. — *Monarchy*

"But if any one of those present, being able to instruct the ignorance of men, shrink from it, thinking only of his own ease, let him expect to hear this sentence: 'O wicked and slothful servant, thou oughtest to have given my money to the exchangers, and I at my coming should have got my own. Cast out the unprofitable servant into the outer darkness.' [54] And with good reason; 'for,' says He, 'it is thine, O man, to prove my words, as silver and money are proved among the exchangers.' [55] Therefore the multitude of the faithful ought to obey some one, that they may live in harmony. For that which tends to the government of one person, in the form of monarchy, enables the subjects to enjoy peace by means of good order; but in case of all, through desire of ruling, being unwilling to submit to one only, they must altogether fall by reason of division.

Chap. LXII. — *Obedience leads to peace*

"But, further, let the things that are happening before your eyes persuade you; how wars are constantly arising through there being now many kings all over the earth. For each one holds the government of another as a pretext for war. But if one were universal superior, he, having no reason why he should make war, would have perpetual peace. In short, therefore, to those who are thought worthy of eternal life, God appoints one universal King in the world that shall then be, that by means of monarchy there may be unfailing peace. It behoves all, therefore, to follow some one as a leader, honouring him as the image of God; and it behoves the leader to be acquainted with the road that entereth into the holy city.

Chap. LXIII. — *Zaccheus appointed*

"But of those who are present, whom shall I choose but Zaccheus, to whom also the Lord went in [56] and rested, judging him worthy to be saved?" And having said this, he laid his hand upon Zaccheus, who stood by, and forced him to sit down in his own chair. But Zaccheus, falling at his feet, begged that he would permit him to decline the rulership; promising, at the same time, and saying, "Whatever it behoves the ruler to do, I will do; only grant me not to have this name: for I am afraid of assuming the name of the rulership, for it teems with bitter envy and danger."

Chap. LXIV. — *The bishopric*

Then Peter said: "If you are afraid of this, do not be called *ruler*, but the *appointed one*, the Lord having permitted you to be so called, when He said, 'Blessed is that man whom his Lord shall *appoint* to the ministry of his fellow-servants.' [57] But if you wish it to be altogether unknown that you have authority of administration, you seem to me to be ignorant that the acknowledged authority of the president has great influence as regards the respect of the multitude. For every one obeys him who has received authority, having conscience as a great constraint. And are you not well aware that you are not to rule as the rulers of the nations, but as a servant ministering to them, as a father to the oppressed, visiting them as a physician, guarding them as a shepherd, — in short, taking all care for their salvation? And do you think that I am not aware what labours I compel you to undertake, desiring you to be judged by multitudes whom it is impossible for any one to please. But it is most possible for him who does well to please God. Wherefore I entreat you to undertake it heartily, by God, by Christ, for the salvation of the brethren, for their ordering, and your own profit.

Chap. LXV. — *Nolo episcopari*

"And consider this other thing, that in proportion as there is labour and danger in ruling the church of Christ, so much greater is the reward. And yet again the greater is also the punishment to him who can, and refuses. I wish, therefore, knowing that you are the best instructed of my attendants, to turn to account those noble powers of judging with which you have been entrusted by the Lord, in order that you may be saluted with the *Well done, good and faithful servant*, and not be found fault with, and declared liable to punishment, like him who hid the one talent. But if you will not be appointed a good guardian of the church, point out another in your stead, more learned and more faithful than yourself. But you cannot do this; for you associated with the Lord, and witnessed His marvellous doings, and learned the administration of the church.

Chap. LXVI. — *Danger of disobedience*

"And your work is to order what things are proper; and that of the brethren is to submit, and not to disobey. Therefore submitting they shall be saved, but disobeying they shall be punished by the Lord, because the president is entrusted with the place of Christ. Wherefore, indeed, honour or contempt shown to the president is handed on to Christ, and from Christ to God.

And this I have said, that these brethren may not be ignorant of the danger they incur by disobedience to you, because whosoever disobeys your orders, disobeys Christ; and he who disobeys Christ offends God.

Chap. LXVII. — *Duties of church office-hearers*

"It is necessary, therefore, that the church, as a city built upon a hill, have an order approved of God, and good government. In particular, let the bishop, as chief, be heard in the things which he speaks; and let the elders give heed that the things ordered be done. Let the deacons, going about, look after the bodies and the souls of the brethren, and report to the bishop. Let all the rest of the brethren bear wrong patiently; but if they wish judgment to be given concerning wrongs done to them, let them be reconciled in presence of the elders; and let the elders report the reconciliation to the bishop.

Chap. LXVIII. — *"Marriage always honourable."*

"And let them inculcate marriage not only upon the young, but also upon those advanced in years, lest burning lust bring a plague upon the church by reason of whoredom or adultery. For, above every other sin, the wickedness of adultery is hated by God, because it not only destroys the person himself who sins, but those also who eat and associate with him. For it is like the madness of a dog, because it has the nature of communicating its own madness. For the sake of chastity, therefore, let not only the elders, but even all, hasten to accomplish marriage. For the sin of him who commits adultery necessarily comes upon all. Therefore, to urge the brethren to be chaste, this is the first charity. For it is the healing of the soul. For the nourishment of the body is rest.

Chap. LXIX. — *"Not forsaking the assembling of yourselves together"*

"But if you love your brethren, take nothing from them, but share with them such things as ye have. Feed the hungry; give drink to the thirsty; clothe the naked; visit the sick; so far as you can, help those in prison; receive strangers gladly into your own abodes; hate no one. And how you must be pious, your own mind will teach you, judging rightly. But before all else, if indeed I need say it to you, come together frequently, if it were every hour, especially on the appointed days of meeting. For if you do this, you are within a wall of safety. For disorderliness is the beginning of perdition. Let no one therefore forsake the assembly on the ground of envy towards a brother. For if any one of you forsake the assembly, he shall be regarded as of those who scatter the church of Christ, and shall be cast out with adulterers. For as an adulterer, under the influence of the spirit that is in him, he separates himself on some pretext, and gives place to the wicked one against himself, — a sheep for the stealing, as one found outside the fold. [58]

Chap. LXX. — *"Hear the bishop"*

"However, hear your bishop, and do not weary of giving all honour to him; knowing that, by showing it to him, it is borne to Christ, and from Christ it is borne to God; and to him who offers it, is requited manifold. [59] Honour, therefore, the throne of Christ. For you are commanded even to honour the chair of Moses, and that although they who occupy it are accounted sinners. [60] And now I have said enough to you; and I deem it superfluous to say to him how he is to live unblameably, since he is an approved disciple of Him who taught me also.

Chap. LXXI. — *Various duties of Christians*

"But, brethren, there are some things that you must not wait to hear, but must consider of yourselves what is reasonable. Zaccheus alone having given himself up wholly to labour for you, and needing sustenance, and not being able to attend to his own affairs, how can he procure necessary support? Is it not reasonable that you are to take forethought for his living? not waiting for his asking you, for this is the part of a beggar. But he will rather die of hunger than submit to do this. And shall not you incur punishment, not considering that the workman is worthy of his hire? And let no one say: Is, then, the word sold which was freely given? Far be it. For if any one has the means of living, and takes anything, he sells the word; but if he who has not takes support in order to live — as the Lord also took at supper and among His friends, having nothing, though He alone is the owner of all things — he sins not. Therefore suitably honour elders, catechists, useful deacons, widows who have lived well, orphans as children of the church. But wherever there is need of any provision for an emergency, contribute all together. Be kind one to another, not shrinking from the endurance of anything whatever for your own salvation."

Chap. LXXII. — *Ordination*

And having thus spoken, he placed his hand upon Zaccheus, saying, "O Thou Ruler and Lord of all. Father and God, do Thou guard the shepherd with the flock. Thou art the cause, Thou the power. We are that which is helped; Thou the helper, the physician, the saviour, the wall, the life, the hope, the refuge, the joy, the expectation, the rest. In a word, Thou art all things to us. In order to the eternal attainment of salvation, do Thou co-operate, preserve, protect. Thou canst do all things. For Thou art the Ruler of rulers, the Lord of lords, the Governor of kings. Do Thou give power to the president to loose what ought to be loosed, to bind what ought to be bound. Do Thou make him wise. Do Thou, as by His name, protect the church of Thy Christ as a fair bride. For Thine is eternal glory. Praise to the Father and the Son and the Holy Ghost to all ages. Amen."

Chap. LXXIII. — *Baptisms*

And having thus spoken, he afterwards said: "Whoever of you wish to be baptized, begin from to-morrow to fast, and have hands laid upon you day by day, and inquire about what matters you please. For I mean still to remain with you ten days." And after three days, having begun to baptize, he called me, and Aquila, and Nicetas, and said to us: "As I am going to set out for Tyre after seven days, I wish you to go away this very day, and to lodge secretly with Bernice the Canaanite, the daughter of Justa, and to learn from her, and write accurately to me what Simon is about. For this is of great consequence to me, that I may prepare myself accordingly. Therefore depart straightway in peace." And leaving him baptizing, as he commanded, we preceded him to Tyre of Phoenicia.

[1] The text manifestly corrupt.
[2] Perhaps, rather, "the greater part."
[3] Matt. XXIV. 2, 34; Luke XIX. 43.
[4] Deut. XXXII. 7.
[5] Matt. XXII. 2.
[6] From a conjectural reading by Neander.
[7] Matt, XXIII. 37; Luke XIII. 34; Luke XXIII. 34.
[8] Matt. V. 44.
[9] Gen. II. 20.
[10] That is, the present world is female, and is under the rule of the female; the world to come is male, and is under the rule of the male.
[11] The allusion is to the fact that John the Baptist is called the greatest of those born of woman, while Christ is called the Son of man.
[12] Literally, "Let there be to us two genuine prophecies."
[13] Qu. "towards Abel"?
[14] Matt. X. 12; Mark VI. 11; Luke X. 5.
[15] This is rather a paraphrase than a strict translation.
[16] Various reading, "assigning it [the sea] as a habitation for aquatic animals."
[17] Literally, "of their life," according to the idea prevalent of old, that the heavenly bodies were living creatures.
[18] Gen. XVIII. 21.
[19] Gen. III. 22.
[20] Gen. VI. 6.
[21] Gen. VIII. 21.
[22] Gen. XXII. 1.
[23] The text of this passage in all the editions is meaningless. It becomes clear by a change of punctuation.
[24] Gen. XV. 13-16.
[25] That is, Kibroth-Hattaavah; Num. XI. 34.
[26] Septuagint version of Deut. xxxiv. 8.
[27] Gen. XLIX. 10.
[28] From the amended reading of Davis.
[29] Matt. XXII. 29.
[30] This is frequently quoted as a saying of Christ. It is probably from one of the apocryphal gospels.
[31] Matt. V. 17.
[32] Matt. V. 18.
[33] Matt. XV. 13.
[34] John X. 9.
[35] Matt. XI. 28.
[36] John X. 3.
[37] Matt. VII. 7.
[38] Matt. XVII. 5.
[39] Matt. XIII. 17; Luke X. 24.
[40] Deut. XVIII. 15-19; Acts III. 22, VII. 37.
[41] Matt. XIX. 8; Mark X. 5.
[42] Matt. V. 37.
[43] Matt. XXII. 32; Mark XII. 27; Luke XX. 38.

[44] Perhaps Matt. XIII. 39.
[45] Matt. VI. 8, 32.
[46] Matt. VI. 6.
[47] Matt. VII. 9-11.
[48] Matt. V. 34, 35.
[49] Matt IX. 13, XII. 7.
[50] Matt. XIX. 17; Mark X. 18; Luke XVIII. 19.
[51] Matt. V. 44, 45.
[52] Mark XII. 29.
[53] Matt. XXIV. 45-50.
[54] Matt. XXV. 27-30.
[55] Probably from an apocryphal gospel.
[56] Luke XIX. 5.
[57] Luke XII. 42.
[58] There seems to be a corruption of the text here, but the general meaning is evident enough.
[59] There are several conjectural readings of this sentence. We have not exactly followed any one of them, but have ventured on a conjecture of our own.
[60] Matt, XXIII. 2.

Homily IV

Chap. I. — *Bernice's hospitality*

Thus I Clement, departing from Caesarea Stratonis, together with Nicetas and Aquila, entered into Tyre of Phoenicia; and according to the injunction of Peter, who sent us, we lodged with Bernice, the daughter of Justa the Canaanitess. She received us most joyfully; and striving with much honour towards me, and with affection towards Aquila and Nicetas, and speaking freely as a friend, through joy she treated us courteously, and hospitably urged us to take bodily refreshment. Perceiving, therefore, that she was endeavouring to impose a short delay upon us, I said: "You do well, indeed, to busy yourself in fulfilling the part of love; but the fear of our God must take the precedence of this. For, having a combat on hand on behalf of many souls, we are afraid of preferring our own ease before their salvation.

Chap. II. — *Simon's practices*

"For we hear that Simon the magician, being worsted at Caesarea in the discussion with our lord Peter, immediately hastened hither, and is doing much mischief. For he is slandering Peter, in opposition to truth, to all the adversarijes, and stealing away the souls of the multitude. For he being a magician, calls him a magician; and he being a deceiver, proclaims him as a deceiver. And although in the discussions he was beaten in all points, and fled, yet he says that he was victorious; and he constantly charges them that they ought not to listen to Peter, — as if, forsooth, he were anxious that they may not be fascinated by a terrible magician.

Chap. III. — *Object of the mission*

"Therefore our lord Peter, having learned these things, has sent us to be investigators of the things that have been told him; that if they be so, we may write to him and let him know, so that he may come and convict him face to face of the accusations that he has uttered against him. Since, therefore, danger on the part of many souls lies before us, on this account we must neglect bodily rest for a short time; and we would learn truly from you who live here, whether the things which we have heard be true. Now tell us particularly."

Chap. IV. — *Simon's doings*

But Bernice, being asked, said: "These things are indeed as you have heard; and I will tell you other things respecting this same Simon, which perhaps you do not know. For he astonishes the whole city every day, by making spectres and ghosts appear in the midst of the market-place; and when he walks abroad, statues move, and many shadows go before him, which, he says, are souls of the dead. And many who attempted to prove him an impostor he speedily reconciled to him; and afterwards, under pretence of a banquet, having slain an ox, and given them to eat of it, he infected them with various diseases, and subjected them to demons. And in a word, having injured many, and being supposed to be a god, he is both feared and honoured.

Chap. V. — *Discretion the better part of valour*

"Wherefore I do not think that any one will be able to quench such a fire as has been kindled. For no one doubts his promises; but every one affirms that this is so. Wherefore, lest you should expose yourselves to danger, I advise you not to attempt anything against him until Peter come, who alone shall be able to resist such a power, being the most esteemed disciple of our Lord Jesus Christ. For so much do I fear this man, that if he had not elsewhere been vanquished in disputing with my lord Peter, I should counsel you to persuade even Peter himself not to attempt to oppose Simon."

Chap. VI. — *Simon's departure*

Then I said: "If our lord Peter did not know that he himself alone can prevail against this power, he would not have sent us before him with orders to get information secretly concerning Simon, and to write to him." Then, as evening had come on, we took supper, [1] and went to sleep. But in the morning, one of Bernice's friends came and said that Simon had set sail for Sidon, and that he had left behind him Appion Pleistonices, [2] — a man of Alexandria, a grammarian by profession, whom I knew as being a friend of my father; and a certain astrologer, Annubion the Diospolitan, and Athenodorus the Athenian, attached to the doctrine of Epicurus. And we, having learned these things concerning Simon, in the morning wrote and despatched a letter to Peter, and went to take a walk.

Chap. VII. — *Appion's salutation*

And Appion met us, not only with the two companions just named, but with about thirty other men. And as soon as he saw me, he saluted and kissed me, and said, "This is Clement, of whose noble birth and liberal education I have often told you; for he, being related to the family of Tiberius Caesar, and equipped with all Grecian learning, has been seduced by a certain barbarian called Peter to speak and act after the manner of the Jews. Wherefore I beg of you to strive together with me for the setting of him right. And in your presence I now ask him. Let him tell me, since he thinks that he has devoted himself to piety, whether he is not acting most impiously, in forsaking the customs of his country, and falling away to those of the barbarians."

Chap. VIII. — *A challenge*

I answered: "I accept, indeed, your kindly affection towards me, but I take exception to your ignorance. For your affection is kindly, because you wish me to continue in those [customs] which you consider to be good. But your inaccurate knowledge strives to lay a snare for me, under the guise of friendship." Then said Appion: "Does it seem to you to be ignorance, that one should observe the customs of his fathers, and judge after the manner of the Greeks?" Then I answered: "It behoves one who desires to be pious not altogether to observe the customs of his fathers; but ta observe them if they be pious, and to shake them off if they be impious. For it is possible that one who is the son of an impious father, if he wishes to be pious, should not desire to follow the religion of his father." [3] Then answered Appion: "What then? Do you say that your father was a man of an evil life?" Then said I: "He was not of an evil life, but of an evil opinion." Then Appion: "I should like to know what was his evil apprehension." Then said I: "Because he believed the false and wicked myths of the Greeks." Then Appion asked: "What are these false and evil myths of the Greeks?" Then I said: "The wrong opinion concerning the gods, which, if you will bear with me, you shall hear, with those who are desirous to learn.

Chap. IX. — *Unworthy ends of philosophers*

"Wherefore, before beginning our conversation, let us now" withdraw into some quieter place, and there I shall converse with you. And the reason why I wish to speak privately is this, because neither the multitude, nor even all the philosophers, approach honestly to the judgment of things as they are. For we know many, even of those who pride themselves on their philosophy, who are vainglorious, or who have put on the philosopher's robe for the sake of gain, and not for the sake of virtue itself; and they, if they do not find that for which they take to philosophy, turn to mockery. Therefore, on account of such as these, let us choose some place fit for private conference."

Chap. X. — *A cool retreat*

And a certain one amongst them — a rich man, and possessing a garden of evergreen plants [4] — said: "Since it is very hot, let us retire for a little from the city to my gardens." Accordingly they went forth, and sat down in a place where there were pure streams of cool water, and a green shade of all sorts of trees. There I sat pleasantly, and the others round about me; and they being silent, instead of a verbal request made to me, showed by their eager looks to me that they required the proof of my assertion. And therefore I proceeded to speak thus:

Chap. XI. — *Truth and custom*

"There is a certain great difference, O men of Greece, between truth and custom. For truth is found when it is honestly sought; but custom, whatsoever be the character of the custom received, whether true or false, is strengthened by itself without the exercise of judgment; and he who has received it is neither pleased with it as being true, nor grieved with it as false. For such an one has believed not by judgment, but by prejudice, resting his own hope on the opinion of those who have lived before him on a mere peradventure. And it is not easy to cast off the ancestral garment, though it be shown to himself to be wholly foolish and ridiculous.

Chap. XII. — *Genesis*

"Therefore I say that the whole learning of the Greeks is a most dreadful fabrication of a wicked demon. For they have introduced many gods of their own, and these wicked, and subject to all kinds of passion; so that he who wishes to do the like things may not be ashamed, which belongs to a man, having as an example the wicked and unquiet lives of the mythological gods. And through his not being ashamed, such an one affords no hope of his repenting. And others have introduced fate, which is called genesis, contrary to which no one can suffer or do anything. This, therefore, also is like to the first. For any one who thinks that no one has aught to do or suffer contrary to genesis easily falls into sin; and having sinned, he does not repent of his impiety, holding it as his apology that he was borne on by genesis to do these things. And as he cannot rectify genesis, he has no reason to be ashamed of the sins he commits.

Chap. XIII. — *Destiny*

"And others introduce an unforeseeing destiny, as if all things revolved of their own accord, without the superintendence of any master. But thus to think these things is, as we have said, the most grievous of all opinions. For, as if there were no one superintending and fore-judging and distributing to every one according to his deserving, they easily do everything as they can through fearlessness. Therefore those who have such opinions do not easily, or perhaps do not at all, live virtuously; for they do not foresee the danger which might have the effect of converting them. But the doctrine of the barbarous Jews, as you call them, is most pious, introducing One as the Father and Creator of all this world, by nature good and righteous; good, indeed, as pardoning sins to those who repent; but righteous, as visiting to every one after repentance according to the worthiness of his doings.

Chap. XIV. — *"Doctrine according to godliness."*

"This doctrine, even if it also be mythical, being pious, would not be without advantage for this life. For every one, in expectation of being judged by the all-seeing God, receives the greater impulse towards virtue. But if the doctrine be also true, it withdraws him who has lived virtuously from eternal punishment, and endows him with eternal and unspeakable blessings from God.

Chap. XV. — Wickedness of the gods

"But I return to the foremost doctrine of the Greeks, that which states in stories [5] that there are gods many, and subject to all kinds of passions. And not to spend much time upon things that are clear, referring to the impious deeds of every one of those who are called gods, I could not tell all their amours: those of Zeus and Poseidon, of Pluto and Apollo, of Dionysus and Hercules, and of them all singly. And of these you are yourselves not ignorant, and have been taught their manners of life, being instructed in the Grecian learning, that, as competitors with the gods, you might do like things.

Chap. XVI. — Wickedness of Jupiter

"But I shall begin with the most royal Zeus, whose father Kronos, having, as you say, devoured his own children, and having shorn off the members of his father Uranus with a sickle of adamant, showed to those who are zealous for the mysteries of the gods an example of piety towards parents and of love towards children. And Jupiter himself bound his own father, and imprisoned him in Tartarus; and he also punishes the other gods. [6] And for those who wish to do things not to be spoken of, he begat Metis, and devoured her. But Metis was seed; for it is impossible to devour a child. And for an excuse to abusers of themselves with mankind, he carries away Ganymedes. And as a helper of adulterers in their adultery, he is often found an adulterer. And to those who wish to commit incest with sisters, he sets the example in his intercourse with his sisters Hera and Demeter, and the heavenly Aphrodite, whom some call Dodona. [7] And to those who wish to commit incest with their daughters, there is a wicked example from his story, in his committing incest with Persephone. But in myriads of instances he acted impiously, that by reason of his excessive wickedness the fable of his being a god might be received by impious men.

Chap. XVII. — *"Their makers are like unto them."*

"You would hold it reasonable for ignorant men to be moderately indignant at these fancies. But what must we say to the learned, some of whom, professing themselves to be grammarians and sophists, affirm that these acts are worthy of gods? For, being themselves incontinent, they lay hold of this mythical pretext; and as imitators of the gods, [8] they practise unseemly things with freedom.

Chap. XVIII. — *Second nature.*

"On this account, they who live in the country sin much less than they do, not having been indoctrinated in those things in which they have been indoctrinated who dare do these things, having learned from evil instruction to be impious. For they who from their childhood learn letters by means of such fables, while their soul is yet pliant, engraft the impious deeds of those who are called gods into their own minds; whence, when they are grown up, they ripen fruit, like evil seeds cast into the soul. And what is worst of all, the rooted impurities cannot be easily cut down, when they are perceived to be bitter by them when they have attained to manhood. For every one is pleased to remain in those habits which he forms in childhood; and thus, since custom is not much less powerful than nature, they become difficult to be converted to those good things which were not sown in their souls from the beginning.

Chap. XIX. — *"Where ignorance is bliss"*

"Wherefore it behoves the young not to be satisfied with those corrupting lessons, and those who are in their prime should carefully avoid listening to the mythologies of the Greeks. For lessons about their gods are much worse than ignorance, as we have shown from the case of those dwelling in the country, who sin less through their not having been instructed by Greeks. Truly, such fables of theirs, and spectacles, and books, ought to be shunned, and if it were possible, even their cities. For those who are full of evil learning, even with their breath infect as with madness those who associate with them, with their own passions. And what is worst, whoever is most instructed among them, is so much the more turned from the judgment which is according to nature.

Chap. XX. — *False theories of philosophers*

"And some of those amongst them who even profess to be philosophers, assert that such sins are indifferent, and say that those who are indignant at such practices are senseless. For they say that such things are not sins by nature, but have been proscribed by laws made by wise men in early times, through their knowing that men, through the instability of their minds, being greatly agitated on these accounts, wage war with one another; for which reason, wise men have made laws to proscribe such things as sins. But this is a ridiculous supposition. For how can they be other than sins, which are the cause of tumults, and murders, and every confusion? For do not shortenings of life [9] and many more evils proceed from adultery?

Chap. XXI. — *Evils of adultery*

"But why, it is said, if a man is ignorant of his wife's being an adulteress, is he not indignant, enraged, distracted? why does he not make war? Thus these things are not evil by nature, but the unreasonable opinion of men make them terrible. But I say, that even if these dreadful things do not occur, it is usual for a woman, through association with an adulterer, either to forsake her husband, or if she continue to live with him, to plot against him, or to bestow upon the adulterer the goods procured by the labour of her husband; and having conceived by the adulterer while her husband is absent, to attempt the destruction of that which is in her womb, through shame of conviction, and so to become a child-murderer; or even, while destroying it, to be destroyed along with it. But if while her husband is at home she conceives by the adulterer and bears a child, the child when he grows up does not know his father, and thinks that he is his father who is not; and thus he who is not the father, at his death leaves his substance to the child of another. And how many other evils naturally spring from adultery! And the secret evils we do not know. For as the mad dog destroys all that he touches, infecting them with the unseen madness, so also the hidden evil of adultery, though it be not known, effects the cutting off of posterity.

Chap. XXII. — *A more excellent way*

"But let us pass over this now. But this we all know, that universally men are beyond measure enraged on account of it, that wars have been waged, that there have been overthrows of houses, and captures of cities, and myriads of other evils. On this account I betook myself to the holy God and law of the Jews, putting my faith in the well-assured conclusion that the law has been assigned by the righteous judgment of God, and that the soul must at some time receive according to the desert of its deeds."

Chap. XXIII. — *"Whither shall I go from Thy presence?"*

When I had thus spoken, Appion broke in upon my discourse. "What!" said he; "do not the laws of the Greeks also forbid wickedness, and punish adulterers?" Then said I: "Then the gods of the Greeks, who acted contrary to the laws, deserve punishment. But how shall I be able to restrain myself, if I suppose that the gods themselves first practised all wickednesses as well as adultery, and did not suffer punishment; whereas they ought the rather to have suffered, as not being slaves to lust? But if they were subject to it, how were they gods?" Then Appion said: "Let us have in our eye not the gods, but the judges; and looking to them, we shall be afraid to sin." Then I said: "This is not fitting, O Appion: for he who has his eye upon men will dare to sin, in hope of escaping detection; but he who sets before his soul the all-seeing God, knowing that he cannot escape His notice; will refrain from sinning even in secret."

Chap. XXIV. — *Allegory*

When Appion heard this, he said: "I knew, ever since I heard that you were consorting with Jews, that you had alienated your judgment. For it has been well said by some one, 'Evil communications corrupt good manners.'" Then said I: "Therefore good communications correct evil manners." And Appion said: "To-day I am fully satisfied to have learned your position; therefore I permitted you to speak first. But to-morrow, in this place, if it is agreeable to you, I will show, in the presence of these friends when they meet, that our gods are neither adulterers, nor murderers, nor corrupters of children, nor guilty of incest with sisters or daughters. But the ancients, wishing that only lovers of learning should know the mysteries, veiled them with those fables of which you have spoken. For they speak physiologically of boiling substance under the name of Zen, and of time under that of Kronos, and of the ever-flowing nature of water under that of Rhea. However, as I have promised, I shall to-morrow exhibit the truth of things, explaining them one by one to you when you come together in the morning." In reply to this I said: "To-morrow, as you have promised, so do. But now hear something in opposition to what you are going to say.

Chap. XXV. — *An engagement for to-morrow*

"If the doings of the gods, being good, have been veiled with evil fables, the wickedness of him who wove the veil is shown to have been great, because he concealed noble things with evil narratives, that no one imitate them. But if they really did things impious, they ought, on the contrary, to have veiled them with good narratives, lest men, regarding them as their superiors, should set about sinning in like manner." As I spoke thus, those present were evidently beginning to be well-disposed towards the words spoken by me; for they repeatedly and earnestly asked me to come on the following day, and departed.

[1] Literally, "partook of salt."

[2] This epithet means, "the conqueror of very many." Suidas makes Appion the son of Pleistonices.

[3] We have adopted the emendation of Wieseler, who reads σεβάσματι for σεβάσματα. He also proposes ἔθει (habit) instead of σεβάσματι. The readings in the MSS. vary.

[4] The text here is corrupt. If we adopt Lobeck's emendation of παμμιούσων into παμπλούιον, the literal translation is, "possessing a property around him continually rich in leaves."

[5] μυθολογοῦσαν.

[6] Wieseler proposes θείους instead of θεούς; and he punishes his uncles also, as in VI. 2, 21.

[7] This is properly regarded as a mistake for Dione, or Didone, which is another form of the name Dione.

[8] Lit. "of those who are superior or better."

[9] The Vatican MS. inserts here, "upturning of houses, magic practices, deceptions, perplexities."

Homily V

Chap. I. — *Appion does not appear*

The next day, therefore, in Tyre, as we had agreed, I came to the quiet place, and there I found the rest, with some others also. Then I saluted them. But as I did not see Appion, I asked the reason of his not being present; and some one said that he had been unwell ever since last evening. Then, when I said that it was reasonable that we should immediately set out to visit him, almost all begged me first to discourse to them, and that then we could go to see him. Therefore, as all were of one opinion, I proceeded to say:

Chap. II. — *Clements previous knowledge of Appion*

"Yesterday, when I left this, O friends, I confess that, through much anxiety about the discussion that was to take place with Appion, I was not able to get any sleep. And while I was unable to sleep, I remembered a trick that I played upon him in Rome. It was this. From my boyhood I Clement was a lover of truth, and a seeker of the things that are profitable for the soul, and spending my time in raising and refuting theories; but being unable to find anything perfect, through distress of mind I fell sick. And while I was confined to bed Appion came to Rome, and being my father's friend, he lodged with me; and hearing that I was in bed, he came to me, as being not unacquainted with medicine, and inquired the cause of my being in bed. But I, being aware that the man exceedingly hated the Jews, as also that he had written many books against them, and that he had formed a friendship with this Simon, not through desire of learning, but because he knew that he was a Samaritan and a hater of the Jews, and that he had come forth in opposition to the Jews, therefore he had formed an alliance with him, that he might learn something from him against the Jews; —

Chap. III. — *Clement's trick*

"I, knowing this before concerning Appion, as soon as he asked me the cause of my sickness, answered feignedly, that I was suffering and distressed in my mind after the manner of young men. And to this he said, 'My son, speak freely as to a father: what is your soul's ailment?' And when I again groaned feignedly, as being ashamed to speak of love, by means of silence and down-looking I conveyed the impression of what I wished to intimate. But he, being persuaded that I was in love with a woman, said: 'There is nothing in life which does not admit of help. For indeed I myself, when I was young, being in love with a most accomplished woman, not only thought it impossible to obtain her, but did not even hope ever to address her. And yet, having fallen in with a certain Egyptian who was exceedingly well versed in magic, and having become his friend, I disclosed to him my love, and not only did he assist me in all that I wished, but, honouring me more bountifully, he hesitated not to teach me an incantation by means of which I obtained her; and as soon as I had obtained her, by means of his secret instruction, being persuaded by the liberality of my teacher, I was cured of love.

Chap. IV. — *Appion's undertaking*

"'Whence, if you also suffer any such thing after the manner of men, use freedom with me with all security; for within seven days I shall put you fully in possession of her.' When I heard this, looking at the object I had in view, I said: 'Pardon me that I do not altogether believe in the existence of magic; for I have already tried many who have made many promises, and have deceived me. However, your undertaking influences me, and leads me to hope. But when I think of the matter, I am afraid that the demons are sometimes not subject to the magicians with respect to the things that are commanded them.'

Chap. V. — *Theory of magic*

"Then Appion said: 'Admit that I know more of these things than you do. However, that you may not think that there is nothing in what you have heard from me in reference to what you have said, I will tell you how the demons are under necessity to obey the magicians in the matters about which they are commanded. For as it is impossible for a soldier to contradict his general, and impossible for the generals themselves to disobey the king — for if any one oppose those set over him, he is altogether deserving of punishment — so it is impossible for the demons not to serve the angels who are their generals; and when they are adjured by them, they yield trembling, well knowing that if they disobey they shall be fully punished. But the angels also themselves, being adjured by the magicians in the name of their ruler, obey, lest, being found guilty of disobedience, they be destroyed. For unless all things that are living and rational foresaw vengeance from the ruler, confusion would ensue, all revolting against one another.'

Chap. VI. — *Scruples*

"Then said I: 'Are those things correct, then, which are spoken by poets and philosophers, that in Hades the souls of the wicked are judged and punished for their attempts; such as those of Ixion, and Tantalus, and Tityus, and Sisyphus, and the daughters of Danaus, and as many others as have been impious here? And how, if these things are not so, is it possible that magic can subsist?' Then he having told me that these things are so in Hades, I asked him: 'Why are not we ourselves afraid of magic, being persuaded of the punishment in Hades for adultery? For I do not admit that it is a righteous thing to compel to adultery a woman who is unwilling; but if any one will engage to persuade her, I am ready for that, besides confessing my thanks.'

Chap. VII. — *A distinction with a difference*

"Then Appion said: 'Do you not think it is the same thing, whether you obtain her by magic, or by deceiving her with words?' Then said I: 'Not altogether the same: for these differ widely from one another. For he who constrains an unwilling woman by the force of magic, subjects himself to the most terrible punishment, as having plotted against a chaste woman; but he who persuades her with words, and puts the choice in her own power and will, does not force her. And I am of opinion, that he who has persuaded [a woman] will not suffer so great punishment as he who has forced her. Therefore, if you can persuade her, I shall be thankful to you when I have obtained her; but otherwise, I had rather die than force her against her will.'

Chap. VIII. — *Flattery or magic*

"Then Appion, being really puzzled, said: 'What am I to say to you? For at one time, as one perturbed with love, you pray to obtain her; and anon, as if you loved her not, you make more account of your fear than your desire: and you think that if you can persuade her you shall be blameless, as without sin; but obtaining her by the power of magic, you will incur punishment. But do you not know that it is the end of every action that is judged, the fact that it has been committed, and that no account is made of the means by which it has been effected? And if you commit adultery, being enabled by magic, shall you be judged as having done wickedly; and if by persuasion, shall you be absolved from sin in respect of the adultery?' Then I said: * On account of my love, there is a necessity for me to choose one or other of the means that are available to procure the object of my love; and I shall choose, as far as possible, to cajole her rather than to use magic. But neither is it easy to persuade her by flattery, for the woman is very much of a philosopher.'

Chap. IX. — *A love-letter*

"Then Appion said: 'I am all the more hopeful to be able to persuade her, as you wish, provided only we be able to converse with her.' 'That,' said I, 'is impossible.' Then Appion asked if it were possible to send a letter to her. Then I said: 'That indeed may be done.' Then Appion said: 'This very night I shall write a paper on encomiums of adultery, which you shall get from me and despatch to her; and I hope that she shall be persuaded, and consent.' Appion accordingly wrote the paper, and gave it to me; audi thought of it this very night, and I remembered that fortunately I have it by me, along with other papers which I carry about with me." Having thus spoken, I showed the paper to those who were present, and read it to them as they wished to hear it; and having read it, I said: "This, O men, is the instruction of the Greeks, affording a bountiful licence to sin without fear. The paper was as follows:

Chap. X. — *The lover to the beloved one*

"'Anonymously, on account of the laws of foolish men. At the bidding of Love, the first-born of all, salutation: I know that you are devoted to philosophy, and for the sake of virtue you affect the life of the noble. But who are nobler then the gods among all, and philosophers among men? For these alone know what works are good or evil by nature, and what, not being so, are accounted so by the imposition of laws. Now, then, some have supposed that the action which is called adultery is evil, although it is in every respect good. For it is by the appointment of Eros for the increase of life. And Eros is the eldest of all the gods. For without Eros there can be no mingling or generation either of elements, or gods, or men, or irrational animals, or aught else. For we are all instruments of Eros. He, by means of us, is the fabricator of all that is begotten, the mind inhabiting our souls. Hence it is not when we ourselves wish it, but when we are ordered by him, that we desire to do his will. But if, while we desire according to his will, we attempt to restrain the desire for the sake of what is called chastity, what do we do but the greatest impiety, when we oppose the oldest of all gods and men?

Chap. XI. — *"All uncleanness with greediness."*

"But let all doors be opened to him, and let all baneful and arbitrary laws be set aside, which have been ordained by fanatical men, who, under the power of senselessness, and not willing to understand what is reasonable, and, moreover, suspecting those who are called adulterers, are with good reason mocked with arbitrary laws by Zeus himself, through Minos and Rhadamanthus. For there is no restraining of Eros dwelling in our souls; for the passion of lovers is not voluntary. Therefore Zeus himself, the giver of these laws, approached myriads of women; and, according to some wise men, he sometimes had intercourse with human beings, as a benefactor for the production of children. But in the case of those to whom he knew that his being unknown would be a favour, [1] he changed his form, in order that he might neither grieve them, nor seem to act in opposition to the laws given by himself. It becomes you, therefore, who are debaters of philosophy, for the sake of a good life, to imitate those who are acknowledged to be the nobler, who have had sexual intercourse ten thousand times.

Chap. XII. — *Jupiter's amours*

"'And not to spend the time to no purpose in giving more examples, I shall begin with mentioning some embraces of Zeus himself, the father of gods and men. For it is impossible to mention all, on account of their multitude. Hear, therefore, the amours of this great Jupiter, which he concealed by changing his form, on account of the fanaticism of senseless men. For, in the first place, wishing to show to wise men that adultery is no sin, when he was going to marry, being, according to the multitude, knowingly an adulterer, in his first marriage, but not being so in reality, by means, as I said, of a seeming sin he accomplished a sinless marriage. [2] For he married his own sister Hera, assuming the likeness of a cuckoo's wing; and of her were born Hebe and Ilithyia. For he gave birth to Metis without copulation with any one, as did also Hera to Vulcan.

Chap. XIII. — *Jupiter's amours continued*

"'Then he committed incest with his sister, who was born of Kronos and Thalasse, after the dismemberment of Kronos, and of whom were born Eros and Cypris, whom they call also Dodone. Then, in the likeness of a satyr, he had intercourse with Antiope the daughter of Nycteus, of whom were born Amphion and Zethus. And he embraced Alcmene, the wife of Amphitryon, in the form of her husband Amphitryon, of whom was born Hercules. And, changed into an eagle, he approached Aegina, the daughter of Asclepius, of whom Aeacus was born. And in the form of a bear he lay with Amalthea the daughter of Phocus; and in a golden shower he fell upon Danae, the daughter of Acrisius, of whom sprang Perseus. He became wild as a lion to Callisto the daughter of Lycaon, and begat Arcus the second. And with Europa the daughter of Phoenix he had intercourse by means of a bull, of whom sprang Minos, and Rhadamanthus, and Sarpedon; and with Eurymedusa the daughter of Achelous, changing himself into an ant, of whom was born Myrmidon. With a nymph of Hersaeus, in the form of a vulture, from whom sprang the wise men of old in Sicily. He came to Juno the earth-born in Rhodes, and of her were born Pargaeus, Kronius, Kytis. And he deflowered Ossia, taking the likeness of her husband Phoenix, of whom Anchinous was born to him. Of Nemesis the daughter of Thestius, who is also thought to be Leda, he begot Helena, in the form of a swan or goose; and again, in the form of a star, he produced Castor and Polydeuces. With Lamia he was transformed into a hoopoo.

Chap. XIV. — *Jupiter's undisguised amours*

"'In the likeness of a shepherd he made Mnemosyne mother of the Muses. Setting himself on fire, he married Semele, the daughter of Cadmus, of whom he begat Dionysus. In the likeness of a dragon he deflowered his daughter Persephone, thought to be the wife of his brother Pluto. He had intercourse with many other women without undergoing any change in his form; for the husbands had no ill-will to him as if it were a sin, but knew well that in associating with their wives he bountifully produced children for them, bestowing upon them the Hermeses, the Apollos, the Dionysi, the Endymions, and others whom we have spoken of, most excellent in beauty through his fatherhood.

Chap. XV. — *Unnatural lusts*

"'And not to spend the time in an endless exposition, you will find numerous unions with Jupiter of all the gods. But senseless men call these doings of the gods adulteries; even of those gods who did not refrain from the abuse of males as disgraceful, but who practised even this as seemly. For instance, Jupiter himself was in love with Ganymede; Poseidon with Pelops; Apollo with Cinyras, Zacynthus, Hyacinthus, Phorbas, Hylas, Admetus, Cyparissus, Amyclas, Troilus, Branchus the Tymnsean, Parus the Potnian, Orpheus; Dionysus with Laonis, Ampelus, Hymenaeus, Hermaphrodites, Achilles; Asclepius with Hippolytus, and Hephaestus with Peleus; Pan with Daphnis; Hermes with Perseus, Chrysas, Theseus, Odrysus; Hercules with Abderus, Dryops, Jocastus, Philoctetes, Hylas, Polyphemus, Haemon, Chonus, Eurystheus.

Chap. XVI. — *Praise of unchastity*

"'Thus have I in part set before you the amours of all the more noted gods, beloved, that you may know that fanaticism respecting this thing is confined to senseless men. Therefore they are mortal, and spend their lives sadly, because through their zeal they proclaim those things to be evil which the gods esteem as excellent. Therefore for the future you will be blessed, imitating the gods, and not men. For men, seeing you preserving that which is thought to be chastity, on account of what they themselves feel, praise you indeed, but do not help you. But the gods, seeing you like unto themselves, will both praise and help.

Chap. XVII. — *The constellations*

"'For reckon to me how many mistresses they have rewarded, some of whom they have placed among the stars; and of some they have blessed both the children and the associates. Thus Zeus made Callisto a constellation, called the Little Bear, which some also call the Dog's Tail. Poseidon also placed the dolphin in the sky for the sake of Amphitrlte; and he gave a place among the stars to Orion the son of Euryale, the daughter of Minos, for the sake of his mother Euryale. And Dionysus made a constellation of the crown of Ariadne, and Zeus invested the eagle which assisted him in the rape of Ganymede, and Ganymede himself with the honour of the Water-pourer. Also he honoured the bull for the sake of Europa; and also having bestowed Castor, and Polydeuces, and Helena upon Leda, he made them stars. Also Perseus for the sake of Danae; and Arcus for the sake of Callisto. The virgin who also is Dice, for the sake of Themis; and Heracles for the sake of Alcmene. But I do not enlarge further; for it were long to tell particularly how many others the gods have blessed for the sake of their many mistresses, in their intercourse with human beings, which senseless men repudiate as evil deeds, not knowing that pleasure is the great advantage among men.

Chap. XVIII. — *The philosophers advocates of adultery*

"'But why? Do not the celebrated philosophers extol pleasure, and have they not had intercourse with what women they would? Of these the first was that teacher of Greece, of whom Phoebus himself said, "Of all men, Socrates is the wisest." Does not he teach that in a well-regulated state women should be common? [3] and did he not conceal the fair Alcibiades under his philosopher's gown? And the Socratic Antisthenes writes of the necessity of not abandoning what is called adultery. And even his disciple Diogenes, did not he freely associate with Lais, for the hire of carrying her on his shoulders in public? Does not Epicurus extol pleasure? Did not Aristippus anoint himself with perfumes, and devote himself wholly to Aphrodite? Does not Zeno, intimating indifference, say that the deity pervades all things, that it may be known to the intelligent, that with whomsoever a man has intercourse, it is as with himself; and that it is superfluous to forbid what are called adulteries, or intercourse with mother, or daughter, or sister, or children. And Chrysippus, in his erotic epistles, makes mention of the statue in Argos, representing Hera and Zeus in an obscene position.

Chap. XIX. — *Close of the love-letter*

"'I know that to those uninitiated in the truth these things seem dreadful and most base; but not so to the gods and the philosophers of the Greeks, nor to those initiated in the mysteries of Dionysus and Demeter. But above all these, not to waste time in speaking of the lives of all the gods, and all the philosophers, let the two chief be your marks — Zeus the greatest of the gods, and Socrates of philosophic men. And the other things which I have mentioned in this letter, understand and attend to, that you may not grieve your lover; since, if you act contrarily to gods and heroes, you will be judged wicked, and will subject yourself to fitting punishment. But if you offer yourself to every lover, then, as an imitator of the gods, you shall receive benefits from them. For the rest, dearest one, remember what mysteries I have disclosed to you, and inform me by letter of your choice. Fare thee well.'

Chap. XX. — *The use made of it*

"I therefore, having received this billet from Appion, as though I were really going to send it to a beloved one, pretended as if she had written in answer to it; and the next day, when Appion came, I gave him the reply, as if from her, as follows:

Chap. XXI. — *Answer to Appion's letter*

"'I wonder how, when you commend me for wisdom, you write to me as to a fool. For, wishing to persuade me to your passion, you make use of examples from the mythologies of the gods, that Eros is the eldest of all, as you say, and above all gods and men, not being afraid to blaspheme, that you might corrupt my soul and insult my body. For Eros is not the leader of the gods, — he, I mean, who has to do with lusts. For if he lusts willingly, he is himself his own suffering and punishment; and he who should suffer willingly could not be a god. But if against his will he lust for copulation, and, pervading our souls as through the members of our bodies, is borne into intermeddling with our minds, then he that impels him to love is greater than he. And again, he who impels him, being himself impelled by another desire, another greater than he is found impelling him. And thus we come to an endless succession of lovers, [4] which is impossible. Thus, neither is there an impeller nor an impelled; but it is the lustful passion of the lover himself, which is increased by hope and diminished by despair.

Chap. XXII. — *Lying fables*

"'But those who will not subdue base lusts belie the gods, that, by representing the gods as first doing the things which they do, they may be set free from blame. For if those who are called gods committed adulteries for the sake of begetting children, and not through lasciviousness, why did they also debauch males? But it is said they complimented their mistresses by making them stars. Therefore before this were there no stars, until such time as, by reason of wantonness, the heaven was adorned with stars by adulterers? And how is it that the children of those who have been made stars are punished in Hades, — Atlas loaded, Tantalus tortured with thirst, Sisyphus pushing a stone, Tityus thrust through the bowels, Ixion continually rolled round a wheel? How is it that these divine lovers made stars of the women whom they defiled, but gave no such grace to these?

Chap. XXIII. — *The gods no gods*

"'They were not gods, then, but representations of tyrants. For a certain tomb is shown among the Caucasian mountains, not in heaven, but in earth, as that of Kronus, a barbarous man and a devourer of children. Further, the tomb of the lascivious Zeus, so famed in story, who in like manner devoured his own daughter Metis, is to be seen in Crete, and those of Pluto and Poseidon in the Acherusian lake; and that of Helius in Astra, and of Selene in Carrae, of Hermes in Hermopolis, of Ares in Thrace, of Aphrodite in Cyprus, of Dionysus in Thebes, and of the rest in other places. At all events, the tombs are shown of those that I have named: for they were men, and in respect of these things, wicked men and magicians. For else they should not have become despots — I mean Zeus, renowned in story, and Dionysus — but that by changing their forms they prevailed over whom they pleased, for whatever purpose they designed.

Chap. XXIV. — *If a principle he goody carry it out*

"'But if we must emulate their lives, let us imitate not only their adulteries, but also their banquets. For Kronus devoured his own children, and Zeus in like manner his own daughter. And what must I say? Pelops served as a supper for all the gods. Wherefore let us also, before unhallowed marriages, perpetrate a supper like that of the gods; for thus the supper would be worthy of the marriages. But this you would never consent to; no more will I to adultery. Besides this, you threaten me with the anger of Eros as of a powerful god. Eros is not a god, as I conceive him, but a desire occurring from the temperament of the living creature in order to the perpetuation of life, according to the foresight of Him who worketh all things, that the whole race may not fail, but by reason of pleasure another may be produced out of the substance of one who shall die, springing forth by lawful marriage, that he may know to sustain his own father in old age. And this those born from adultery cannot do, not having the nature of affection towards those who have begotten them.

Chap. XXV. — *Better to marry than to burn*

"'Since, therefore, the erotic desire occurs for the sake of continuation and legitimate increasing, as I have said, it behoves parents providing for the chastity of their children to anticipate the desire, by imbuing them with instruction by means of chaste books, and to accustom them beforehand by excellent discourses; for custom is a second nature. And in addition to this, frequently to remind them of the punishments appointed by the laws, that, using fear as a bridle, they may not run on in wicked pleasures. And it behoves them also, before the springing of the desire, to satisfy the natural passion of puberty by marriage, first persuading them not to look upon the beauty of another woman.

Chap. XXVI. — *Close of the answer*

"'For our mind, whenever it is impressed delightfully with the image of a beloved one, always seeing the form as in a mirror, is tormented by the recollection; and if it do not obtain its desire, it contrives ways of obtaining it; but if it do obtain it, it is rather increased, like fire having a supply of wood, and especially when there is no fear impressed upon the soul of the lover before the rise of passion. For as water extinguishes fire, so fear is the extinguisher of unreasonable desire. Whence I, having learned from a certain Jew both to understand and to do the things that are pleasing to God, am not to be entrapped into adultery by your lying fables. But may God help you in your wish and efforts to be chaste, and afford a remedy to your soul burning with love.'

Chap. XXVII. — *A reason for hatred*

"When Appion heard the pretended answer, he said: 'Is it without reason that I hate the Jews? Here now some Jew has fallen in with her, and has converted her to his religion, and persuaded her to chastity, and it is henceforth impossible that she ever have intercourse with another man; for these fellows, setting God before them as the universal inspector of actions, are extremely persistent in chastity, as being unable to be concealed from Him.'

Chap. XXVIII. — *The hoax confessed*

"When I heard this, I said to Appion: 'Now I shall confess the truth to you. I was not enamoured of the woman, or of any one else, my soul being exceedingly spent upon other desires, and upon the investigation of true doctrines. And till now, although I have examined many doctrines of philosophers, I have inclined to none of them, excepting only that of the Jews, — a certain merchant of theirs having sojourned here in Rome, selling linen clothes, and a fortunate meeting having set simply before me the doctrine of the unity of God.'

Chap. XXIX. — *Appion's resentment*

"Then Appion, having heard from me the truth, with his unreasonable hatred of the Jews, and neither knowing nor wishing to know what their faith is, being senselessly angry, forthwith quitted Rome in silence. And as this is my first meeting with him since then, I naturally expect his anger in consequence. However, I shall ask him in your presence what he has to say concerning those who are called gods, whose lives, fabled to be filled with all passions, are constantly celebrated to the people, in order to their imitation; while, besides their human passions, as I have said, their graves are also shown in different places."

Chap. XXX. — *A discussion promised*

The others having heard these things from me, and desiring to learn what would ensue, accompanied me to visit Appion. And we found him bathed, and sitting at a table furnished. Wherefore we inquired but little into the matter concerning the gods. But he, understanding, I suppose, our wish, promised that next day he would have something to say about the gods, and appointed to us the same place where he would converse with us. And we, as soon as he had promised, thanked him, and departed, each one to his home.

[1] We have adopted the punctuation of Wieseler.
[2] I have no doubt that this is the general meaning; but the text is hopelessly corrupt.
[3] This from a marginal reading.
[4] I suspect it should rather be *impellers,* reading φερόντων for ἐρώντων.

Homily VI

Chap. I. — *Clement meets Appion*

And on the third day, when I came with my friends to the appointed place in Tyre, I found Appion sitting between Anubion and Athenodorus, and waiting for us, along with many other learned men. But in no wise dismayed, I greeted them, and sat down opposite Appion. And in a little he began to speak: "I wish to start from the following point, and to come with all speed at once to the question. Before you, my son Clement, joined us, my friend Anubion here, and Athenodorus, who yesterday were among those who heard you discourse, were reporting to me what you said of the numerous false accusations I brought against the gods when I was visiting you in Rome, at the time you were shamming love, how I charged them with paederasty, lasciviousness, and numerous incests of all kinds. But, my son, you ought to have known that I was not in earnest when I wrote such things about the gods, but was concealing the truth, from my love to you. That truth, however, if it so please you, you may hear from me now.

Chap. II. — *The myths are not to be taken literally*

"The wisest of the ancients, men who had by hard labour learned all truth, kept the path of knowledge hid from those who were unworthy and had no taste for lessons in divine things. For it is not really true that from Ouranos and his mother Ge were born twelve children, as the myth counts them: six sons, Okeanos, Koios, Krios, Hyperion, Japetos, Kronos; and six daughters, Thea, Themis, Mnemosyne, Demeter, Tethys, and Rhea. Nor that Kronos, with the knife of adamant, mutilated his father Ouranos, as you say, and threw the part into the sea; nor that Aphrodite sprang from the drops of blood which flowed from it; nor that Kronos associated with Rhea, and devoured his first-begotten son Pluto, because a certain saving of Prometheus led him to fear that a child born from him would wax stronger than himself, and spoil him of his kingdom; nor that he devoured in the same way Poseidon, his second child; nor that, when Zeus was born next, his mother Rhea concealed him, and when Kronos asked for him that he might devour him, gave him a stone instead; nor that this, when it was devoured, pressed those who had been previously devoured, and forced them out, so that Pluto, who was devoured first, came out first, and after him Poseidon, and then Zeus; [1] nor that Zeus, as the story goes, preserved by the wit of his mother, ascended into heaven, and spoiled his father of the kingdom; nor that he punished his father's brothers; nor that he came down to lust after mortal women; nor that he associated with his sisters, and daughters, and sisters-in-law, and was guilty of shameful paederasty; nor that he devoured his daughter Metis, in order that from her he might make Athene be born out of his own brain (and from his thigh might bear Dionysos, [2] who is said to have been rent in pieces by the Titans); nor that he held a feast at the marriage of Peleus and Thetis; nor that he excluded Eris (discord) from the marriage; nor that Eris on her part, thus dishonoured, contrived an occasion of quarrelling and discord among the feasters: nor that she took a golden apple from the gardens of the Hesperides, and wrote on it 'For the fair.' And then they fable how Hera, and Athena, and Aphrodite, found the apple, and quarrelling about it, came to Zeus; and he did not decide it for them, but sent them by Hermes to the shepherd Paris, to be judged of their beauty. But there was no such judging of the goddesses; nor did Paris give the apple to Aphrodite; nor did Aphrodite, being thus honoured, honour him in return, by giving him Helen to wife. For the honour bestowed by the goddess could never have furnished a pretext for a universal war, and that to the ruin of him who was honoured, himself nearly related to the race of Aphrodite. But, my son, as I said, such stories have a peculiar and philosophical meaning, which can be allegorically set forth in such a way that you yourself would listen with wonder." And I said, "I beseech you not to torment me with delay." And he said, "Do not be afraid; for I shall lose no time, but commence at once.

Chap. III. — *Appion proceeds to interpret the myths*

"There was once a time when nothing existed but chaos and a confused mixture of orderless elements, which were as yet simply heaped together. This nature testifies, and great men have been of opinion that it was so. Of these great men I shall bring forward to you him who excelled them all in wisdom, Homer, where he says, with a reference to the original confused mass, 'But may you all become water and earth;' [3] implying that from these all things had their origin, and that all things return to their first state, which is chaos, when the watery and earthy subtances are separated. And Hesiod in the *Theogony* says, 'Assuredly chaos was the very first to come into being.' [4] Now, by 'come into being,' he evidently means that chaos came into being, as having a beginning, and did not always exist, without beginning. And Orpheus likens chaos to an egg, in which was the confused mixture of the primordial elements. This chaos, which Orpheus calls an egg, is taken for granted by Hesiod, having a beginning, produced from infinite matter, and originated in the following way.

Chap. IV. — *Origin of chaos*

"This matter, of four kinds, and endowed with life, was an entire infinite abyss, so to speak, in eternal stream, borne about without order, and forming every now and then countless but ineffectual combinations (which therefore it dissolved again from want of order); ripe indeed, but not able to be bound so as to generate a living creature. And once it chanced that this infinite sea, which was thus by its own nature driven about with a natural motion, flowed in an orderly manner from the same to the same (back on itself), like a whirlpool, mixing the substances in such a way that from each [5] there flowed down the middle of the universe (as in the funnel of a mould) precisely that which was most useful and suitable for the generation of a living creature. This was carried down by the all-carrying whirlpool, drew to itself the surrounding spirit, and having been so conceived that it was very fertile, formed a separate substance. For just as a bubble is usually formed in water, so everything round about contributed to the conception of this ball-like globe. Then there came forth to the light, after it had been conceived in itself, and was borne upwards by the divine spirit which surrounded it, [6] perhaps the greatest thing ever born; a piece of workmanship, so to speak, having life in it which had been conceived from that entire infinite abyss, in shape like an egg, and as swift as a bird.

Chap. V. — *Kronos and Rhea explained*

"Now you must think of Kronos as time (*chronos*) and Rhea as the flowing (*rheon*) of the watery substance. For the whole body of matter was borne about for some time, before it brought forth, like an egg, the sphere-like, all-embracing heaven (*ouranos*), which at first was full of productive marrow, so that it was able to produce out of itself elements and colours of all sorts, while from the one substance and the one colour it produced all kinds of forms. For as a peacock's egg seems to have only one colour, while potentially it has in it all the colours of the animal that is to be, so this living egg, conceived out of infinite matter, when set in motion by the underlying and ever-flowing matter, produces many different forms. For within the circumference a certain living creature, which is both male and female, is formed by the skill of the indwelling divine spirit. This Orpheus calls Phanes, because when it appeared (*phaneis*) the universe shone forth from it, with the lustre of that most glorious of the elements, fire, perfected in moisture. Nor is this incredible, since in glowworms nature gives us to see a moist light.

Chap. VI. — *Phanes and Pluto*

"This egg, then, which was the first substance, growing somewhat hot, was broken by the living creature within, and then there took shape and came forth something; [7] such as Orpheus also speaks of, where he says, 'when the capacious egg was broken,' [8] etc. And so by the mighty power of that which appeared (*phaneis*) and came forth, the globe attained coherency, and maintained order, while it itself took its seat, as it were, on the summit of heaven, there in ineffable mystery diffusing light through endless ages. But the productive matter left inside the globe, separated the substances of all things. For first its lower part, just like dregs, sank downwards of its own weight; and this they called Pluto from its gravity, and weight, and great quantity (*polu*) of underlying matter, styling it the king of Hades and the dead.

Chap. VII. — *Poseidon, Zeus, and Metis*

"When, then, they say that this primordial substance, although most filthy and rough, was devoured by Kronos, that is, time, this is to be understood in a physical sense, as meaning that it sank downwards. And the water which flowed together after this first sediment, and floated on the surface of the first substance, they called Poseidon. And then what remained, the purest and noblest of all, for it was translucent fire, they called Zeus, from its glowing (*zeousa*) nature. Now since fire ascends, this was not swallowed, and made to descend by time or Kronos; but, as I said, the fiery substance, since it has life in it, and naturally ascends, flew right up into the air, which from its purity is very intelligent. By his own proper heat, then, Zeus — that is, the glowing substance — draws up what is left in the underlying moisture, to wit, that very strong [9] and divine spirit which they called Metis.

Chap. VIII. — *Pallas and Hera*

"And this, when it had reached the summit of the aether, was devoured by it (moisture being mixed with heat, so to say); and causing in it that ceaseless palpitation, it begat intelligence, which they call Pallas from this palpitating (*pallesthai*). And this is artistic wisdom, by which the aetherial artificer wrought out the whole world. And from all-pervading Zeus, that is, from this very hot aether, air (*aer*) extends all the way to our earth; and this they call Hera. Wherefore, because it has come below the aether, which is the purest substance (just as a woman, as regards purity, is inferior), when the two were compared to see which was the better, she was rightly regarded as the sister of Zeus, in respect of her origin from the same substance, but as his spouse, as being inferior like a wife.

Chap. IX. — *Artemis*

"And Hera we understand to be a happy tempering of the atmosphere, and therefore she is very fruitful; but Athena, as they call Pallas, was reckoned a virgin, because on account of the intense heat she could produce nothing. And in a similar fashion Artemis is explained: for her they take as the lowest depth of air, and so they called her a virgin, because she could not bear any thing on account of the extreme cold. And that troubled and drunken composition which arises from the upper and lower vapours they called Dionysus, as troubling the intellect. And the water under the earth, which is in nature indeed one, but which flows through all the paths of earth, and is divided into many parts, they called Osiris, as being cut in pieces. And they understand Adonis as favourable seasons. Aphrodite as coition and generation, Demeter as the earth, the Girl (Proserpine) as seeds; and Dionysus some understand as the vine.

Chap. X. — *All such stories are allegorical*

"And I must ask you to think of all such stories as embodying some such allegory. Look on Apollo as the wandering Sun (*peri-polôn*), a son of Zeus, who was also called Mithras, as completing the period of a year. And these said transformations of the all-pervading Zeus must be regarded as the numerous changes of the seasons, while his numberless wives you must understand to be years, or generations. For the power which proceeds from the aether and passes through the air unites with all the years and generations in turn, and continually varies them, and so produces or destroys the crops.

And ripe fruits are called his children, the barrenness of some seasons being referred to unlawful unions."

Chap. XI. — *Clement has heard all this before*

While Appion was allegorizing in this way, I became plunged in thought, and seemed not to be following what he was saying. So he interrupted his discourse, and said to me, "If you do not follow what I am saying, why should I speak at all?" And I answered, "Do not suppose that I do not understand what you say. I understand it thoroughly; and that the more that this is not the first time I have heard it. And that you may know that I am not ignorant of these things, I shall epitomize what you have said, and supply in their order, as I have heard them from others, the allegorical interpretations of those stories you have omitted." And Appion said: "Do so."

Chap. XII. — *Epitome of Appion's explanation*

And I answered: "I shall not at present speak particularly of that living egg, which was conceived by a happy combination out of infinite matter, and from which, when it was broken, the masculo-feminine Phanes leaped forth, as some say. I say little about all that, up to the point when this broken globe attained coherency, there being left in it some of its marrow-like matter; and I shall briefly run over the description of what took place in it by the agency of this matter, with all that followed. For from Kronos and Rhea were born, as you say — that is, by time and matter — first Pluto, who represents the sediment which settled down; and then Poseidon, the liquid substance in the middle, [10] which floated over the heavier body below; and the third child — that is, Zeus — is the aether, and is highest of all. It was not devoured; but as it is a fiery power, and naturally ascends, it flew up as with a bound to the very highest aether.

Chap. XIII. — *Kronos and Aphrodite*

"And the bonds of Kronos are the binding together of heaven and earth, as I have heard others allegorizing; and his mutilation is the separation and parting of the elements; for they all were severed and separated, according to their respective natures, that each kind might be arranged by itself. And time no longer begets anything; but the things which have been begotten of it, by a law of nature, produce their successors. And the Aphrodite who emerged from the sea is the fruitful substance which arises out of moisture, with which the warm spirit mixing, causes that sexual desire, and perfects the beauty of the world.

Chap. XIV. — *Peleus and Thetis, Prometheus, Achilles, and Polyxena.*

"And the marriage banquet, at which Zeus held the feast on the occasion of the marriage of the Nereid Thetis and the beautiful Peleus, has in it this allegory, — that you may know, Appion, that you are not the only one from whom I have heard this sort of thing. the banquet, then, is the world, and the twelve are these heavenly props of the Fates, [11] called the Zodiac. Prometheus is foresight (*prometheia*), by which all things arose: Peleus is clay (*pelos*), namely, that which was collected [12] from the earth and mixed with Nereis, or water, to produce man; and from the mixing of the two, i.e. water and earth, the first offspring was not begotten, but fashioned complete, and called Achilles, because he never put his lips (*cheile*) to the breast. [13] Still in the bloom of life, he is slain by an arrow while desiring to have Polyxena, that is, something other than the truth, and foreign (*xene*) to it, death stealing on him through a wound in his foot.

Chap. XV. — *The judgment of Paris*

"Then Hera, and Athena, and Aphrodite, and Eris, and the apple, and Hermes, and the judgment, and the shepherd, have some such hidden meaning as the following: — Hera is dignity; Athena, manliness; Aphrodite, pleasure; Hermes, language, which interprets (*hermeneutikos*) thought; the shepherd Paris, unreasoned and brutish passion. Now if, in the prime of life, reason, that shepherd of the soul, is brutish, does not regard its own advantage, will have nothing to do with manliness and temperance, chooses only pleasure, and gives the prize to lust alone, bargaining that it is to receive in return from lust what may delight it, — he who thus judges incorrectly will choose pleasure to his own destruction and that of his friends. And Eris is jealous spite; and the golden apples of the Hesperides are perhaps riches, by which occasionally even temperate persons like Hera are seduced, and manly ones like Athena are made jealous, so that they do things which do not become them, and the soul's beauty like Aphrodite is destroyed under the guise of refinement. To speak briefly, in all men riches provoke evil discord.

Chap. XVI. — *Hercules*

"And Hercules, who slew the serpent which led and guarded riches, is the true philosophical reason which, free from all wickedness, wanders all over the world, visiting the souls of men, and chastising all it meets, — namely, men like fierce lions, or timid stags, or savage boars, or multiform hydras; and so with all the other fabled labours of Hercules, they all have a hidden reference to moral valour. But these instances must suffice, for all our time would be insufficient if we were to go over each one.

Chap. XVII. — *They are blameworthy who invented such stories*

"Now, since these things can be clearly, profitably, and without prejudice to piety, set forth in an open and straightforward manner, I wonder you call those men sensible and wise who concealed them under crooked riddles, and overlaid them with filthy stories, and thus, as if impelled by an evil spirit, deceived almost all men. For either these things are not riddles, but real crimes of the gods, in which case they should not have been exposed to contempt, nor should these their deeds have been set before men at all as models; or things falsely attributed to the gods were set forth in an allegory, and then, Appion, they whom you call wise erred, in that, by concealing under unworthy stories things in themselves worthy, they led men to sin, and that not without dishonouring those whom they believed to be gods.

Chap. XVIII. — *The same*

"Wherefore do not suppose that they were wise men, but rather evil spirits, who could cover honourable actions with wicked stories, in order that they who wish to imitate their betters may emulate these deeds of so-called gods, which yesterday in my discourse I spoke so freely of, — namely, their parricides, their murders of their children, their incests of all kinds, their shameless adulteries and countless impurities. The most impious of them are those who wish these stories to be believed, in order that they may not be ashamed when they do the like. If they had been disposed to act reverently, they ought, as I said a little ago, even if the gods really did the things which are sung of them, to have veiled their indecencies under more seemly stories, and not, on the contrary, as you say they did, when the deeds of the gods were honourable, clothed them in wicked and indecent forms, which, even when interpreted, can only be understood by much labour; and when they were understood by some, they indeed got for their much toil the privilege of not being deceived, which they might have had without the toil, while they who were deceived were utterly ruined. (Those, however, who trace the allegories to a more honourable source I do not object to; as, for instance, those who explain one allegory by saying that it was wisdom which sprang from the head of Zeus.) On the whole, it seems to me more probable that wicked men, robbing the gods of their honour, ventured to promulgate these insulting stories.

Chap. XIX. — *None of these allegories are consistent*

"Nor do we find the poetical allegory about any of the gods consistent with itself. To go no further than the fashioning of the universe, the poets now say that nature was the first cause of the whole creation, now that it was mind. For, say they, the first moving and mixing of the elements came from nature, but it was the foresight of mind which arranged them in order. Even when they assert that it was nature which fashioned the universe, being unable absolutely to demonstrate this on account of the traces of design in the work, they inweave the foresight of mind in such a way that they are able to entrap even the wisest. But we say to them: If the world arose from self-moved nature, how did it ever take proportion and shape, which cannot come but from a superintending wisdom, and can be comprehended only by knowledge, which alone can trace such things? If, on the other hand, it is by wisdom that all things subsist and maintain order, how can it be that those things arose from self-moved chance?

Chap. XX. — *These gods were really wicked magicians*

"Then those who chose to make dishonourable allegories of divine things — as, for instance, that Metis was devoured by Zeus — have fallen into a dilemma, because they did not see that they who in these stories about the gods indirectly taught physics, denied the very existence of the gods, resolving all kinds of gods into mere allegorical representations of the various substances of the universe. And so it is more likely that the gods these persons celebrate were some sort of wicked magicians, who were in reality wicked men, but by magic assumed different shapes, committed adulteries, and took away life, and thus to the men of old who did not understand magic seemed to be gods by the things they did; and the bodies and tombs of these men are to be seen in many towns.

Chap. XXI. — *Their graves are still to be seen*

"For instance, as I have mentioned already, in the Caucasian mountains there is shown the tomb of a certain Kronos, a man, and a fierce monarch who slew his children. And the son of this man, called Zeus, became worse [than his father]; and having by the power of magic been declared ruler of the universe, he committed many adulteries, and inflicted punishment on his father and uncles, and so died; and the Cretans show his tomb. And in Mesopotamia there lie buried a certain Helios at Atir, and a certain Selene at Carrhae. A certain Hermes, a man, lies buried in Egypt; Ares in Thrace; Aphrodite in Cyprus; Aesculapius in Epidaurus; and the tombs of many other such persons are to be seen.

Chap. XXII. — *Their contemporaries, therefore, did not look on them as gods*

"Thus, to right thinking men, it is clear that they were admitted to be mortals. And their contemporaries, knowing that they were mortal, when they died paid them no more heed; and it was length of time which clothed them with the glory of gods. Nor need you wonder that they who lived in the times of Aesculapius and Hercules were deceived, or the contemporaries of Dionysus or any other of the men of that time, when even Hector in Ilium, and Achilles in the island of Leuce, are worshipped by the inhabitants of those places; and the Opuntines worship Patroclus, and the Rhodians Alexander of Macedon.

Chap. XXIII. — *The Egyptians pay divine honours to a man*

"Moreover, among the Egyptians even to the present day, a man is worshipped as a god before his death. And this truly is a small impiety, that the Egyptians give divine honours to a man in his lifetime; but what is of all things most absurd is, that they worship birds and creeping things, and all kinds of beasts. For the mass of men neither think nor do anything with discretion. But look, I pray you, at what is most disgraceful of all: he who is with them the father of gods and men is said by them to have had intercourse with Leda; and many of them set up in public a painting of this, writing above it the name Zeus. To punish this insult, I could wish that they would paint their own present king in such base embraces as they have dared to do with Zeus, and set it up in public, that from the anger of a temporary monarch, and him a mortal, they might learn to render honour where it is due. This I say to you, not as myself already knowing the true God; but I am happy to say that even if I do not know who is God, I think I at least know clearly what God is.

Chap. XXIV. — *What is not God*

"And first, then, the four original elements cannot be God, because they have a cause. Nor can that mixing be God, nor that compounding, nor that generating, nor that globe which surrounds the visible universe; nor the dregs which flow together in Hades, nor the water which floats over them; nor the fiery substance, nor the air which extends from it to our earth. For the four elements, if they lay outside one another, could not have been mixed together so as to generate animal life without some great artificer. If they have always been united, even in this case they are fitted together by an artistic mind to what is requisite for the limbs and parts of animals, that they may be able to preserve their respective proportions, may have a clearly defined shape, and that all the inward parts may attain the fitting coherency. In the same way also the positions suitable for each are determined, and that very beautifully, by the artificer mind. To be brief, in all other things which a living creature must have, this great being of the world is in no respect wanting.

Chap. XXV. — *The universe is the product of mind*

"Thus we are shut up to the supposition that there is an unbegotten artificer, who brought the elements together, if they were separate; or, if they were together, artistically blended them so as to generate life, and perfected from all one work. For it cannot be that a work which is completely wise can be made without a mind which is greater than it. Nor will it do to say that love is the artificer of all things, or desire, or power, or any such thing. All these are liable to change, and transient in their very nature. Nor can that be God which is moved by another, much less what is altered by time and nature, and can be annihilated."

Chap. XXVI. — *Peter arrives from Caesarea*

While I was saying these things to Appion, Peter drew near from Caesarea, and in Tyre the people were flocking together, hurrying to meet him and unite in an expression of gratification at his visit. And Appion withdrew, accompanied by Anubion and Athenodorus only; but the rest of us hurried to meet Peter, and I was the first to greet him at the gate, and I led him towards the inn. When we arrived, we dismissed the people; and when he deigned to ask what had taken place, I concealed nothing, but told him of Simon's slanders, and the monstrous shapes he had taken, and all the diseases he had sent after the sacrificial feast, and that some of the sick persons were still there in Tyre, while others had gone on with Simon to Sidon just as I arrived, hoping to be cured by him, but that I had heard that none of them had been cured by him. I also told Peter of the controversy I had had with Appion; and he, from his love to me, and desiring to encourage me, praised and blessed me. Then, having supped, he betook himself to the rest the fatigues of his journey rendered so necessary.

[1] The passage seems to be corrupt.
[2] The common story about Dionysus is, that he was the unborn son, not of Metis, but of Semele. Wieseler supposes that some words have fallen out, or that the latter part of the sentence is a careless interpolation.
[3] *Iliad,* VII. 99.
[4] L. 116.
[5] This is the emendation of Davisius. The Greek has ἐξ ἀχουστοῦ; the Latin, "mirum in raodum."' Wieseler suggests ἐξαχονιστόν.
[6] This is Wieseler's emendation for "received."
[7] Wieseler corrects to "some such being," etc.; and below, "of him who appeared," etc.; and "he took his seat."
[8] The first word of this quotation gives no sense, and has been omitted in the translation. Lobeck suggests "at its prime;" Hermann, "Heracapeian;" Duentzer, "ancient;" and Wieseler, "white."
[9] The Paris MS. has "very fine."
[10] This is "Wieseler's conjecture.
[11] The Latin takes "moira" in the sense of "district," and translates, "these props of the districts of the sky."
[12] This is Wieseler's conjecture for the reading of the MSS., "contrived."
[13] This is Schwegler's restoration of the passage. Davisius proposes, "He is in the bloom of life, at which tune if any one desires," etc.

Homily VII

Chap. I. — *Peter addresses the people*

And on the fourth day of our stay in Tyre, Peter went out about daybreak, and there met him not a few of the dwellers round about, with very many of the inhabitants of Tyre itself, who cried out, and said, "God through you have mercy upon us, God through you heal us!" And Peter stood on a high stone, that all might see him; and having greeted them in a godly manner, thus began;

Chap. II. — *Reason of Simon's power*

"God, who created the heavens and the whole universe, does not want occasion for the salvation of those who would be saved. Wherefore let no one, in seeming evils, rashly charge Him with unkindness to man. For men do not know the issue of those things which happen to them, nay, suspect that the result will be evil; but God knows that they will turn out well. So is it in the case of Simon. He is a power of the left hand of God, and has authority to do harm to those who know not God, so that he has been able to involve you in diseases; but by these very diseases, which have been permitted to come upon you by the good providence of God, you, seeking and finding him who is able to cure, have been compelled to submit to the will of God on the occasion of the cure of the body, and to think of believing, in order that in this way you may have your souls as well as your bodies in a healthy state.

Chap. III. — *The remedy*

"Now I have been told, that after he had sacrificed an ox he feasted you in the middle of the forum, and that you, being carried away with much wine, made friends with not only the evil demons, but their prince also, and that in this way the most of you were seized by these sicknesses, unwittingly drawing upon yourselves with your own hands the sword of destruction. For the demons would never have had power over you, had not you first supped with their prince. For thus from the beginning was a law laid by God, the Creator of all things, on each of the two princes, him of the right hand and him of the left, that neither should have power over any one whom they might wish to benefit or to hurt, unless first he had sat down at the same table with them. As, then, when you partook of meat offered to idols, you became servants to the prince of evil, in like manner, if you cease from these things, and flee for refuge to God through the good Prince of His right hand, honouring Him without sacrifices, by doing whatsoever He wills, know of a truth that not only will your bodies be healed, but your souls also will become healthy. For He only, destroying with His left hand, can quicken with His right; He only can both smite and raise the fallen.

Chap. IV. — *The golden rule*

"Wherefore, as then ye were deceived by the forerunner Simon, and so became dead in your souls to God, and were smitten in your bodies; so now, if you repent, as I said, and submit to those things which are well-pleasing to God, you may get new strength to your bodies, and recover your soul's health. And the things which are well-pleasing to God are these: to pray to Him, to ask from Him, recognising that He is the giver of all things, and gives with discriminating law; to abstain from the table of devils, not to taste dead flesh, not to touch blood; to be washed from all pollution; and the rest in one word, — as the God-fearing Jews have heard, do you also hear, and be of one mind in many bodies; let each man be minded to do to his neighbour those good things he wishes for himself. And you may all find out what *is* good, by holding some such conversation as the following with yourselves: You would not like to be murdered; do not murder another man: you would not like your wife to be seduced by another; do not you commit adultery: you would not like any of your things to be stolen from you; steal nothing from another. And so understanding by yourselves what is reasonable, and doing it, you will become dear to God, and will obtain healing; otherwise in the life which now is your bodies will be tormented, and in that which is to come your souls will be punished."

Chap. V. — *Peter departs for Sidon*

After Peter had spent a few days in teaching them in this way, and in healing them, they were baptized. And after that, [1] all sat down together in the market-places in sackcloth and ashes, grieving because of his other wondrous works, and repenting their former sins. And when they of Sidon heard it, they did likewise, and sent to beseech Peter, since they could not come themselves for their diseases. And Peter did not spend many days in Tyre; but when he had instructed all its inhabitants, and freed them from all manners of diseases, and had founded a church, and set over it as bishop one of the elders who were with him, he departed for Sidon. But when Simon heard that Peter was coming, he straightway fled to Beyrout with Appion and his friends.

Chap. VI. — *Peter in Sidon*

And as Peter entered Sidon, they brought many in couches, and laid them before him. And he said to them: "Think not, I pray you, that I can do anything to heal you, who am a mortal man, myself subject to many evils. But I shall not refuse to show you the way in which you must be saved. For I have learned from the Prophet of truth the conditions fore-ordained of God before the foundation of the world; that is to say, the evil deeds which if men do He has ordained that they shall be injured by the prince of evil, and in like manner the good deeds for which He has decreed that they who have believed in Him as their Physician shall have their bodies made whole, and their souls established in safety.

Chap. VII. — *The two paths*

"Knowing, then, these good and evil deeds, I make known unto you as it were two paths, and I shall show you by which travellers are lost and by which they are saved, being guided of God. The path of the lost, then, is broad and very smooth — it ruins them without troubling them; but the path of the saved is narrow, rugged, and in the end it saves, not without much toil, those who have journeyed through it. And these two paths are presided over by unbelief and faith; and these journey through the path of unbelief, those who have preferred pleasure, on account of which they have forgotten the day of judgment, doing that which is not pleasing to God, and not caring to save their souls by the word, and have not anxiously sought their own good. Truly they know not that the counsels of God are not like men's counsels; for, in the first place. He knows the thoughts of all men, and all must give an account not only of their actions, but also of their thoughts. And their sin is much less who strive to understand well and fail, than that of those who do not at all strive after good things. Because it has pleased God that he who errs in his knowledge of good, as men count errors, should be saved after being slightly punished. But they who have taken no care at all to know the better way, even though they may have done countless other good deeds, if they have not stood in the service He has Himself appointed, come under the charge of indifference, and are severely punished, and utterly destroyed.

Chap. VIII. — *The service of God's appointment*

"And this is the service He has appointed: To worship Him only, and trust only in the Prophet of truth, and to be baptized for the remission of sins, and thus by this pure baptism to be born again unto God by saving water; to abstain from the table of devils, that is, from food offered to idols, from dead carcasses, from animals which have been suffocated or caught by wild beasts, and from blood; not to live any longer impurely; to wash after intercourse; that the women on their part should keep the law of purification; that all should be sober-minded, given to good works, refraining from wrong-doing looking for eternal life from the all-powerful God, and asking with prayer and continual supplication that they may win it." Such was Peter's counsel to the men of Sidon also. And in few days many repented and believed, and were healed. And Peter having founded a church, and set over it as bishop one of the elders who were with him, left Sidon.

Chap. IX. — *Simon attacks Peter*

No sooner had he reached Beyrout than an earthquake took place; and the multitude, running to Peter, said, "Help us, for we are afraid we shall all utterly perish." Then Simon ventured, along with Appion and Anubion and Athenodorus, and the rest of his companions, to cry out to the people against Peter in public: "Flee, friends, from this man! he is a magician; trust us, he it was who caused this earthquake: he sent us these diseases to terrify us, as if he were God Himself." And many such false charges did Simon and his friends bring against Peter, as one who could do things above human power. But as soon as the people gave him a moment's quiet, Peter with surprising boldness gave a little laugh, and said, "Friends, I admit that I can do, God willing, what these men say; and more than that, I am ready, if you do not believe what I say, to overturn your city from top to bottom."

Chap. X. — *Simon is driven away*

And the people were afraid, and promised to do whatever he should command. "Let none of you, then," said Peter, "either hold conversation with these sorcerers, or have anything to do with them." And as soon as the people heard this concise command, they took up sticks, and pursued them till they had driven them wholly out of the town. And they who were sick and possessed with devils came and cast themselves at Peter's feet. And he seeing all this, and anxious to free them from their terror, said to them:

Chap. XI. — *The way of salvation*

"Were I able to cause earthquakes, and do all that I wish, I assure you I would not destroy Simon and his friends (for not to destroy men am I sent), but would make him my friend, that he might no longer, by his slanders against my preaching the truth, hinder the salvation of many. But if you believe me, he himself is a magician; he is a slanderer; he is a minister of evil to them who know not the truth. Therefore he has power to bring diseases on sinners, having the sinners themselves to help him in his power over them. But I am a servant of God the Creator of all things, and a disciple of His Prophet who is at His right hand. Wherefore I, being His apostle, preach the truth: to serve a good man I drive away diseases, for I am His second messenger, since first the disease comes, but after that the healing. By that evil-working magician, then, you were stricken with disease because you revolted from God. By me, if you believe on Him ye shall be cured; and so having had experience that He is able, you may turn to good works, and have your souls saved."

Chap. XII. — *Peter goes to Byblus and Tripolis*

As he said these things, all fell on their knees before his feet. And he, lifting up his hands to heaven, prayed to God, and healed them all by his simple prayer alone. And he remained not many days in Beyrout; but after he had accustomed many to the service of the one God, and had baptized them, and had set over them a bishop from the elders who were with him, he went to Byblus. And when he came there, and learned that Simon had not waited for them for a day, but had gone straightway to Tripolis, he remained there only a few days; and after that he had healed not a few, and exercised them in the Scriptures, he followed in Simon's track to Tripolis, preferring to pursue him rather than flee from him.

[1] We have adopted Wieseler's emendation. The text may be translated thus: "And after that, among his other -wondrous deeds, all the rest (who had not been baptized) sat down," etc.

Homily VIII

Chap. I. — *Peters arrival at Tripolis*

Now, as Peter was entering Tripolis, the people from Tyre and Siclon, Berytus and Byblas, who were eager [1] to get instruction, and many from the neighbourhood, entered along with him; and not least were there gatherings of the multitudes from the city itself wishing to see him. Therefore there met with us in the suburbs the brethren who had been sent forth by him to ascertain as well other particulars respecting the city, as the proceedings of Simon, and to come and explain them. They received him, and conducted him to the house of Maroones.

Chap. II. — *Peter's thoughtfulness*

But he, when he was at the very gate of his lodging, turned round, and promised to the multitudes that after the next day he would converse with them on the subject of religion. And when he had gone in, the forerunners assigned lodgings to those who had come with him. And the hosts and the entertainers did not fall short of the desire of those who sought hospitality. But Peter, knowing nothing of this, being asked by us to partake of food, said that he would not himself partake until those who had come with him were settled. And on our assuring him that this was already done, all having received them eagerly by reason of their affection towards him, so that those were grieved beyond measure who had no guests to entertain, — Peter hearing this, and being pleased with their eager philanthropy, blessed them and went out, and having bathed in the sea, partook of food with the forerunners; and then, the evening having come, he slept.

Chap. III. — *A conversation interrupted*

But awaking about the second cock-crowing, he found us astir. We were in all sixteen, viz. Peter himself, and I Clement, Nicetas and Aquila, and the twelve who bad preceded us. Having therefore saluted us, he said, "To-day, not being occupied with those without, we are free to be occupied with one another. Wherefore I shall tell you the things that happened after your departure from Tyre; and do you minutely relate to me what have been the doings of Simon here." While, therefore, we were answering one another by narratives on either side, one of our friends entered, and announced to Peter that Simon, learning of his arrival, had set off for Syria, and that the multitudes, thinking this one night to be like a year's time, and not able to wait for the appointment which he had made, were standing before the doors conversing with one another in knots and circles about the accusation brought by Simon, and how that, having raised their expectations, and promised that he would charge Peter when he came with many evils, he had fled by night when he knew of his arrival. "However," said he, "they are eager to hear you; and I know not whence some rumour has reached them to the effect that you are going to address them to-day. In order, therefore, that they may not when they are very tired be dismissed without reason, you yourself know what it is proper for you to do."

Chap. IV. — *Many called*

Then Peter, wondering at the eagerness of the multitudes, answered, "You see, brethren, how the words of our Lord are manifestly fulfilled. For I remember His saying, * Many shall come from the east and from the west, the north and the south, and shall recline on the bosoms of Abraham, and Isaac, and Jacob.' [2] 'But many,' said He also, 'are called, but few chosen.' [3] The coming, therefore, of these called ones is fulfilled. But inasmuch as it is not of themselves, but of God who has called them and caused them to come, on this account alone they have no reward, since it is not of themselves, but of Him who has wrought in them. But if, after being called, they do things that are excellent, for this is of themselves, then for this they shall have a reward.

Chap. V. — *Faith the gift of God*

"For even the Hebrews who believe Moses, and do not observe the things spoken by him, are not saved, unless they observe the things that were spoken to them. For their believing Moses was not of their own will, but of God, who said to Moses, 'Behold, I come to thee in a pillar of cloud, that the people may hear me speaking to thee, and may believe thee for ever.' [4] Since, therefore, both to the Hebrews and to those who are called from the Gentiles, believing in the teachers of truth is of God, while excellent actions are left to every one to do by his own judgment, the reward is righteously bestowed upon those who do well. For there would have been no need of Moses, or of the coming of Jesus, if of themselves they would have understood what is reasonable. Neither is there salvation in believing in teachers and calling them lords.

Chap. VI. — *Concealment and revelation*

"For on this account Jesus is concealed from the Jews, who have taken Moses as their teacher, and Moses is hidden from those who have believed Jesus. For, there being one teaching by both, God accepts him who has believed either of these. But believing a teacher is for the sake of doing the things spoken by God. And that this is so our Lord Himself says, 'I thank thee, Father of heaven and earth, because Thou hast concealed these things from the wise and elder, and hast revealed them to sucking babes.' [5] Thus God Himself has concealed a teacher from some, as foreknowing what they ought to do, and has revealed him to others, who are ignorant what they ought to do.

Chap. VII. — *Moses and Christ*

"Neither, therefore, are the Hebrews condemned on account of their ignorance of Jesus, by reason of Him who has concealed Him, if, doing the things [commanded] by Closes, they do not hate Him whom they do not know. Neither are those from among the Gentiles condemned, who know not Moses on account of Him who hath concealed him, provided that these also, doing the things spoken by Jesus, do not hate Him whom they do not know. And some will not be profited by calling the teachers lords, but not doing the works of servants. For on this account our Jesus Himself said to one who often called Him Lord, but did none of the things which He prescribed, 'Why call ye me Lord, Lord, and do not the things which I say?' [6] For it is not saying that will profit any one, but doing. By all means, therefore, is there need of good works. Moreover, if any one has been thought worthy to recognise both as preaching one doctrine, that man has been counted rich in God, understanding both the old things as new in time, and the new things as old."

Chap. VIII. — *A large congregation*

While Peter was thus speaking, the multitudes, as if they had been called by some one, entered into the place where Peter was. Then he, seeing a great multitude, like the smooth current of a river gently flowing towards him, said to Maroones, "Have you any place here that is better able to contain the crowd?" Then Maroones conducted him to a garden-plot in the open air, and the multitudes followed. But Peter, standing upon a base of a statue which was not very high, as soon as he had saluted the multitude in pious fashion, knowing that many of the crowd that stood by were tormented with demons and many sufferings of long standing, and [hearing them] shrieking with lamentation, and falling down [before him] in supplication, rebuked them, and commanded them to hold their peace; and promising healing to them after the discourse, began to speak on this wise: —

Chap. IX. — *"Vindicate the ways of God to men."*

"While beginning to discourse on the worship of God to those who are altogether ignorant of everything, and whose minds have been corrupted by the accusations of our adversary Simon, I have thought it necessary first of all to speak of the blamelessness of the God who hath made all things, starting from the occasion seasonably afforded by Him according to His providence, that it may be known how with good reason many are held by many demons, and subjected to strange sufferings, that in this the justice of God may appear; and that those who through ignorance blame Him, now may learn by good speaking and well-doing what sentiments they ought to hold, and recall themselves from their previous accusation, assigning ignorance as the cause of their evil presumption, in order that they may be pardoned.

Chap. X. — *The original law*

"But thus the matter stands. The only good God having made all things well, and having handed them over to man, who was made after His image, he who had been made breathing of the divinity of Him who made him, being a true prophet and knowing all things, for the honour of the Father who had given all things to him, and for the salvation of the sons born of him, as a genuine father preserving his affection towards the children born of him, and wishing them, for their advantage, to love God and be loved of Him, showed them the way which leads to His friendship, teaching them by what deeds of men the one God and Lord of all is pleased; and having exhibited to them the things that are pleasing to Him, appointed a perpetual law to all, which neither can be abrogated by enemies, nor is vitiated by any impious one, nor is concealed in any place, but which can be read by all. To them, therefore, by obedience to the law, all things were in abundance, — the fairest of fruits, fulness of years, freedom from grief and from disease, bestowed upon them without fear, with all salubrity of the air.

Chap. XI. — *Cause of the fall of man*

"But they, because they had at first no experience of evils, being insensible to the gift of good things, were turned to ingratitude by abundance of food and luxuries, so that they even thought that there is no Providence, since they had not by previous labour got good things as the reward of righteousness, inasmuch as no one of them had fallen into any suffering or disease, or any other necessity; so that, as is usual for men afflicted on account of wicked transgression, they should look about for the God who is able to heal them. [7] But immediately after their despite, which proceeded from fearlessness and secure luxury, a certain just punishment met them, as following from a certain arranged harmony, removing from them good things as having hurt them, and introducing evil things instead, as advantageous.

Chap. XII. — *Metamorphoses of the angels*

"For of the spirits who inhabit the heaven, the angels who dwell in the lowest region, being grieved at the ingratitude of men to God, asked that they might come into the life of men, that, really becoming men, by more intercourse they might convict those who had acted ungratefully towards Him, and might subject every one to adequate punishment. When, therefore, their petition was granted, they metamorphosed themselves into every nature; for, being of a more godlike substance, they are able easily to assume any form. So they became precious stones, and goodly pearl, and the most beauteous purple, and choice gold, and all matter that is held in most esteem. And they fell into the hands of some, and into the bosoms of others, and suffered themselves to be stolen by them. They also changed themselves into beasts and reptiles, and fishes and birds, and into whatsoever they pleased. These things also the poets among yourselves, by reason of fearlessness, sing, as they befell, attributing to one the many and diverse doings of all.

Chap. XIII. — *The fall of the angels*

"But when, having assumed these forms, they convicted as covetous those who stole them, and changed themselves into the nature of men, in order that, living holily, and showing the possibility of so living, they might subject the ungrateful to punishment, yet having become in all respects men, they also partook of human lust, and being brought under its subjection they fell into cohabitation with women; and being involved with them, and sunk in defilement and altogether emptied of their first power, were unable to turn back to the first purity of their proper nature, their members turned away from their fiery substance: [8] for the fire itself, being extinguished by the weight of lust, [and changed] into flesh, they trode the impious path downward. For they themselves, being fettered with the bonds of flesh, were constrained and strongly bound; wherefore they have no more been able to ascend into the heavens.

Chap. XIV. — *Their discoveries*

"For after the intercourse, being asked to show what they were before, and being no longer able to do so, on account of their being unable to do aught else after their defilement, yet wishing to please their mistresses, instead of themselves, they showed the bowels [9] of the earth; I mean, the choice metals, [10] gold, brass, silver, iron, and the like, with all the most precious stones. And along with these charmed stones, they delivered the arts of the things pertaining to each, and imparted the discovery of magic, and taught astronomy, and the powers of roots, and whatever was impossible to be found out by the human mind; also the melting of gold and silver, and the like, and the various dyeing of garments. And all things, in short, which are for the adornment and delight of women, are the discoveries of these demons bound in flesh.

Chap. XV. — *The giants*

"But from their unhallowed intercourse spurious men sprang, much greater in stature than [ordinary] men, whom they afterwards called giants: not those dragon-footed giants who waged war against God, as those blasphemous myths of the Greeks do sing, but wild in manners, and greater than men in size, inasmuch as they were sprung of angels; yet less than angels, as they were born of women. Therefore God, knowing that they were barbarized to brutality, and that the world was not sufficient to satisfy them (for it was created according to the proportion of men and human use), that they might not through want of food turn, contrary to nature, to the eating of animals, and yet seem to be blameless, as having ventured upon this through necessity, the Almighty God rained manna upon them, suited to their various tastes; and they enjoyed all that they would. But they, on account of their bastard nature, not being pleased with purity of food, longed only after the taste of blood. Wherefore they first tasted flesh.

Chap. XVI. — *Cannibalism*

"And the men who were with them there for the first time were eager to do the like. Thus, although we are born neither good nor bad, we become [one or the other]; and having formed habits, we are with difficulty drawn from them. But when irrational animals fell short, these bastard men tasted also human flesh. For it was not a long step to the consumption of flesh like their own, having first tasted it in other forms.

Chap. XVII. — *The flood*

"But by the shedding of much blood, the pure air being defiled with impure vapour, and sickening those who breathed it, rendered them liable to diseases, so that thenceforth men died prematurely. But the earth being by these means greatly defiled, these first teemed with poison-darting and deadly creatures. All things, therefore, going from bad to worse, on account of these brutal demons, God wished to cast them away like an evil leaven, lest each generation from a wicked seed, being like to that before it, and equally impious, should empty the world to come of saved men. And for this purpose, having warned a certain righteous man, with his three sons, together with their wives and their children, to save themselves in an ark, He sent a deluge of water, that all being destroyed, the purified world might be handed over to him who was saved in the ark, in order to a second beginning of life. And thus it came to pass.

Chap. XVIII. — *The law to the survivors*

"Since, therefore, the souls of the deceased giants were greater than human souls, inasmuch as they also excelled their bodies, they, as being a new race, were called also by a new name. And to those who survived in the world a law was prescribed of God through an angel, how they should live. For being bastards in race, of the fire of angels and the blood of women, and therefore liable to desire a certain race of their own, they were anticipated by a certain righteous law. For a certain angel was sent to them by God, declaring to them His will, and saying:

Chap. XIX. — *The law to the giants or demons*

"'These things seem good to the all-seeing God, that you lord it over no man; that you trouble no one, unless any one of his own accord subject himself to you, worshipping you, and sacrificing and pouring libations, and partaking of your table, or accomplishing aught else that they ought not, or shedding blood, or tasting dead flesh, or filling themselves with that which is torn of beasts, or that which is cut, or that which is strangled, or aught else that is unclean. But those who betake themselves to my law, you not only shall not touch, but shall also do honour to, and shall flee from, their presence. For whatsoever shall please them, being just, respecting you, that you shall be constrained to suffer. But if any of those who worship me go astray, either committing adultery, or practising magic, or living impurely, or doing any other of the things which are not well-pleasing to me, then they will have to suffer something at your hands or those of others, according to my order. But upon them, when they repent, I, judging of their repentance, whether it be worthy of pardon or not, shall give sentence. These things, therefore, ye ought to remember and to do, well knowing that not even your thoughts shall be able to be concealed from Him.'

Chap. XX. — *Willing captives*

"Having charged them to this effect, the angel departed. But you are still ignorant of this law, that every one who worships demons, or sacrifices to them, or partakes with them of their table, shall become subject to them and receive all punishment from them, as being under wicked lords. And you who, on account of ignorance of this [law], have been corrupted beside their altars, [11] and have been satiated with [food offered to] them, have come under their power, and do not know how you have been in every way injured in respect of your bodies. But you ought to know that the demons have no power over any one, unless first he be their table-companion; since not even their chief can do anything contrary to the law imposed upon them by God, wherefore he has no power over any one who does not worship him; but neither can any one receive from them any of the things that he wishes, nor in anything be hurt by them, as you may learn from the following statement.

Chap. XXI. — *Temptation of Christ*

"For once the king of the present time came to our King of righteousness, using no violence, for this was not in his power, but inducing and persuading, because the being persuaded lies in the power of every one. Approaching him, therefore, as being king of things present, he said to the King of things future, 'All the kingdoms of the present world are subject to me; also the gold and the silver and all the luxury of this world are under my power. Wherefore fall down and worship me, and I will give you all these things.' And this he said, knowing that after He worshipped him he would have power also over Him, and thus would rob Him of the future glory and kingdom. But He, knowing all things, not only did not worship him, but would not receive aught of the things that were offered by him. For He pledged Himself with those that are His, to the effect that it is not lawful henceforth even to touch the things that are given over to him. Therefore He answered and said, 'Thou shalt fear the Lord thy God, and Him only shalt thou serve.' [12]

Chap. XXII. — *The marriage supper*

"However, the king of the impious, striving to bring over to his own counsel the King of the pious, and not being able, ceased his efforts, undertaking to persecute Him for the remainder of His life. But you, being ignorant of the foreordained law, are under his power through evil deeds. Wherefore you are polluted in body and soul, and in the present life you are tyrannized over by sufferings and demons, but in that which is to come you shall have your souls to be punished. And this not you alone suffer through ignorance, but also some of our nation, who by evil deeds having been brought under the power of the prince of wickedness, like persons invited to a supper by a father celebrating the marriage of his son, have not obeyed. [13] But instead of those who through preoccupation disobeyed, the Father celebrating the marriage of his Son, has ordered us, through the Prophet of the truth, to come into the partings of the ways, that is, to you, and to invest you with the clean wedding-garment, which is baptism, which is for the remission of the sins done by you, and to bring the good to the supper of God by repentance, although at the first they were left out of the banquet.

Chap. XXIII. — *The assembly dismissed*

"If, therefore, ye wish to be the vesture of the Divine Spirit, hasten first to put off your base presumption, which is an unclean spirit and a foul garment. And this you cannot otherwise put off, than by being first baptized in good works. And thus being pure in body and in soul, you shall enjoy the future eternal kingdom. Therefore neither believe in idols, nor partake with them of the impure table, nor commit murder, nor adultery, nor hate those whom it is not right to hate, nor steal, nor set upon any evil deeds; since, being deprived of the hope of future blessings in the present life, you shall be subjected to evil demons and terrible sufferings, and in the world to come you shall be punished with eternal fire. Now, then, what has been said is enough for to-day. For the rest, those of you who are afflicted with ailments remain for healing; and of the others, you who please go in peace."

Chap. XXIV. — *The sick healed*

When he had thus spoken, all of them remained, some in order to be healed, and others to see those who obtained cures. But Peter, only laying his hands upon them, and praying, healed them; so that those who were straightaway cured were exceeding glad, and those who looked on exceedingly wondered, and blessed God, and believed with a firm hope, and with those who had been healed departed to their own homes, having received a charge to meet early on the following day. And when they had gone, Peter remained there with his associates, and partook of food, and refreshed himself with sleep.

[1] Lit.: more willing to learn [than the others].
[2] Matt. VIII. 11; Luke XIII. 29.
[3] Matt. XX. 16.
[4] Ex. XIX. 9.
[5] Matt. XI. 25.
[6] Matt VII. 21.
[7] The general meaning seems to be as given; but the text is undoubtedly corrupt, and scarcely intelligible.
[8] The text is somewhat obscure; but the following sentence shows this to be the meaning of it.
[9] Literally, "the marrow."
[10] Literally, "the flowers of metals."
[11] τοῖς αὐτῶν βωμοῖς προσφθαρέντες χαὶ αὐτῶν ἐχπληρωθέντες.
[12] Matt. iv.; Luke IV.
[13] Matt. xxii.

Homily IX

Chap. I. — *Peter's discourse resumed*

Therefore on the next day, Peter going out with his companions, and coming to the former place, and taking his stand, proceeded to say: "God having cut off by water all the impious men of old, having found one alone amongst them all that was pious, caused him to be saved in an ark, with his three sons and their wives. Whence may be perceived that it is His nature not to care for a multitude of wicked, nor to be indifferent to the salvation of one pious. Therefore the greatest impiety of all is forsaking the sole Lord of all, and worshipping many, who are no gods, as if they were gods.

Chap. II. — *Monarchy and polyarchy*

"If, therefore, while I expound and show you that this is the greatest sin, which is able to destroy you all, it occur to your mind that you are not destroyed, being great multitudes, you are deceived. For you have the example of the old world deluged. And yet their sin was much less than that which is chargeable against you. For they were wicked with respect to their equals, murdering or committing adultery. But you are wicked against the God of all, worshipping lifeless images instead of Him or along with Him, and attributing His divine name to every kind of senseless matter. In the first place, therefore, you are unfortunate in not knowing the difference between monarchy and polyarchy — that monarchy, on the one hand, is productive of concord, but polyarchy is effective of wars. For unity does not fight with itself, but multitude has occasion of undertaking battle one against another.

Chap. III. — *Family of Noe*

"Therefore, straightway after the flood, Noe continued to live three hundred and fifty years with the multitude of his descendants in concord, being a king according to the image of the one God. But after his death many of his descendants were ambitious of the kingdom, and being eager to reign, each one considered how it might be effected; and one attempted it by war, another by deceit, another by persuasion, and one in one way and another in another; one of whom was of the family of Ham, whose descendant was Mestren, from whom the tribes of the Egyptians and Babylonians and Persians were multiplied.

Chap. IV. — *Zoroaster*

"Of this family there was born in due time a certain one, who took up with magical practices, by name Nebrod, who chose, giant-like, to devise things in opposition to God. Him the Greeks have called Zoroaster. He, after the deluge, being ambitious of sovereignty, and being a great magician, by magical arts compelled the world-guiding star of the wicked one who now rules, to the bestowal of the sovereignty [as a gift] from him. But he, [1] being a prince, and having authority over him who compelled him, [2] wrathfully poured out the fire of the kingdom, that he might both bring to allegiance, and might punish him who at first constrained him.

Chap. V. — *Hero-worship*

"Therefore the magician Nebrod, being destroyed by this lightning falling on earth from heaven, for this circumstance had his name changed to Zoroaster, on account of the living (ξῶσαν) stream of the star (ἀστέρος) being poured upon him. But the unintelligent amongst the men who then were, thinking that through the love of God his soul had been sent for by lightning, buried the remains of his body, and honoured his burial-place with a temple among the Persians, where the descent of the fire occurred, and worshipped him as a god. By this example also, others there bury those who die by lightning as beloved of God, and honour them with temples, and erect statues of the dead in their own forms. Thence, in like manner, the rulers in different places were emulous [of like honour], and very many of them honoured the tombs of those who were beloved of them, though not dying by lightning, with temples and statues, and lighted up altars, and ordered them to be adored as gods. And long after, by the lapse of time, they were thought by posterity to be really gods.

Chap. VI. — *Fire-worship*

"Thus, in this fashion, there ensued many partitions of the one original kingdom. The Persians, first taking coals from the lightning which fell from heaven, preserved them by ordinary fuel, and honouring the heavenly fire as a god, were honoured by the fire itself with the first kingdom, as its first worshippers. After them the Babylonians, stealing coals from the fire that was there, and conveying it safely to their own home, and worshipping it, they themselves also reigned in order. And the Egyptians, acting in like manner, and calling the fire in their own dialect *Phthaë*, which is translated *Hephaistus* or *Osiris*, he who first reigned amongst them is called by its name. Those also who reigned in different places, acting in this fashion, and making an image, and kindling altars in honour of fire, most of them were excluded from the kingdom.

Chap. VII. — *Sacrificial orgies*

"But they did not cease to worship images, by reason of the evil intelligence of the magicians, who found excuses for them, which had power to constrain them to the foolish worship. For, establishing these things by magical ceremonies, they assigned them feasts from sacrifices, libations, flutes, and shoutings, by means of which senseless men, being deceived, and their kingdom being taken from them, yet did not desist from the worship that they had taken up with. To such an extent did they prefer error, on account of its pleasantness, before truth. they also howl after their sacrificial surfeit, their soul from the depth, as it were by dreams, forewarning them of the punishment that is to befall such deeds of theirs.

Chap. VIII. — *The best merchandise*

"Many forms of worship, then, having passed away in the world, we come, bringing to you, as good merchantmen, the worship that has been handed down to us from our fathers, and preserved; showing you, as it were, the seeds of plants, and placing them under your judgment and in your power. Choose that which seems good unto you. If, therefore, ye choose our wares, not only shall ye be able to escape demons, and the sufferings which are inflicted by demons, but yourselves also putting them to flight, and having them reduced to make supplication to you, shall for ever enjoy future blessings.

Chap. IX. — *How demons get power over men*

"Since, on the other hand, you are oppressed by strange sufferings inflicted by demons, on your removal from the body you shall have your souls also punished for ever; not indeed by God's inflicting vengeance, but because such is the judgment of evil deeds. For the demons, having power by means of the food given to them, are admitted into your bodies by your own hands; and lying hid there for a long time, they become blended with your souls. And through the carelessness of those who think not, or even wish not, to help themselves, upon the dissolution of their bodies, their souls being united to the demon, are of necessity borne by it into whatever places it pleases. And what is most terrible of all, when at the end of all things the demon is first consumed to the purifying fire, the soul which is mixed with it is under the necessity of being horribly punished, and the demon of being pleased. For the soul, being made of light, and not capable of bearing the heterogeneous flame of fire, is tortured; but the demon, being in the substance of his own kind, is greatly pleased, becoming the strong chain of the soul that he has swallowed up.

Chap. X. — *How they are to be expelled*

"But the reason why the demons delight in entering into men's bodies is this. Being spirits, and having desires after meats and drinks, and sexual pleasures, but not being able to partake of these by reason of their being spirits, and wanting organs fitted for their enjoyment, they enter into the bodies of men, in order that, getting organs to minister to them, they may obtain the things that they wish, whether it be meat, by means of men's teeth, or sexual pleasure, by means of men's members. Hence, in order to the putting of demons to flight, the most useful help is abstinence, and fasting, and suffering of affliction. For if they enter into men's bodies for the sake of sharing [pleasures], it is manifest that they are put to flight by suffering. But inasmuch as some, [3] being of a more malignant kind, remain by the body that is undergoing punishment, though they are punished with it, therefore it is needful to have recourse to God by prayers and petitions, refraining from every occasion of impurity, that the hand of God may touch him for his cure, as being pure and faithful.

Chap. XI. — *Unbelief the demon's stronghold*

"But it is necessary in our prayers to acknowledge that we have had recourse to God, and to bear witness, not to the apathy, but to the slowness of the demon. For all things are done to the believer, nothing to the unbeliever. Therefore the demons themselves, knowing the amount of faith of those of whom they take possession, measure their stay proportionately. Wherefore they stay permanently with the unbelieving, tarry for a while with the weak in faith; but with those who thoroughly believe, and who do good, they cannot remain even for a moment. For the soul being turned by faith, as it were, into the nature of water, quenches the demon as a spark of fire. The labour, therefore, of every one is to be solicitous about the putting to flight of his own demon. For, being mixed up with men's souls, they suggest to every one's mind desires after what things they please, in order that he may neglect his salvation.

Chap. XII. — *Theory of disease*

"Whence many, not knowing how they are influenced, consent to the evil thoughts suggested by the demons, as if they were the reasoning of their own souls. Wherefore they become less active to come to those who are able to save them, and do not know that they themselves are held captive by the deceiving demons. Therefore the demons who lurk in their souls induce them to think that it is not a demon that is distressing them, but a bodily disease, such as some acrid matter, or bile, or phlegm, or excess of blood, or inflammation of a membrane, or something else. But even if this were so, the case would not be altered of its being a kind of demon. For the universal and earthly soul, which enters on account of all kinds of food, being taken to excess by overmuch food, is itself united to the spirit, as being cognate, which is the soul of man; and the material part of the food being united to the body, is left as a dreadful poison to it. Wherefore in all respects moderation is excellent.

Chap. XIII. — *Deceits of the demons*

"But some of the maleficent demons deceive in another way. For at first they do not even show their existence, in order that care may not be taken against them; but in due time, by means of anger, love, or some other affection, they suddenly injure the body, by sword, or halter, or precipice, or something else, and at last bring to punishment the deceived souls of those who have been mixed up with them, as we said, withdrawing into the purifying fire. But others, who are deceived in another way, do not approach us, being seduced by the instigations of maleficent demons, as if they suffered these things at the hands of the gods themselves, on account of their neglect of them, and were able to reconcile them by sacrifices, and that it is not needful to come to us, but rather to flee from and hate us. And at the same time [4] they hate and flee from those who have greater compassion for them, and who follow after them in order to do good to them.

Chap. XIV. — *More tricks*

"Therefore shunning and hating us they are deceived, not knowing how it happens that they devise things opposed to their health. For neither can we compel them against their will to incline towards health, since now we have no such power over them, nor are they able of themselves to understand the evil instigation of the demon; for they know not whence these evil instigations are suggested to them. And these are they whom the demons affright, appearing in such forms as they please. And sometimes they prescribe remedies for those who are diseased, and thus they receive divine honours from those who have previously been deceived. And they conceal from many that they are demons, but not from us, who know their mystery, and why they do these things, changing themselves in dreams against those over whom they have power; and why they terrify some, and give oracular responses to others, and demand sacrifices from them, and command them to eat with them, that they may swallow up their souls.

Chap. XV. — *Test of idols*

"For as dire serpents draw sparrows to them by their breath, so also these draw to their own will those who partake of their table, being mixed up with their understanding by means of food and drink, changing themselves in dreams according to the forms of the images, that they may increase error. For the image is neither a living creature, nor has it a divine spirit, but the demon that appeared abused the form. [5] How many, in like manner, have been seen by others in dreams; and when they have met one another when awake, and compared them with what they saw in. their dream, they have not accorded: so that the dream is not a manifestation, but is either the production of a demon or of the soul, giving forms to present fears and desire. For the soul, being struck with fear, conceives forms in dreams. But if you think that images, as being alive, can accomplish such things, place them on a beam accurately balanced, and place an equipoise in the other scale, then ask them to become either heavier or lighter; and if this be done, then they are alive. But it does not so happen. But if it were so, this would not prove them to be gods. For this might be accomplished by the finger of the demon. Even maggots move, yet they are not called gods.

Chap. XVI. — *Powers of the demons*

"But that the soul of each man embodies the forms of demons after his own preconceptions, and that those who are called gods do not appear, is manifest from the fact that they do not appear to the Jews. But some one will say, How then do they give oracular responses, forecasting future things? This also is false. But suppose it were true, this does not prove them to be gods; for it does not follow, if anything prophesies, that it is a god. For pythons prophesy, yet they are cast out by us as demons, and put to flight. But some one will say. They work cures for some persons. It is false. But suppose it were true, this is no proof of Godhead; for physicians also heal many, yet are not gods. But, says one, physicians do not completely heal those of whom they take charge, but these heal oracularly. But the demons know the remedies that are suited to each disease. Wherefore, being skilful physicians, and able to cure those diseases which can be cured by men, and also being prophets, and knowing when each disease is healed of itself, they so arrange their remedies that they may gain the credit of producing the cure.

Chap. XVII. — *Reasons why their deceits are not detected*

"For why do they oracularly foretell cures after a long time? And why, if they are almighty, do they not effect cures without administering any medicine? And for what reason do they prescribe remedies to some of those who pray to them, while to some, and it may be more suitable cases, they give no response? Thus, whenever a cure is going to take place spontaneously, they promise, in order that they may get the credit of the cure; and others, having been sick, and having prayed, and having recovered spontaneously, attributed the cure to those whom they had invoked, and make offerings to them. Those, however, who, after praying, have failed, are not able to offer their sacrifices. But if the relatives of the dead, or any of their children, inquired into the losses, you would find the failures to be more than the successes. But no one who has been taken in by them is willing to exhibit an accusation against them, through shame or fear; but, on the other hand, they conceal the crimes which they believe them to be guilty of.

Chap. XVIII. — *Props of the system*

"And how many also falsify the responses given and the cures effected by them, and confirm them with an oath! And how many give themselves up to them for hire, undertaking falsely to suffer certain things, and thus proclaiming their suffering, and being restored by remedial means, they say that they oracularly promised them healing, in order that they may assign as the cause the senseless worship! And how many of these things were formerly done by magical art, in the way of interpreting dreams, and divining! Yet in course of time these things have disappeared. And how many are there now, who, wishing to obtain such things, make use of charms! However, though a thing be prophetical or healing, it is not divine.

Chap. XIX. — *Privileges of the baptized*

"For God is almighty. For He is good and righteous, now long-suffering to all, that those who will, repenting of the evils which they have done, and living well, may receive a worthy reward in the day in which all things are judged. Wherefore now begin to obey God by reason of good knowledge, and to oppose your evil lusts and thoughts, that you may be able to recover the original saving worship which was committed to humanity. For thus shall blessings straightway spring up to you, which, when you receive, you will thenceforth quit the trial of evils. But give thanks to the Giver; being kings for ever of unspeakable good things, with the King of peace. But in the present life, washing in a flowing river, or fountain, or even in the sea, with the thrice-blessed invocation, you shall not only be able to drive away the spirits which lurk in you; but yourselves no longer sinning, and undoubtingly believing God, you shall drive out evil spirits and dire demons, with terrible diseases, from others. And sometimes they shall flee when you but look on them. For they know those who have given themselves up to God. Wherefore, honouring them, they flee affrighted, as you saw yesterday, how, when after the address I delayed praying for those who were suffering these maladies, through respect towards the worship they cried out, not being able to endure it for a short hour.

Chap. XX. — *"Not almost, but altogether such as I am."*

"Do not then suppose that we do not fear demons on this account, that we are of a different nature [from you]. For we are of the same nature, but not of the same worship. Wherefore, being not only much but altogether superior to you, we do not grudge you becoming such [as we are]; but, on the other hand, counsel you, knowing that all these [demons] beyond measure honour and fear those who are reconciled to God.

Chap. XXI. — *The demons subject to the believer*

"For, in like manner as the soldiers who are put under one of Caesar's captains know to honour him who has received authority on account of him who gave it, so that the commanders say to this one, Come, and he comes, and to another, Go, and he goes; so also he who has given himself to God, being faithful, is heard when he only speaks to demons and diseases; and the demons give place, though they be much stronger than they who command them. For with unspeakable power God subjects the mind of every one to whom He pleases. For as many captains, with whole camps and cities, fear Caesar, who is but a man, every one's heart being eager to honour the image of all; [6] for by the will of God, all things being enslaved by fear, do not know the cause; so also all disease-producing spirits, being awed in some natural way, honour and flee from him who has had recourse to God, and who carries right faith as His image in his heart.

Chap. XXII. — *"Rather rejoice"*

"But still, though all demons, with all diseases, flee before you, you are not to rejoice in this only, but in that, through grace, your names, as of the everliving, are written in heaven. Thus also the Divine Holy Spirit rejoices, because man hath overcome death; for the putting of the demons to flight makes for the safety of another. But this we say, not as denying that we ought to help others, but that we ought not to be inflated by this and neglect ourselves. It happens, also, that the demons flee before some wicked men by reason of the honoured name, and both he who expels the demon and he who witnesses it are deceived: he who expels him, as if he were honoured on account of righteousness, not knowing the wickedness of the demon. For he has at once honoured the name, and by his flight has brought the wicked man into a thought of his righteousness, and so deceived him away from repentance. But the looker-on, associating with the expeller as a pious man, hastens to a like manner of life, and is ruined. Sometimes also they pretend to flee before adjurations not made in the name of God, that they may deceive men, and destroy them whom they will.

Chap. XXIII. — *The sick healed*

"This then we would have you know, that unless any one of his own accord give himself over as a slave to demons, as I said before, the demon has no power against him. Choosing, therefore, to worship one God, and refraining from the table of demons, and undertaking chastity with philanthropy and righteousness, and being baptized with the thrice-blessed invocation for the remission of sins, and devoting yourselves as much as you can to the perfection of purity, you can escape everlasting punishment, and be constituted heirs of eternal blessings."

Having thus spoken, he ordered those to approach who were distressed with diseases; and thus many approached, having come together through the experience of those who had been healed yesterday. And he having laid his hands upon them and prayed, and immediately healed them, and having charged them and the others to come earlier, he bathed and partook of food, and went to sleep.

[1] That is, I suppose, the wicked one.
[2] I suppose Nimrod, or Zoroaster.
[3] The gender is here changed, but the sense shows that the reference is still to the demons. I suppose the author forgot that in the preceding sentences he had written ὀαίμονες (*masc.*) and not ὀαιμόνια (*neut.*).
[4] Some read οὔτως, thus.
[5] The meaning is: "the idols or images of the heathen deities are not living, but the demons adopt the forms of these images when they appear to men in dreams."
[6] I prefer here the common text to any of the proposed emendations, and suppose that the author represents Caesar, though but one man, as the image or personification of the whole empire.

Homily X

Chap. I. — *The third day in Tripolis*

Wherefore on the third day in Tripolis, Peter rose early and went into the garden, where there was a great water-reservoir, into which a full stream of water constantly flowed. There having bathed, and then having prayed, he sat down; and perceiving us sitting around and eagerly observing him, as wishing to hear something from him, he said:

Chap. II. — *Ignorance and error*

"There seems to me to be a great difference between the ignorant and the erring. For the ignorant man seems to me to be like a man who does not wish to set out for a richly stored city, through his not knowing the excellent things that are there; but the erring man to be like one who has learned indeed the good things that are in the city, but who has forsaken the highway in proceeding towards it, and so has wandered. Thus, therefore, it seems to me that there is a great difference between those who worship idols and those who are faulty in the worship of God. For they who worship idols are ignorant of eternal life, and therefore they do not desire it; for what they do not know, they cannot love. But those who have chosen to worship one God, and who have learned of the eternal life given to the good, if they either believe or do anything 'different from what is pleasing to God, are like to those who have gone out from the city of punishment, and are desirous to come to the well-stored city, and on the road have strayed from the right path."

Chap. III. — *Man the lord of all*

While he was thus discoursing to us, there entered one of our people, who had been appointed to make the following announcement to him, and said: "My lord Peter, there are great multitudes standing before the doors." With his consent, therefore, a great multitude entered. Then he rose up, and stood on the basis, as he had done the day before; and having saluted them in religious fashion, he said: "God having formed the heaven and the earth, and having made all things in them, as the true Prophet has said to us, man, being made after the image and likeness of God, was appointed to be ruler and lord of things, I say, in air and earth and water, as may be known from the very fact that by his intelligence he brings down the creatures that are in the air, and brings up those that are in the deep, hunts those that are on the earth, and that although they are much greater in strength than he; I mean elephants, and lions, and such like.

Chap. IV. — *Faith and duty*

"While, therefore, he was righteous, he was also superior to all sufferings, as being unable by his immortal body to have any experience of pain; but when he sinned, as I showed you yesterday and the day before, becoming as it were the servant of sin, he became subject to all sufferings, being by a righteous judgment deprived of all excellent things. For it was not reasonable, the Giver having been forsaken, that the gifts should remain with the ungrateful. Whence, of His abundant mercy, in order to our receiving, with the first, also future blessings, He sent His Prophet. And the Prophet has given in charge to us to tell you what you ought to think, and what to do. Choose, therefore; and this is in your power. What, therefore, you ought to think is this, to worship the God who made all things; whom if you receive in your minds, you shall receive from Him, along with the first excellent things, also the future eternal blessings.

Chap. V. — *The fear of God*

"Therefore you shall be able to persuade yourselves with respect to the things that are profitable, if, like charmers, you say to the horrible serpent which lurks in your heart, 'The Lord God thou shalt fear, and Him alone thou shalt serve.' [1] On every account it is advantageous to fear Him alone, not as an unjust, but as a righteous God. For one fears an unjust being, lest he be wrongfully destroyed, but a righteous one, lest he be caught in sin and punished. You can therefore, by fear towards Him, be freed from many hurtful fears. For if you do not fear the one Lord and Maker of all, you shall be the slaves of all evils to your own hurt, I mean of demons and diseases, and of everything that can in any way hurt you.

Chap. VI. — *Restoration of the divine image*

"Therefore approach with confidence to God, you who at first were made to be rulers and lords of all things: ye who have His image in your bodies, have in like manner the likeness of His judgment in your minds. Since, then, by acting like irrational animals, you have lost the soul of man from your soul, becoming like swine, you are the prey of demons. If, therefore, you receive the law of God, you become men. For it cannot be said to irrational animals, 'Thou shalt not kill, thou shalt not commit adultery, thou shalt not steal,' and so forth. Therefore do not refuse, when invited, to return to your first nobility; for it is possible, if ye be conformed to God by good works. And being accounted to be sons by reason of your likeness to Him, you shall be reinstated as lords of all.

Chap. VII. — *Unprofitableness of idols*

"Begin, then, to divest yourselves of the injurious fear of vain idols, that you may escape unrighteous bondage. For they have become your masters, who even as servants are unprofitable to you. I speak of the material of the lifeless images, which are of no use to you as far as service is concerned. For they neither hear nor see nor feel, nor can they be moved. For is there any one of you who would like to see as they see, and to hear as they hear, and to feel as they feel, and to be moved as they are? God forbid that such a wrong should be done to any man bearing the image of God, though he have lost His likeness.

Chap. VIII. — *No gods which are made with hands*

"Therefore reduce your gods of gold and silver, or any other material, to their original nature; I mean into cups and basins and all other utensils, such as may be useful to you for service; and those good things which were given you at first shall be able to be restored. But perhaps you will say. The laws of the emperors do not permit us to do this. You say well that it is the law, and not the power of the vain idols themselves, which is nothing. How, then, have ye regarded them as gods, who are avenged by human laws, guarded by dogs, kept by multitudes? — and that if they are of gold, or silver, or brass. For those of wood or earthenware are preserved by their worthlessness, because no man desires to steal a wooden or earthenware god! So that your gods are exposed to danger in proportion to the value of the material of which they are made. How, then, can they be gods, which are stolen, molten, weighed, guarded?

Chap. IX. — *"Eyes have they, but they see not," etc.*

"Oh the minds of wretched men, who fear things deader than dead men! For I cannot call them even dead, which have never lived, unless they are the tombs of ancient men. For sometimes a person, visiting unknown places, does not know whether the temples which he sees are monuments of dead men, or whether they belong to the so-called gods; but on inquiring and hearing that they belong to the gods, he worships, without being ashamed that if he had not learned on inquiring, he would have passed them by as the monument of a dead man, on account of the strictness of the resemblance. However, it is not necessary that I should adduce much proof in regard to such superstition. For it is easy for any one who pleases to understand that it [an idol] is nothing, unless there be any one who does not see. However, now at least hear that it does not hear, and understand that it does not understand. For the hands of a man who is dead made it. If, then, the maker is dead, how can it be that that which was made by him shall not be dissolved? Why, then, do you worship the work of a mortal which is altogether senseless? whereas those who have reason do not worship animals, nor do they seek to propitiate the elements which have been made by God, — I mean the heaven, the sun, the moon, lightning, the sea, and all things in them, — rightly judging not to worship the things that He has made, but to reverence the Maker and Sustainer of them. For in this they themselves also rejoice, that no one ascribes to them the honour that belongs to their Maker.

Chap. X. — *Idolatry a delusion of the serpent*

"For His alone is the excellent glory of being alone uncreated, while all else is created. As, therefore, it is the prerogative of the uncreated to be God, so whatever is created is not God indeed. Before all things, therefore, you ought to consider the evil-working suggestion of the deceiving serpent that is in you, which seduces you by the promise of better reason, creeping from your brain to your spinal marrow, and setting great value upon deceiving you.

Chap. XI. — *Why the serpent tempts to sin*

"For he knows the original law, that if he bring you to the persuasion of the so-called gods, so that you sin against the one good of monarchy, your overthrow becomes a gain to him. And that for this reason, because he being condemned eats earth, he has power to eat him who through sin being dissolved into earth, has become earth, your souls going into his belly of fire. In order, therefore, that you may suffer these things, he suggests every thought to your hurt.

Chap. XII. — *Ignorantia neminem excusat*

"For all the deceitful conceptions against the monarchy are sown in your mind by him to your hurt. First, that you may not hear the discourses of piety, and so drive away ignorance, which is the occasion of evils, he ensnares you by a pretence of knowledge, giving in the first instance, and using throughout this presumption, which is to think and to be unhappily advised, that if any one do not hear the word of piety, he is not subject to judgments. Wherefore also some, being thus deceived, are not willing to hear, that they may be ignorant, not knowing that ignorance is of itself a sufficient deadly drug. For if any one should take a deadly drug in ignorance, does he not die? So naturally sins destroy the sinner, though he commit them in ignorance of what is right.

Chap. XIII. — *Condemnation of the ignorant*

"But if judgment follows upon disobedience to instruction, much more shall God destroy those who will not undertake His worship. For he who will not learn, lest that should make him subject to judgment, is already judged as knowing, for he knew what he will not hear; so that that imagination avails nothing as an apology in presence of the heart-knowing God. Wherefore avoid that cunning thought suggested by the serpent to your minds. But if any one end this life in real ignorance, this charge will lie against him, that, having lived so long, he did not know who was the bestower of the food supplied to him; and as a senseless, and ungrateful, and very unworthy servant, he is rejected from the kingdom of God.

Chap. XIV. — *Polytheistic illustration*

"Again, the terrible serpent suggests this supposition to you, to think and to say that very thing which most of you do say; viz., We know that there is one Lord of all, but there also are gods. For in like manner as there is one Caesar, but he has under him procurators, proconsuls, prefects, commanders of thousands, and of hundreds, and of tens; in the same way, there being one great God, as there is one Caesar, there also, after the manner of inferior powers, are gods, inferior indeed to Him, but ruling over us. Hear, therefore, ye who have been led away by this conception as by a terrible poison — I mean the evil conception of this illustration — that you may know what is good and what is evil. For you do not yet see it, nor do you look into the things that you utter.

Chap. XV. — *Its inconclusiveness*

"For if you say that, after the manner of Caesar, God has subordinate powers — those, namely, which are called gods — you do not thus go by your illustration. For if you went by it, you must of necessity know that it is not lawful to give the name of Caesar to another, whether he be consul, or prefect, or captain, or any one else, and that he who gives such a name shall not live, and he who takes it shall be cut off. Thus, according to your own illustration, the name of God must not be given to another; and he who is tempted either to take or give it is destroyed. Now, if this insult of a man induces punishment, much more they who call others gods shall be subject to eternal punishment, as insulting God. And with good reason; because you subject to all the insult that you can the name which it was committed to you to honour, in order to His monarchy. For God is not properly His name; but you having in the meantime received it, insult what has been given you, that it may be accounted as done against the real name, according as you use that. But you subject it to every kind of insult.

Chap. XVI. — *Gods of the Egyptians*

"Therefore you ringleaders among the Egyptians, boasting of meteorology, and promising to judge the natures of the stars, by reason of the evil opinion lurking in them, subjected that name to all manner of dishonour as far as in them lay. For some of them taught the worship of an ox called Apis, some that of a he-goat, some of a cat, some of a serpent; yea, even of a fish, and of onions, and rumblings in the stomach, [2] and common sewers, and members of irrational animals, and to myriads of other base abominations [they gave the name of god]."

Chap. XVII. — *The Egyptians' defence of their system*

On Peter's saying this, the surrounding multitude laughed. Then Peter said to the laucrhino; multitude: "You laugh at their proceedings, not knowing that you are yourselves much more objects of ridicule to them. But you laugh at one another's proceedings; for, being led by evil custom into deceit, you do not see your own. But I admit that you have reason to laugh at the idols of the Egyptians, since they, being rational, worship irrational animals, and these altogether dying. But listen to what they say when they deride you. Aye, they say, though we worship dying creatures, yet still such as have once had life; but you reverence things that never lived. And in addition to this, they say, We wish to honour the form of the one God, but we cannot find out what it is, and so we choose to give honour to every form. And so, making some such statements as these, they think that they judge more rightly than you do.

Chap. XVIII. — *Answer to the Egyptians*

"Wherefore answer them thus: You lie, for you do not worship these things in honour of the true God, for then all of you would worship every form; not as ye do. For those of you who suppose the onion to be the divinity, and those who worship rumblings in the stomach, contend with one another; and thus all in like manner preferring some one thing, revile those that are preferred by others. And with diverse judgments, one reverences one and another, another of the limbs of the same animal. Moreover, those of them who still have a breath of right reason, being ashamed of the manifest baseness, attempt to drive these things into allegories, wishing by another vagary to establish their deadly error. But we should confute the allegories, if we were there, the foolish passion for which has prevailed to such an extent as to constitute a great disease of the understanding. For it is not necessary to apply a plaster to a whole part of the body, but to a diseased part. Since then, you, by your laughing at the Egyptians, show that you are not affected with their disease, with respect to your own disease it were reasonable I should afford to you a present cure of your own malady.

Chap. XIX. — *God's peculiar attribute*

"He who would worship God ought before all things to know what alone is peculiar to the nature of God, which cannot pertain to another, that, looking at His peculiarity, and not finding it in any other, he may not be seduced into ascribing godhead to another. But this is peculiar to God, that He alone is, as the Maker of all, so also the best of all. That which makes is indeed superior in power to that which is made; that which is boundless is superior in magnitude to that which is bounded: in respect of beauty, that which is comeliest; in respect of happiness, that which is most blessed; in respect of understanding, that which is most perfect. And in like manner, in other respects. He has incomparably the pre-eminence. Since then, as I said, this very thing, viz. to be the best of all, is peculiar to God, and the all-comprehending world was made by Him, none of the things made by Him can come into equal comparison with Him.

Chap. XX. — *Neither the world nor any of its parts can be God*

"But the world, not being incomparable and unsurpassable, and altogether in all respects without defect, cannot be God. But if the whole world cannot be God, in respect of its having been made, how much more should not its parts be reasonably called God; I mean the parts that are by you called gods, being made of gold and silver, brass and stone, or of any other material whatsoever; and they constructed by mortal hand. However, let us further see how the terrible serpent through man's mouth poisons those who are seduced by his solicitations.

Chap. XXI. — *Idols not animated by the Divine Spirit*

"For many say, We do not worship the gold or the silver, the wood or the stone, of the objects of our worship. For we also know that these are nothing but lifeless matter, and the art of mortal man. But the spirit that dwells in them, that we call God. Behold the immorality of those who speak thus! For when that which appears is easily proved to be nothing, they have recourse to the invisible, as not being able to be convicted in respect of what is non-apparent. However, they agree with us in part, that one half of their images is not God, but senseless matter. It remains for them to show how we are to believe that these images have a divine spirit. But they cannot prove to us that it is so, for it is not so; and we do not believe them [when they say that they] have seen it. "We shall afford them proofs that they have not a divine spirit, that lovers of truth, hearing the refutation of the thought that they are animated, may turn away from the hurtful delusion.

Chap. XXII. — *Confutation of idol-worship*

"In the first place, indeed, if you worship them as being animated, why do you also worship the sepulchres of memorable men of old, who confessedly had no divine spirit? Thus you do not at all speak truth respecting this. But if your objects of worship were really animated, they would move of themselves; they would have a voice; they would shake off the spiders that are on them; they would thrust forth those that wish to surprise and to steal them; they would easily capture those who pilfer the offerings. But now they do none of these things, but are guarded, like culprits, and especially the more costly of them, as we have already said. But what? Is it not so, that the rulers demand of you imposts and taxes on their account, as if you were greatly benefited by them? But what? Have they not often been taken as plunder by enemies, and been broken and scattered? And do not the priests, more than the outside worshippers, carry off many of the offerings, thus acknowledging the uselessness of their worship?

Chap. XXIII. — *Folly of idolatry*

"Nay, it will be said; but they are detected by their foresight. It is false; for how many of them have not been detected? And if on account of the capture of some it be said that they have power, it is a mistake. For of those who rob tombs, some are found out and some escape; but it is not by the power of the dead that those who are apprehended are detected. And such ought to be our conclusion with respect to those who steal and pilfer the gods. But it will be said, The gods that are in them take no care of their images. Why, then, do you tend them, wiping them, and washing them, and scouring them, crowning them, and sacrificing to them? Wherefore agree with me that you act altogether without right reason. For as you lament over the dead, so you sacrifice and make libations to your gods.

Chap. XXIV. — *Impotence of idols*

"Nor yet is that in harmony with the illustration of Caesar, and of the powers under him, to call them administrators; whereas you take all care of them, as I said, tending your images in every respect. For they, having no power, do nothing. Wherefore tell us what do they administer? what do they of that sort which rulers in different places do? and what influence do they exert, as the stars of God? Do they show anything like the sun, or do you light lamps before them? Are they able to bring showers, as the clouds bring rain, — they which cannot even move themselves, unless men carry them? Do they make the earth fruitful to your labours, these to whom you supply sacrifices? Thus they can do nothing.

Chap. XXV. — *Servants become masters*

"But if they were able to do something, you should not be right in calling them gods: for it is not right to call the elements gods, by which good things are supplied; but only Him who ordereth them, to accomplish all things for our use, and who commandeth them to be serviceable to man, — Him alone we call God in propriety of speech, whose beneficence you do not perceive, but permit those elements to rule over you which have been assigned to you as your servants. And why should I speak of the elements, when you not only have made and do worship lifeless images, but deign to be subject to them in all respects as servants? Wherefore, by reason of your erroneous judgments, you have become subject to demons. However, by acknowledgment of God Himself, by good deeds you can again become masters, and command the demons as slaves, and as sons of God be constituted heirs of the eternal kingdom."

Chap. XXVI. — *The sick healed*

Having said this, he ordered the demoniacs, and those taken with diseases, to be brought to him; and when they were brought, he laid his hands on them, and prayed, and dismissed them healed, reminding them and the rest of the multitude to attend upon him there every day that he should discourse. Then, when the others had withdrawn, Peter bathed in the reservoir that was there, with those who pleased; and then ordering a table to be spread on the ground under the thick foliage of the trees, for the sake of shade, he ordered us each to recline, according to our worth; and thus we partook of food. Therefore having blessed and having given thanks to God for the enjoyment, according to the accustomed faith of the Hebrews; and there being still a long time before us, he permitted us to ask him questions about whatever we pleased; and thus, though there were twenty of us putting questions to him all round, he satisfied every one. And now evening having descended, we all went with him into the largest apartment of the lodging, and there we all slept.

[1] Matt. iv. 10. **[2]** γαστρῶν πνεύματα.

Homily XI

Chap. I. — *Morning exercises*

Therefore on the fourth day at Tripolis, Peter rising and finding us awake, saluted us and went out to the reservoir, that he might bathe and pray; and we also did so after him. To us, therefore, when we had prayed together, and were set down before him, he gave a discourse touching the necessity of purity. And when thereafter it was day, he permitted the multitudes to enter. Then, when a great crowd had entered, he saluted them according to custom, and began to speak.

Chap. II. — *"Giving all diligence"*

"Inasmuch as, by long-continued neglect on your part, to your own injury, your mind has caused to sprout many hurtful conceptions about religion, and ye have become like land fallow by the carelessness of the husbandman, you need a long time for your purification, that your mind, receiving like good seed the true word that is imparted to you, may not choke it with evil cares, and render it unfruitful with respect to works that are able to save you. Wherefore it behoves those who are careful of their own salvation to hear more constantly, that their sins which have been long multiplying may, in the short time that remains, be matched with constant care for their purification. Since, therefore, no one knows the time of his end, hasten to pluck out the many thorns of your hearts; but not by little and little, for then you cannot be purified, for you have been long fallow.

Chap. III. — *"Behold what indignation."*

"But not otherwise will you endure to undertake much care for your purification unless you be angry with yourselves, and chastise yourselves for those things with which, as unprofitable servants, you have been ensnared, consenting to your evil lusts, that you may be able to let in your righteous indignation upon your mind, as fire upon a fallow field. If, therefore, ye have not righteous fire, I mean indignation, against evil lusts, learn from what good things ye have been seduced, and by whom ye have been deceived, and for what punishment ye are prepared; and thus, your mind being sober, and kindled into indignation like fire by the teaching of Him who sent us, may be able to consume the evil things of lust. Believe me, that if you will, you can rectify all things.

Chap. IV. — *The golden rule*

"Ye are the image of the invisible God. Whence let not those who would be pious say that idols are images of God, and therefore that it is right to worship them. For the image of God is man. He who wishes to be pious towards God does good to man, because the body of man bears the image of God. But all do not as yet bear His likeness, but the pure mind of the good soul does.

However, as we know that man was made after the image and after the likeness of God, we tell you to be pious towards him, that the favour may be accounted as done to God, whose image he is. Therefore it behoves you to give honour to the image of God, which is man — in this wise; food to the hungry, drink to the thirsty, clothing to the naked, care to the sick, shelter to the stranger, and visiting him who is in prison, to help him as you can. And not to speak at length, whatever good things any one wishes for himself, so let him afford to another in need, and then a good reward can be reckoned to him as being pious towards the image of God. And by like reason, if he will not undertake to do these things, he shall be punished as neglecting the image.

Chap. V. — *Forasmuch as ye did it unto one of these*

"Can it therefore be said that, for the sake of piety towards God, ye worship every form, while in all things ye injure man who is really the image of God, committing murder, adultery, stealing, and dishonouring him in many other respects? But you ought not to do even one evil thing on account of which man is grieved. But now you do all things on account of which man is disheartened, for wrong is also distress. Wherefore you murder and spoil his goods, and whatever else you know which you would not receive from another. But you, being seduced by some malignant reptile to malice, by the suggestion of polytheistic doctrine, are impious towards the real image, which is man, and think that ye are pious towards senseless things.

Chap. VI. — *Why God suffers objects of idolatry to subsist*

"But some say, Unless He wished these things to be, they should not be, but He would take them away. But I say this shall assuredly be the case, when all shall show their preference for Him, and thus there shall be a change of the present world. However, if you wished him to act thus, so that none of the things that are worshipped should subsist, tell me what of existing things you have not worshipped. Do not some of you worship the sun, and some the moon, and some water, and some the earth, and some the mountains, and some plants, and some seeds, and some also man, as in Egypt? Therefore God must have suffered nothing, not even you, so that there should have been neither worshipped nor worshipper. Truly this is what the terrible serpent which lurks in you would have, and spares you not. But so it shall not be. For it is not the thing that is worshipped that sins; for it suffers violence at the hands of him who will worship it. For though unjust judgment is passed by all men, yet not by God. For it is not just that the sufferer and the disposer receive the same punishment, unless he willingly receive the honour which belongs only to the Most Honourable.

Chap. VII. — *"Let both grow together till the harvest"*

"But it will be said that the worshippers themselves ought to be taken away by the true God, that others may not do it. But you are not wiser than

God, that you should give Him counsel as one more prudent than He. He knows what He does; for He is long-suffering to all who are in impiety, as a merciful and philanthropic father, knowing that impious men become pious. And of those very worshippers of base and senseless things, many becoming sober have ceased to worship these things and to sin, and many Greeks have been saved so as to pray to the true God.

Chap. VIII. — *Liberty and necessity*

"But, you say, God ought to have made us at first so that we should not have thought at all of such things. You who say this do not know what is free-will, and how it is possible to be really good; that he who is good by his own choice is really good; but he who is made good by another under necessity is not really good, because he is not what he is by his own choice. Since therefore every one's freedom constitutes the true good, and shows the true evil, God has contrived that friendship or hostility should be in each man by occasions. But no, it is said; everything that we think He makes ns to think. Stop! Why do you blaspheme more and more, in saying this? For if we are under His influence in all that we think, you say that He is the cause of fornications, lusts, avarice, and all blasphemy. Cease your evil-speaking, ye -who ought to speak well of Him, and to bestow all honour upon Him. And do not say that God does not claim any honour; for if He Himself claims nothing, you ought to look to what is right, and to answer with thankful voice Him who does you good in all things.

Chap. IX. — *God a jealous God*

"But, you say, we do better when we are thankful at once to Him and to all others. Now, when you say this, you do not know the plot that is formed against you. For as, when many physicians of no powder promise to cure one patient, one who is really able to cure him does not apply his remedy, considering that, if he should cure him, the others would get the credit; so also God does not do you good, when He is asked along with many who can do nothing. What! it will be said, is God enraged at this, if, when He cures, another gets the credit? I answer: Although He be not indignant, at all events He will not be an accomplice in deceit; for when He has conferred a benefit, the idol, which has done nothing, is credited with the power. But also I say to you, if he who crouches in adoration before senseless idols had not been injured naturally, perhaps He (God) would have endured even this. Wherefore watch ye that you may attain to a reasonable understanding on the matter of salvation. [1] For God being without want, neither Himself needs anything, nor receives hurt; for it belongs to us to be profited or injured. For in like manner as Caesar is neither hurt when he is evil spoken of, nor profited when he is thanked, but safety accrues to the renderer of thanks, and ruin to the evil-speaker, so they who speak well of God indeed profit Him nothing, but save themselves; and in like manner, those who blaspheme Him do not indeed injure Him, but themselves perish.

Chap. X. — *The creatures avenge God's cause*

"But it will be said that the cases are not parallel between God and man; and I admit that they are not parallel: for the punishment is greater to him who is guilty of impiety against the greater, and less to him who sins against the less. As, therefore, God is greatest of all, so he who is impious against Him shall endure greater punishment, as sinning against the greater; not through His defending Himself with His own hand, but the whole creation being indignant at him, and naturally taking vengeance on him. For to the blasphemer the sun will not give his light, nor the earth her fruits, nor the fountain its water, nor in Hades shall he who is there constituted prince give rest to the soul; since even now, while the constitution of the world subsists, the whole creation is indignant at him. Wherefore neither do [the clouds] afford sufficient rains, nor the earth fruits, whereby many perish; yea, even the air itself, inflamed with anger, is turned to pestilential courses. However, whatsoever good things we enjoy, He of His mercy compels the creature to our benefits. Still, against you who dishonour the Maker of all, the whole creation is hostile.

Chap. XI. — *Immortality of the soul*

"And though by the dissolution of the body you should escape punishment, how shall you be able by corruption to flee from your soul, which is incorruptible? For the soul even of the wicked is immortal, for whom it were better not to have it incorruptible. For, being punished with endless torture under unquenchable fire, and never dying, it can receive no end of its misery. But perhaps some one of you will say, 'You terrify us, O Peter.' Teach us then how we can be silent [about these things, and yet] tell you things as they are, for not otherwise can we tell you them. But if we should be silent, you should be ensnared by evils through ignorance. But if we speak, we are suspected of terrifying you with a false theory. How then shall we charm that wicked [serpent] that lurks in your [soul], and subtilely insinuates suspicions hostile to God, under the guise of love to God? Be reconciled with yourselves; for in order to your salvation recourse is to Him with well-doing. Unreasonable lust in you is hostile to God, for by conceit of wisdom it strengthens ignorance.

Chap. XII. — *Idols unprofitable*

"But others say, God does not care for us. This also is false. For if really He did not care. He would neither cause His sun to rise on the good and the evil, nor send His rain on the just and the unjust. But others say, We are more pious [than you], since we worship both him and images. I do not think, if one were to say to a king, 'I give you an equal share of honour with that which I give to corpses and to worthless dung' — I do not think that he would profit by it. But some one will say, Do you call our objects of worship dung? I say Yes, for you have made them useless to yourselves by setting them aside for worship, whereas their substance might perhaps have been serviceable for some other purpose, or for the purpose of manure. But now it is not useful even for this purpose, since you have changed its shape and worship it. And how do you say that you are more pious, you who are the most wicked of all, who deserve destruction of your souls by this very one incomparable sin, at the hands of Him who is true, if you abide in it? For as if any son having received many benefits from his father, give to another, who is not his father, the honour that is due to his father, he is certainly disinherited; but if he live according to the judgment of his father, and so thanks him for his kindnesses, he is with good reason made the heir.

Chap. XIII. — *Arguments in favour of idolatry answered*

"But others say, We shall act impiously if we forsake the objects of worship handed down to us by our fathers; for it is like the guarding of a deposit. But on this principle the son of a robber or a debauchee ought not to be sober and to choose the better part, lest he should act impiously, and sin by doing differently from his parents! How foolish, then, are they who say, "We worship these things that we may not be troublesome to Him; as if God were troubled by those who bless Him, and not troubled by those who ungratefully blaspheme Him. Why is it, then, that when there is a withholding of rain, you look only to heaven and pour out prayers and supplications; and when you obtain it, you quickly forget? For when you have reaped your harvest or gathered your vintage, you distribute your first-fruits among those idols which are nothing, quickly forgetting God your benefactor; and thus you go into groves and temples, and offer sacrifices and feasts. Wherefore some of you say, These things have been excellently devised for the sake of good cheer and feasting.

Chap. XIV. — *Heathen orgies*

"Oh men without understanding! Judge ye rightly of what is said. For if it were necessary to give one's self to some pleasure for the refreshment of the body, whether were it better to do so among the rivers and woods and groves, where there are entertainments and convivialities and shady places, or where there is the madness of demons, and cuttings of hands, and emasculations, and fury and mania, and dishevelling of hair, and shoutings and enthusiasms and bowlings, and all those things which are done with hypocrisy for the confounding of the unthinking, when you offer your prescribed prayers and thanksgivings even to those who are deader than the dead?

Chap. XV. — *Heathen worshippers under the power of the demon*

"And why do ye take pleasure in these doings? Since the serpent which lurks in you, which has sown in you fruitless lust, will not tell you, I shall speak and put it on record. Thus the case stands. According to the worship of God, the proclamation is made to be sober, to be chaste, to restrain passion, not to pilfer other men's goods, to live uprightly, moderately, fearlessly, gently; rather to restrain one's self in necessities, than to supply his wants by wrongfully taking away the property of another. But with the so-called gods the reverse is done. And ye renounce some things [as done by you], in order to the admiration of [your] righteousness; whereas, although you did all that you are commanded, ignorance with respect to God is alone sufficient for your condemnation. But meeting together in the places which you have dedicated to them, you delight in making yourselves drunk, and you kindle your altars, of which the diffused odour through its influence attracts the blind and deaf spirits to the place of their fumigation. And thus, of those who are present, some are filled with inspirations, and some with strange fiends, and some betake themselves to lasciviousness, and some to theft and murder. For the exhalation of blood, and the libation of wine, satisfies even these unclean spirits, which lurk within you and cause you to take pleasure in the things that are transacted there, and in dreams surround you with false phantasies, and punish you with myriads of diseases. For under the show of the so-called sacred victims you are filled with dire demons, which, cunningly concealing themselves, destroy you, so that you should not understand the plot that is laid for you. For, under the guise of some injury, or love, or anger, or grief, or strangling you with a rope, or drowning you, or throwing you from a precipice, or by suicide, or apoplexy, or some other disease, they deprive you of life.

Chap. XVI. — *All things work for good to them that love God*

"But no one of us can suffer such a thing; but they themselves are punished by us, when, having entered into any one, they entreat us that they may go out slowly. But some one will say perhaps, Even some of the worshippers of God fall under such sufferings. I say that that is impossible. For he is a worshipper of God, of whom I speak, who is truly pious, not one who is such only in name, but who really performs the deeds of the law that has been given him. If any one acts impiously, he is not pious; in like manner as, if he who is of another tribe keeps the law, he is a Jew; bat he who does not keep it is a Greek. For the Jew believes God and keeps the law, by which faith he removes also other sufferings, though like mountains and heavy. [2] But he who keeps not the law is manifestly a deserter through not believing God; and thus as no Jew, but a sinner, he is on account of his sin brought into subjection to those sufferings which are ordained for the punishment of sinners. For, by the will of God prescribed at the beginning, punishment righteously follows those who worship Him on account of transgressions; and this is so, in order that, having reckoned with them by punishment for sin as for a debt, he may set forth those who have turned to Him pure in the universal judgment. For as the wicked here enjoy luxury to the loss of eternal blessings, so punishments are sent upon the Jews who transgress for a settlement of accounts, that, expiating their transgression here, they may there be set free from eternal punishments.

Chap. XVII. — *Speaking the truth in love*

"But you cannot speak thus; for you do not believe that things are then as we say; I mean, when there is a recompense for all. And on this account, you being ignorant of what is advantageous, are seduced by temporal pleasures from taking hold of eternal things. Therefore we attempt to make to you exhibitions of what is profitable, that, being convinced of the promises that belong to piety, you may by good deeds inherit with us the griefless world. Until then you know us, do not be angry with us, as if we spoke falsely of the good things which we desire for you. For the things which are regarded by us as true and good, these we have not scrupled to bring to you, but, on the contrary, have hastened to make you fellow-heirs of good things, which we have considered to be such. For thus it is necessary to speak to the unbelievers. But that we really speak the truth in what we say, you cannot know otherwise than by first listening with love of the truth.

Chap. XVIII. — *Charming of the serpent*

"Wherefore, as to the matter in hand, although in ten thousand ways the serpent that lurks in you suggesting evil reasonings and hindrances, wishes to ensnare you, therefore so much the more ought ye to resist him, and to listen to us assiduously. For it behoves you, consulting, as having been grievously deceived, to know how he must be charmed. But in no other way is it possible. But by charming I mean the setting yourselves by reason in opposition to their evil counsels, remembering that by promise of knowledge he brought death into the world at the first.

Chap. XIX. — *Not peace, but a sword*

"Whence the Prophet of the truth, knowing that the world was much in error, and seeing it ranged on the side of evil, did not choose that there should be peace to it while it stood in error. So that till the end he sets himself against all those who are in concord with wickedness, setting [truth] over against error, sending as it were fire upon those who are sober, namely wrath against the seducer, which is likened to a sword, [3] and by holding forth the word he destroys ignorance by knowledge, cutting, as it were, and separating the living from the dead. Therefore, while wickedness is being conquered by lawful knowledge, war has taken hold of all. For the submissive son is, for the sake of salvation, separated from the unbelieving father, or the father from the son, or the mother from the daughter, or the daughter from the mother, and relatives from relatives, and friends from associates.

Chap. XX. — *What if it he already kindled*

"And let not any one say. How is this just, that parents should be separated from their children, and children from their parents? It is just, even entirely. For if they remained with them, and, after profiting them nothing, were also destroyed along with them, how is it not just that he who wishes to be saved should be separated from him who will not, but who wishes to destroy him along with himself. Moreover, it is not those who judge better that wish to be separated, but they wish to stay with them, and to profit them by the exposition of better things; and therefore the unbelievers, not wishing to hearken to them, make war against them, banishing, persecuting, hating them. But those who suffer these things, pitying those who are ensnared by ignorance, by the teaching of wisdom pray for those who contrive evil against them, having learned that ignorance is the cause of their sin. For the Teacher Himself, being nailed to [the cross], prayed to the Father that the sin of those who slew Him might be forgiven, saying, 'Father, forgive them their sins, for they know not what they do.' [4] They also therefore, being imitators of the Teacher in their sufferings, pray for those who contrive them, as they have been taught. Therefore they are not separated as hating their parents, since they make constant prayers even for those who are neither parents nor relatives, but enemies, and strive to love them, as they have been commanded.

Chap. XXI. — *"If I be a father, where is my fear?"*

"But tell me, how do you love your parents? If, indeed, you do it as always regarding what is right, I congratulate you; but if you love them as it happens, then not so, for then you may on a small occasion become their enemies. But if you love them intelligently, tell me, what are parents? You will say they are the sources of our being. Why, then, do ye not love the [source of the] being of all things, if indeed you have with right understanding elected to do this? But you will now say again, we have not seen Him. Why, then, do ye not seek for Him, but worship senseless things? But what? If it were even difficult for you to know what God is, you cannot fail to know what is not God, so as to reason that God is not wood, nor stone, nor brass, nor anything else made of corruptible matter.

Chap. XXII. — *"The gods that have not made the heavens."*

"For are not they graven with iron? And has not the graving iron been softened by fire? And is not the fire itself extinguished with water? And has not the water its motion from the spirit? And has not the spirit the beginning of its course from the God who hath made all things? For thus said the prophet Moses: 'In the beginning God made the heaven and the earth. And the earth was unsightly, and unadorned; and darkness was over the deep: and the Spirit of God was borne above the waters.' Which Spirit, at the bidding of God, as it were His hand, makes all things, dividing light from darkness, and after the invisible heaven spreading out the visible, that the places above might be inhabited by the angels of light, and those below by man, and all the creatures that were made for his use.

Chap. XXIII. — *"To whom much is given."*

"For on thy account, O man, God commanded the water to retire upon the face of the earth, that the earth might be able to bring forth fruits for thee. And He made water-courses, that He might provide for thee fountains, and that river-beds might be disclosed, that animals might teem forth; in a word, that He might furnish thee with all things. For is it not for thee that the winds blow, and the rains fall, and the seasons change for the production of fruits? Moreover, it is for thee that the sun and moon, with the other heavenly bodies, accomplish their risings and settings; and rivers and pools, with all fountains, serve thee. Whence to thee, O senseless one, as the greater honour has been given, so for thee, ungrateful, the greater punishment by fire has been prepared, because thou wouldest not know Him whom it behoved thee before all things to know.

Chap. XXIV. — *"Born of water."*

"And now from inferior things learn the cause of all, reasoning that water makes all things, and water receives the production of its movement from spirit, and the spirit has its beginning from the God of all. And thus you ought to have reasoned, in order that by reason you might attain to God, that, knowing your origin, and being born again by the firstborn water, you may be constituted heir of the parents who have begotten you to incorruption.

Chap. XXV. — *Good works to be well done*

"Wherefore come readily, as a son to a father, that God may assign ignorance as the cause of your sins. But if after being called you will not, or delay, you shall be destroyed by the just judgment of God, not being willed, through your not willing. And do not think, though you were more pious than all the pious that ever were, but if you be unbaptized, that you shall ever obtain hope. For all the more, on this account, you shall endure the greater punishment, because you have done excellent works not excellently. For well-doing is excellent when it is done as God has commanded. But if you will not be baptized according to His pleasure, you serve your own will and oppose His counsel.

Chap. XXVI. — *Baptism*

"But perhaps some one will say, What does it contribute to piety to be baptized with water? In the first place, because you do that which is pleasing to God; and in the second place, being born again to God of water, by reason of fear you change your first generation, which is of lust, and thus you are able to obtain salvation. But otherwise it is impossible. For thus the prophet has sworn to us, saying, "Verily I say to you. Unless ye be regenerated by living water into the name of Father, Son, and Holy Spirit, you shall not enter the kingdom of heaven. [5] Wherefore approach. For there is there something that is merciful from the beginning, borne upon the water, and rescues from the future punishment those who are baptized with the thrice-blessed invocation, offering as gifts to God the good deeds of the baptized whenever they are done after their baptism. Wherefore flee to the waters, for this alone can quench the violence of fires. He who will not now come to it still bears the spirit of strife, on account of which he will not approach the living water for his own salvation.

Chap. XXVII. — *All need baptism*

"Therefore approach, be ye righteous or unrighteous. For if you are righteous, baptism alone is lacking in order to salvation. But if you are unrighteous, come to be baptized for the remission of the sins formerly committed in ignorance. And to the unrighteous man it remains that his well-doing after baptism be according to the proportion of his [previous] impiety. Wherefore, be ye righteous or unrighteous, hasten to be born to God, because delay brings danger, on account of the fore-appointment of death being unrevealed; and show by well-doing your likeness to the Father, who begetteth you of water. As a lover of truth, honour the true God as your Father. But His honour is that you live as He, being righteous, would have you live. And the will of the righteous One is that you do no wrong. But wrong is murder, hatred, envy, and such like; and of these there are many forms.

Chap. XXVIII. — *Purification*

"However, it is necessary to add something to these things which has not community with man, but is peculiar to the worship of God. I mean purification, not approaching to a man's own wife when she is in separation, for so the law of God commands. But what? If purity be not added to the service of God, you would roll pleasantly like the dung-flies. Wherefore as man, having something more than the irrational animals, namely, rationality, purify your hearts from evil by heavenly reasoning, and wash your bodies in the bath. For purification according to the truth is not that the purity of the body precedes purification after the heart, but that purity follows goodness. For our Teacher also, [dealing with] certain of the Pharisees and Scribes among us, who are separated, and as Scribes know the matters of the law more than others, still He reproved them as hypocrites, because they cleansed only the things that appear to men, but omitted purity of heart and the things seen by God alone.

Chap. XXIX. — *Outward and inward purity*

"Therefore He made use of this memorable expression, speaking the truth with respect to the hypocrites of them, not with respect to all. For to some He said that obedience was to be rendered, because they were entrusted with the chair of Moses. However, to the hypocrites he said, 'Woe to you, Scribes and Pharisees, hypocrites, for ye make clean the outside of the cup and the platter, but the inside is full of filth. Thou blind Pharisee, cleanse first the inside of the cup and the platter, that their outsides may be clean also.' And truly: for when the mind is enlightened by knowledge, the disciple is able to be good, and thereupon purity follows; for from the understanding within a good care of the body without is produced. As from negligence with respect to the body, care of the understanding cannot be produced, so the pure man can purify both that which is without and that which is within. And he who, purifying the things without, does it looking to the praise of men, and by the praise of those who look on, he has nothing from God.

Chap. XXX. — *"Whatsoever things are pure."*

"But who is there to whom it is not manifest that it is better not to have intercourse with a woman in her separation, but purified and washed. And also after copulation it is proper to wash. But if you grudge to do this, recall to mind how you followed after the parts of purity when you served senseless idols; and be ashamed that now, when it is necessary to attain, I say not more, but to attain the one and whole of purity, you are more slothful. Consider, therefore, Him who made you, and you will understand who He is that casts upon you this sluggishness with respect to purity.

Chap. XXXI. — *"What do ye more than others?"*

"But some one of you will say. Must we then do whatsoever things we did while we were idolaters? I say to you, Not all things; but whatsoever you did well, you must do now, and more: for whatsoever is well done in error hangs upon truth, as if anything be ill done in the truth it is from error. Receive, therefore, from all quarters the things that are your own, and not those that are another's, and do not say, If those who are in error do anything well we are not bound to do it. For, on this principle, if any one who worships idols do not commit murder, we ought to commit murder, because he who is in error does not commit it.

Chap. XXXII. — *"To whom much is given."*

"No; but rather, if those who are in error do not kill, let us not be angry; if he who is in error do not commit adultery, let us not lust even in the smallest degree; if he who is in error loves him who loves him, let us love even those who hate us; if he who is in error lends to those who have, let us [give] to those who have not. Unquestionably we ought — we who hope to inherit eternal life — to do better things than the good things that are done by those who know only the present life, knowing that if their works, being judged with ours in the day of judgment, be found equal in goodness, we shall have shame, and they perdition, having acted against themselves through error. And I say that we shall be put to shame on this account, because we have not done more than they, though we have known more than they. And if we shall be put to shame if we show well-doing equal to theirs, and no more, how much more if we show less than their well-doing?

Chap. XXXIII. — *The queen of the south and the men of Nineveh*

"But that indeed in the day of judgment the doings of those who have known the truth are compared with the good deeds of those who have been in error, the unlying One Himself has taught us, saying to those who neglected to come and listen to Him, 'The queen of the south shall rise up with this generation, and shall condemn it; because she came from the extremities of the earth to hear the wisdom of Solomon: and behold, a greater than Solomon is here,' [6] and ye do not believe Him. And to those amongst the people who would not repent at His preaching He said, 'The men of Nineveh shall rise up with this generation and shall condemn it, for they heard and repented on the preaching of Jonas: and behold, a greater is here, and no one believes.' [7] And thus, setting over against all their impiety those from among the Gentiles who have done [well], in order to condemn those who, possessing the true religion, had not acted so well as those who were in error, he exhorted those having reason not only to do equally with the Gentiles whatsoever things are excellent, but more than they. And this speech has been suggested to me, taking occasion from the necessity of respecting the separation, and of washing after copulation, and of not denying such purity, though those who are in error do the same, since those who in error do well, without being saved, are for the condemnation of those who are in the worship of God, [and do ill]; because their respect for purity is through error, and not through the worship of the true Father and God of all."

Chap. XXXIV. — *Peter's daily work*

Having said this, he dismissed the multitudes; and according to his custom, having partaken of food with those dearest to him, he went to rest. And thus doing and discouraging day by day, he strongly buttressed the law of God, challenging the reputed gods with the reputed genesis, and arguing that there is no automatism, but that the world is governed according to providence.

Chap. XXXV. — *"Beware of false prophets."*

Then after three months were fulfilled, he ordered me to fast for several days, and then brought me to the fountains that are near to the sea, and baptized me as in ever-flowing water. Thus, therefore, when our brethren rejoiced at my God-gifted regeneration, not many days after he turned to the elders in presence of all the church, and charged them, saying: "Our Lord and Prophet, who hath sent us, declared to us that the wicked one, having disputed with Him forty days, and having prevailed nothing against Him, promised that he would send apostles from amongst his subjects, to deceive. Wherefore, above all, remember to shun apostle or teacher or prophet who does not first accurately compare his preaching with [that of] James, who was called the brother of my Lord, and to whom was entrusted to administer the church of the Hebrews in Jerusalem, — and that even though he come to you with witnesses; [8] lest the wickedness which disputed forty days with the Lord, and prevailed nothing, should afterwards, like lightning falling from heaven upon the earth, send a preacher to your injury, as now he has sent Simon upon us, preaching, under pretence of the truth, in the name of the Lord, and sowing error. Wherefore He who hath sent us, said, 'Many shall come to me in sheep's clothing, but inwardly they are ravening wolves. By their fruits ye shall know them.'"

Chap. XXXVI. — *Farewell to Tripolis*

Having spoken thus, he sent the harbingers into Antioch of Syria, bidding them expect him there forthwith. Then when they had gone, Peter having driven away diseases, sufferings, and demons from great multitudes who were persuaded, and having baptized them in the fountains which are near to the sea, and having celebrated [9] the eucharist, and having appointed Maroones, who had received him into his house, and was now perfected, as their bishop, and having set apart twelve elders, and having designated deacons, and arranged matters relating to widows, and having discoursed on the common good what was profitable for the ordering of the church, and having counselled them to obey the bishop Maroones, three months being now fulfilled, he bade those in Tripolis of Phoenicia farewell, and took his journey to Antioch of Syria, all the people accompanying us with due honour.

[1] "We have adopted the reading of Codex O. The reading in the others is corrupt.
[2] Matt. XVII. 19.
[3] Matt. X. 34.
[4] Luke XXIII. 34.
[5] Altered from John III. 5.
[6] Matt. XII. 42.
[7] Luke XI. 32.
[8] A conjectural reading, which, seems probable, is, Unless he come to you with credentials, viz. from James.
[9] Literally, "having broken."

Homily XII

Chap. I. — *Two hands*

Therefore starting from Tripolis of Phoenicia to go to Antioch of Syria, on the same day we came to Orthasia, and there stayed. And on account of its being near the city which we had left, almost all having heard the preaching before, we stopped there only one day, and set out to Antaradus. And as there were many who journeyed with us, Peter, addressing Nicetus and Aquila, said, "Inasmuch as the great crowd of those who journey with us draws upon us no little envy as we enter city after city, I have thought that we must of necessity arrange, so that neither, on the one hand, these may be grieved at being prevented from accompanying us, nor, on the other hand, we, by being so conspicuous, may fall under the envy of the wicked. [1] Wherefore I wish you, Nicetus and Aquila, to go before me in two separate bodies, and enter secretly into the Gentile cities.

Chap. II. — *Love of preachers and their converts*

"I know, indeed, that you are distressed at being told to do this, being separated from me by a space of two days. I would have you know, therefore, that we the persuaders love you the persuaded much more than you love us who have persuaded you. Therefore loving one another as we do by not unreasonably doing what we wish, let us provide, as much as in us lies, for safety. For I prefer, as you also know, [to go] into the more notable cities of the provinces, and to remain some days, and discourse. And for the present lead the way into the neighbouring Laodicea, and, after two or three days, so far as it depends upon my choice, I shall overtake you. And do you alone receive me at the gates, on account of the confusion, that thus we may enter along with you without tumult. And thence, in like manner, after some days' stay, others in your stead will go forward by turns to the places beyond, preparing lodgings for us."

Chap. III. — *Submission*

When Peter had thus spoken they were compelled to acquiesce, saying, "It does not altogether grieve us, my lord, to do this on account of its being your command; in the first place, indeed, because you have been chosen by the providence of God, as being worthy to think and counsel well in all things; and in addition to this, for the most part we shall be separated from you only for two days by the necessity of preceding you. And that were indeed a long time to be without sight of thee, O Peter, did we not consider that they will be more grieved who are sent much farther forward, being ordered to wait for thee longer in every city, distressed that they are longer deprived of the sight of thy longed-for countenance. And we, though not less distressed than they, make no opposition, because you order us to do it for profit." Thus, having spoken, they went forward, having it in charge that at the first stage they should address the accompanying multitude that they should enter the cities apart from one another.

Chap. IV. — *Clement's joy*

When, therefore, they had gone, I, Clement, rejoiced greatly that he had ordered me to remain with himself. Then I answered and said, "I thank God that you have not sent me away as you have done the others, as I should have died of grief." But he said, "But what? If there shall ever be any necessity that you be sent away for the sake of teaching, would you, on account of being separated for a little while from me, and that for an advantageous purpose, would you die for that? Would you not rather impress upon yourself the duty of bearing the things that are arranged for you through necessity, and cheerfully submit? And do you not know that friends are present with one another in their memories, although they are separated bodily; whereas some, being bodily present, wander from their friends in their souls, by reason of want of memory?"

Chap. V. — *Clement's office of service*

Then I answered, "Do not think, my lord, that I should endure that grief foolishly, but with some good reason. For since I hold you, my lord, in place of all, father, mother, brothers, relatives, you who are the means through God of my having the saving truth, holding you in place of all, I have the greatest consolation. And in addition to this, being afraid of my natural youthful lust, I was concerned lest, being left by you (being but a young man, and having now such a resolution that it would be impossible to desert you without incurring the anger of God,) [2] I should be overcome by lust. But since it is much better and safer for me to remain with you, when my mind is with good reason set upon venerating, therefore I pray that I may always remain with you. Moreover, I remember you saying in Caesarea, 'If any one wishes to journey with me, let him piously journey.' And by *piously* you meant, that those who are devoted to the worship of God should grieve no one in respect of God, such as by leaving parents, an attached wife, or any others. [3] Whence I am in all respects a fitting fellow-traveller for you, to whom, if you would confer the greatest favour, you would allow to perform the functions of a servant."

Chap. VI. — *Peter's frugality*

Then Peter, hearing, smiled and said, "What think you, then, O Clement? Do you not think that you are placed by very necessity in the position of my servant? For who else shall take care of those many splendid tunics, with all my changes of rings and sandals? And who shall make ready those pleasant and artistic dainties, which, being so various, need many skilful cooks, and all those things which are procured with great eagerness, and are prepared for the appetite of effeminate men as for some great wild beast? However, such a choice has occurred to you, perhaps, without you understanding or knowing my manner of life, that I use only bread and olives, and rarely pot-herbs; and that this is my only coat and cloak which I wear; and I have no need of any of them, nor of aught else: for even in these I abound. For my mind, seeing all the eternal good things that are there, regards none of the things that are here. However, I accept of your good will; and I admire and commend you, for that you, a man of refined habits, have so easily submitted your manner of living to your necessities. For we, from our childhood, both I and Andrew, my brother, who is also my brother as respects God, not only being brought up in the condition of orphans, but also accustomed to labour through poverty and misfortune, easily bear the discomforts of our present journeys. Whence, if you would obey me, you would allow me, a working man, to fulfil the part of a servant to you."

Chap. VII. — *"Not to he ministered unto, but to minister."*

But I, when I heard this, fell a-trembling and weeping, that such a word should be spoken by a man to whom all the men of this generation are inferior in point of knowledge and piety. But he, seeing me weeping, asked the cause of my tears. Then I said, "In what have I sinned so that you have spoken to me such a word?" Then Peter answered, "If it were wrong of me to speak of being your servant, you were first in fault in asking to be mine." Then I said, "The cases are not parallel; for to do this indeed becomes me well; but it is terrible for you, the herald of God, and who savest our souls, to do this to me." Then Peter answered, "I should agree with you, but that [4] our Lord, who came for the salvation of all the world, being alone noble above all, submitted to the condition of a servant, that He might persuade us not to be ashamed to perform the ministrations of servants to our brethren, however well-born we may be." Then I said, "If I think to overcome you in argument, I am foolish. However, I thank the providence of God, that I have been thought worthy to have you instead of parents."

Chap. VIII. — *Family history*

Then Peter inquired, "Are you really, then, alone in your family?" Then I answered, "There are indeed many and great men, being of the kindred of Caesar. Wherefore Caesar himself gave a wife of his own family to my father, who was his foster-brother; and of her three sons of us were born, two before me, who were twins and very like each other, as my father told me. But I scarcely know either them or our mother, but bear about with me an obscure Image of them, as through dreams. My mother's name was Mattidin, and my father's, Faustin; and of my brothers one was called Faastinus, and the other Faustinianus. Then after I, their third son, was born, my mother saw a vision — so my father told me — [which told her,] that unless she immediately took away her twin sons, and left the city of Rome for exile for twelve years, she and they must die by an all-destructive fate.

Chap. IX. — *The lost ones*

"Therefore my father, being fond of his children, supplying them suitably for the journey with male and female servants, put them on board ship, and sent them to Athens with her to be educated, and kept me alone of his sons with him for his comfort; and for this I am very thankful, that the vision had not ordered me also to depart with my mother from the city of Rome. Then, after the lapse of a year, my father sent money to them to Athens, and at the same time to learn how they did. But those who went on this errand did not return. And in the third year, my father being distressed, sent others in like manner with supplies, and they returned in the fourth year with the tidings that they had seen neither my mother nor my brothers, nor had they ever arrived at Athens, nor had they found any trace of any one of those who set out with them.

Chap. X. — *The seeker lost*

"Then my father, hearing this, and being stupefied with excessive grief, and not knowing where to go in quest of them, used to take me with him and go down to the harbour, and inquire of many where any one of them had seen or heard of a shipwreck four years ago. And one turned one place, and another, another. Then he inquired whether they had seen the body of a woman with [two] children cast ashore. And when they told him that they had seen many corpses in many places, my father groaned at the information. But, with his bowels yearning, he asked unreasonable questions, that he might try to search so great an extent of sea. However, he was pardonable, because, through affection towards those whom he was seeking for, he fed on vain hopes. And at last, placing me under guardians, and leaving me at Home when I was twelve years old, he himself, weeping, went down to the harbour, and went on board ship, and set out upon the search. And from that day till this I have neither received a letter from him, nor do I know whether he be alive or dead. But I rather suspect that he is dead somewhere, either overcome by grief, or perished by shipwreck. And the proof of that is that it is now the twentieth year that I have heard no true intelligence concerning him."

Chap. XI. — *The afflictions of the righteous*

But Peter, hearing this, wept through sympathy, and immediately said to the gentlemen who were present: "If any worshipper of God had suffered these things, such as this man's father hath suffered, he would immediately have assigned the cause of it to be his worship of God, ascribing it to the wicked one. Thus also it is the lot of the wretched Gentiles to suffer; and we worshippers of God know it not. But with good reason I call them wretched, because here they are ensnared, and the hope that is thine they obtain not. For those who in the worship of God suffer afflictions, suffer them for the expiation of their transgressions."

Chap. XII. — *A pleasure trip*

When Peter had spoken thus, a certain one amongst us ventured to invite him, in the name of all, that next day, early in the morning, he should sail to Aradus, an island opposite, distant, I suppose, not quite thirty stadia, for the purpose of seeing two pillars of vine-wood that were there, and that were of very great girth. Therefore the indulgent Peter consented, saying, "When you leave the boat, do not go many of you together to see the things that you desire to see; for I do not wish that the attention of the inhabitants should be turned to you." And so we sailed, and in short time arrived at the island. Then landing from the boat, we went to the place where the vine-wood pillars were, and along with them we looked at several of the works of Phidias.

Chap. XIII. — *A woman of a sorrowful spirit*

But Peter alone did not think it worth while to look at the sights that were there; but noticing a certain woman sitting outside before the doors, begging constantly for her support, he said to her, "O woman, is any of your limbs defective, that you submit to such disgrace — I mean that of begging, — and do not rather work with the hands which God has given you, and procure your daily food?" But she, groaning, answered, "Would that I had hands able to work! But now they retain only the form of hands, being dead and rendered useless by my gnawing of them." Then Peter asked her, "What is the cause of your suffering so terribly?" And she answered, "Weakness of soul; and nought else. For if I had the mind of a man, there was a precipice or a pool whence I should have thrown myself, and have been able to rest from my tormenting misfortunes."

Chap. XIV. — *Balm in Gilead*

Then said Peter, "What then? Do you suppose, O woman, that those who destroy themselves are freed from punishment? Are not the souls of those who thus die punished with a worse punishment in Hades for their suicide?" But she said, "Would that I were persuaded that souls are really found alive in Hades; then I should love death, making light of the punishment, that I might see, were it but for an hour, my longed-for sons!" Then said Peter, "What is it that grieves you? I should like to know, O woman. For if you inform me, in return for this favour, I shall satisfy you that souls live in Hades; and instead of precipice or pool, I shall give you a drug, that you may live and die without torment."

Chap. XV. — *The woman's story*

Then the woman, not understanding what was spoken ambiguously, being pleased with the promise, began to speak thus: — "Were I to speak of my family and my country, I do not suppose that I should be able to persuade any one. But of what consequence is it to you to learn this, excepting only the reason why in my anguish I have deadened my hands by gnawing them? Yet I shall give you an account of myself, so far as it is in your power to hear it. I, being very nobly born, by the arrangement of a certain man in authority, became the wife of a man who was related to him. And first I had twin sons, and afterwards another son. But my husband's brother, being thoroughly mad, was enamoured of wretched me, who exceedingly affected chastity. And I, wishing neither to consent to my lover nor to expose to my husband his brother's love of me, reasoned thus; that I may neither defile myself by the commission of adultery nor disgrace my husband's bed, nor set brother at war with brother, nor subject the whole family, which is a great one, to the reproach of all, as I said. I reasoned that it was best for me to leave the city for some time with my twin children, until the impure love should cease of him who flattered me to my disgrace. The other son, however, I left with his father, to remain for a comfort to him.

Chap. XVI. — *The shipwreck*

"However, that matters might be thus arranged, I resolved to fabricate a dream, to the effect that some one stood by me by night, and thus spoke: 'O Woman, straightway leave the city with your twin children for some time, until I shall charge you to return hither again; otherwise you forthwith shall die miserably, with your husband and all your children.' And so I did. For as soon as I told the false dream to my husband, he being alarmed, sent me off by ship to Athens with my two sons, and with slaves, maids, and abundance of money, to educate the boys, until, said he, it shall please the giver of the oracle that you return to me. But, wretch that I am, while sailing with my children, I was driven by the fury of the winds into these regions, and the ship having gone to pieces in the night, I was wrecked. And all the rest having died, my unfortunate self alone was tossed by a great wave and cast upon a rock; and while I sat upon it in my misery, I was prevented, by the hope of finding my children alive, from throwing myself into the deep then, when I could easily have done it, having my soul made drunk by the waves.

Chap. XVII. — *The fruitless search*

"But when the day dawned, I shouted aloud, and howled miserably, and looked around, seeking for the dead bodies of my hapless children. Therefore the inhabitants took pity on me, and seeing me naked, they first clothed me and then sounded the deep, seeking for my children. And when they found nothing of what they sought, some of the hospitable women came to me to comfort me, and every one told her own misfortunes, that I might obtain comfort from the occurrences of similar misfortunes. But this only grieved me the more; for I said that I was not so wicked that I could take comfort from the misfortunes of others. And so, when many of them asked me to accept their hospitality, a certain poor woman with much urgency constrained me to come into her cottage, saying to me, 'Take courage, woman, for my husband, who was a sailor, also died at sea, while ho was still in the bloom of his youth; and ever since, though many have asked me in marriage, I have preferred living as a widow, regretting the loss of my husband. But we shall have in common whatever we can both earn with our hands.'

Chap. XVIII. — *Trouble upon trouble*

"And not to lengthen out unnecessary details, I went to live with her, on account of her love to her husband. And not long after, my hands were debilitated by my gnawing of them; and the woman who had taken me in, being wholly seized by some malady, is confined in the house. Since then the former compassion of the woman has declined, and I and the woman of the house are both of us helpless. For a long time I have sat here, as you see, begging; and whatever I get I convey to my fellow-sufferer for our support. Let this suffice about my affairs. For the rest, what hinders your fulfilling of your promise to give me the drug, that I may give it to her also, who desires to die; and thus I also, as you said, shall be able to escape from life?"

Chap. XIX. — *Evasions*

While the woman thus spoke, Peter seemed to be in suspense on account of many reasonings. But I came up and said, "I have been going about seeking you for a long time. And now, what is in hand?" But Peter ordered me to lead the way, and wait for him at the boat; and because there was no gainsaying when he commanded, I did as I was ordered. But Peter, as he afterwards related the whole matter to me, being struck in his heart with some slight suspicion, inquired of the woman, saying, "Tell me, O woman, your family, and your city, and the names of your children, and presently I shall give you the drug." But she, being put under constraint, and not wishing to speak, yet being eager to obtain the drug, cunningly said one thing for another. And so she said that she was an Ephesian, and her husband a Sicilian; and in like manner she changed the names of the three children.

Then Peter, supposing that she spoke the truth, said, "Alas! O woman, I thought that this day was to bring you great joy, suspecting that you are a certain person of whom I was thinking, and whose affairs I have heard and accurately know." But she adjured him, saying, "Tell me, I entreat of you, that I may know if there is among women any one more wretched than myself."

Chap. XX. — *Peter's account of the matter*

Then Peter, not knowing that she had spoken falsely, through pity towards her, began to tell her the truth: "There is a certain young man in attendance upon me, thirsting after the discourses on religion, a Roman citizen, who told me how that, having a father and two twin brothers, he has lost sight of them all. For," says he, "my mother, as my father related to me, having seen a vision, left the city Rome for a time with her twin children, lest she should perish by an evil fate, and having gone away with them, she cannot be found; and her husband, the young man's father, having one in search of her, he also cannot be found."

Chap. XXI. — *A disclosure*

"While Peter thus spoke, the woman, who had listened attentively, swooned away as if in stupor. But Peter approached her, and caught hold of her, and exhorted her to restrain herself, persuading her to confess what was the matter with her. But she, being powerless in the rest of her body, as through intoxication, turned her [head] round, being able to sustain the greatness of the hoped-for joy, and rubbing her face: "Where," said she, "is this youth?" And he, now seeing through the whole affair, said, "Tell me first; for otherwise you cannot see him." Then she earnestly said, "I am that youth's mother." Then said Peter, "What is his name?" And she said, "Clement." Then Peter said, "It is the same, and he it was that spoke to me a little while ago, whom I ordered to wait for me in the boat. And she, falling at Peter's feet, entreated him to make haste to come to the boat." Then Peter, "If you will keep terms with me, I shall do so." Then she said, "I will do anything; only show me my only child. For I shall seem to see in him my two children who died here." Then Peter said, "When ye see him, be quiet, until we depart from the island." And she said, "I will."

Chap. XXII. — *The lost found*

Peter, therefore, took her by the hand, and led her to the boat. But I, when I saw him leading the woman by the hand, laughed, and approaching, offered to lead her instead of him, to his honour. But as soon as I touched her hand, she gave a motherly shout, and embraced me violently, and eagerly kissed me as her son. But I, being ignorant of the whole affair, shook her off as a madwoman. But, through my respect for Peter, I checked myself.

Chap. XXIII. — *Reward of Hospitality*

But Peter said, "Alas! What are you doing, my son Clement, shaking off your real mother?" But I, when I heard this, wept, and falling down by my mother, who had fallen, I kissed her. For as soon as this was told me, I in some way recalled her appearance indistinctly. Then great crowds ran together to see the beggar woman, telling one another that her son had recognised her, and that he was a man of consideration. Then, when we would have straightway left the island with my mother, she said to us, "My much longed-for son, it is right that I should bid farewell to the woman who entertained me, who, being poor and wholly debilitated, lies in the house." And Peter hearing this, and all the multitude who stood by, admired the good disposition of the woman. And immediately Peter ordered some persons to go and bring the woman on her couch. And as soon as the couch was brought and set down, Peter said, in the hearing of the whole multitude, "If I be a herald of the truth, in order to the faith of the bystanders, that they may know that there is one God, who made the world, let her straightway rise whole." And while Peter was still speaking, the woman arose healed, and fell down before Peter, and kissed her dear associate, and asked her what it all meant. Then she briefly detailed to her the whole business of the recognition, to the astonishment of the hearers. Then also my mother, seeing her hostess cured, entreated that she herself also might obtain healing. And his placing his hand upon her, cured her also.

Chap. XXIV. — *All well arranged*

And then Peter having discoursed concerning God and the service accorded to Him, he concluded as follows: "If any one wishes to learn these things accurately, let him come to Antioch, where I have resolved to remain some length of time, and learn the things that pertain to his salvation. For if you are familiar with leaving your country for the sake of trading or of warfare, and coming to far-off places, you should not be unwilling to for three days' journey for the sake of eternal salvation." Then, after the address of Peter, I presented the woman who had been healed, in the presence of all the multitude, with a thousand drachmas, for her support, giving her in charge to a certain good man, who was the chief man of the city, and who of his own accord joyfully undertook the charge. Further, having distributed money amongst many other women, and thanked those who at any time had comforted my mother, I sailed away to Antaradus, along with my mother, and Peter, and the rest of our companions; and thus we proceeded to our lodging.

Chap. XXV. — *Philanthropy and friendship*

And when we were arrived and had partaken of food, and given thanks according to our custom, there being still time, I said to Peter: "My lord Peter, my mother has done a work of philanthropy in remembering the woman her hostess." And Peter answered, "Have you indeed, O Clement, thought truly that your mother did a work of philanthropy in respect of her treatment of the woman who took her in after her shipwreck, or have you spoken this word by way of greatly complimenting your mother? But if you spoke truly, and not by way of compliment, you seem to me not to know what the greatness of philanthropy is, which is affection towards any one whatever in respect of his being a man, apart from physical persuasion. But not even do I venture to call the hostess who received your mother after her shipwreck, philanthropic; for she was impelled by pity, and persuaded to become the benefactress of a woman who had been shipwrecked, who was grieving for her children, — a stranger, naked, destitute, and greatly deploring her misfortunes. When, therefore, she was in such circumstances, who that saw her, though he were impious, could but pity her? So that it does not seem to me that even the stranger-receiving woman did a work of philanthropy, but to have been moved to assist her by pity for her innumerable misfortunes. And how much more is it true of your mother, that when she was in prosperous circumstances and requited her hostess, she did a deed, not of philanthropy, but of friendship! for there is much difference between friendship and philanthropy, because friendship springs from requital. But philanthropy, apart from physical persuasion, loves and benefits every man as he is a man. If, therefore, while she pitied her hostess, she also pitied and did good to her enemies who have wronged her, she would be philanthropic; but if, on one account she is friendly or hostile, and on another account is hostile or friendly, such an one is the friend or enemy of some quality, not of man as man."

Chap. XXVI. — *What is philanthropy?*

Then I answered, "Do you not think, then, that even the stranger receiver was philanthropic, who did good to a stranger whom she did not know?" Then Peter said, "Compassionate, indeed, I can call her, but I dare not call her philanthropic, just as I cannot call a mother philoteknic, for she is prevailed on to have an affection for them by her pangs, and by her rearing of them. As the lover also is gratified by the company and enjoyment of his mistress, and the friend by return of friendship, so also the compassionate man by misfortune. However the compassionate man is near to the philanthropic, in that he is impelled, apart from hunting after the receipt of anything, to do the kindness. But he is not yet philanthropic." Then I said, "By what deeds, then, can any one be philanthropic?" And Peter answered, "Since I see that you are eager to hear what is the work of philanthropy, I shall not object to telling you. He is the philanthropic man who does good even to his enemies. And that it is so, listen: Philanthropy is masculo-feminine; and the feminine part of it is called *compassion,* and the male part is named love to our neighbour. But every man is neighbour to every man, and not merely this man or that; for the good and the bad, the friend and the enemy, are alike men. It behoves, therefore, him who practises philanthropy to be an imitator of God, doing good to the righteous and the unrighteous, as God Himself vouchsafes His sun and His heavens to all in the present world. But if you will do good to the good, but not to the evil, or even will punish them, you undertake to do the work of a judge, you do not strive to hold by philanthropy.

Chap. XXVII. — *Who can judge?*

Then I said, "Then even God, who, as you teach us, is at some time to judge, is not philanthropic." Then said Peter, "You assert a contradiction; for because He shall judge, on that very account He is philanthropic. For he who loves and compassionates those who have been wronged, avenges those who have wronged them." Then I said, "If, then, I also do good to the good, and punish the wrong-doers in respect of their injuring men, am I not philanthropic?" And Peter answered, "If along with knowledge [5] you had also authority to judge, you would do this rightly on account of your having received authority to judge those whom God made, and on account of your knowledge infallibly justifying some as the righteous, and condemning some as unrighteous." Then I said, "You have spoken rightly and truly; for it is impossible for any one who has not knowledge to judge rightly. For sometimes some persons seem good, though they perpetrate wickedness in secret, and some good persons are conceived to be bad through the accusation of their enemies. But even if one judges, having the power of torturing and examining, not even so should he altogether judge righteously. For some persons, being murderers, have sustained the tortures, and have come off as innocent; while others, being innocent, have not been able to sustain the tortures, but have confessed falsely against themselves, and have been punished as guilty."

Chap. XXVIII. — *Difficulty of judging*

Then said Peter, "These things are ordinary: now hear what is greater. There are some men whose sins or good deeds are partly their own, and partly those of others; but it is right that each one be punished for his own sins, and rewarded for his own merits. But it is impossible for any one except a prophet, who alone has omniscience, to know with respect to the things that are done by any one, which are his own, and which are not; for all are seen as done by him." Then I said, "I would learn how some of men's wrong-doings or right-doings are their own, and some belong to others."

Chap. XXIX. — *Sufferings of the good*

Then Peter answered, "The prophet of the truth has said, 'Good things must needs come, and blessed, said he, is he by whom they come; in like manner evil things must needs come, but woe to him through whom they come.' [6] But if evil things come by means of evil men, and good things are brought by good men, it must needs be in each man as his own to be either good or bad, and proceeding from what he has proposed, in order to the coming of the subsequent good or evil, [7] which, being of his own choice, are not arranged by the providence of God to come from him. This being so, this is the judgment of God, that he who, as by a combat, comes through all misfortune and is found blameless, he is deemed worthy of eternal life; for those who by their own will continue in goodness, are tempted by those who continue in evil by their own will, being persecuted, hated, slandered, plotted against, struck, cheated, accused, tortured, disgraced, — suffering all these things by which it seems reasonable that they should be enraged and stirred up to vengeance.

Chap. XXX. — *Offences must come*

"But the Master knowing that those who wrongfully do these things are guilty by means of their former sins, and that the spirit of wickedness works these things by means of the guilty, has counselled to compassionate men, as they are men, and as being the instruments of wickedness through sin; [and this counsel] He has given to His disciples as claiming philanthropy, and, as much as in us lies, to absolve the wrong-doers from condemnation, that, as it were, the .temperate may help the drunken, by prayers, fastings, and benedictions, not resisting, not avenging, lest they should compel them to sin more. For when a person is condemned by any one to suffer, it is not reasonable for him to be angry with him by whose means the suffering comes; for he ought to reason, that if he had not ill-used him, yet because he was to be ill-used, he must have suffered it by means of another. Why, then, should I be angry with the dispenser, when I was condemned at all events to suffer? But yet, further: if we do these same things to the evil on pretence of revenge, we who are good do the very things which the evil do, excepting that they do them first, and we second; and, as I said, we ought not to be angry, as knowing that in the providence of God, the evil punish the good. Those, therefore, who are bitter against their punishers, sin, as disdaining the messengers of God; but those who honour them, and set themselves in opposition to those who think to injure them, [8] are pious towards God who has thus decreed."

Chap. XXXI. — *"Howbeit, they meant it not!"*

To this I answered, "Those, therefore, who do wrong are not guilty, because they wrong the just by the judgment of God." Then Peter said, "They indeed sin greatly, for they have given themselves to sin. Wherefore knowing this, [God] chooses from among them [some] to punish those who righteously repented of their former sins, that the evil things done by the just before their repentance may be remitted through this punishment. But to the wicked who punish and desire to ill-use them, and will not repent, it is permitted to ill-use the righteous for the filling up of their own punishment. For without the will of God, not even a sparrow can fall into a girn. [9] Thus even the hairs of the righteous are numbered by God.

Chap. XXXII. — *The golden rule*

"But he is righteous who for the sake of what is reasonable fights with nature. For example, it is natural to all to love those who love them. But the righteous man tries also to love his enemies and to bless those who slander him, and even to pray for his enemies, and to compassionate those who do him wrong. Wherefore also he refrains from doing wrong, and blesses those who curse him, pardons those who strike him, and submits to those who persecute him, and salutes those who do not salute him, shares such things as he has with those who have not, persuades him that is angry with him, conciliates his enemy, exhorts the disobedient, instructs the unbelieving, comforts the mourner; being distressed, he endures; being ungratefully treated, he is not angry. But having devoted himself to love his neighbour as himself, he is not afraid of poverty, but becomes poor by sharing his possessions with those who have none. But neither does he punish the sinner. For he who loves his neighbour as himself, as he knows that when he has sinned he does not wish to be punished, so neither does he punish those who sin. And as he washes to be praised, and blessed, and honoured, and to have all his sins forgiven, thus he does to his neighbour, loving him as himself. [10] In one word, what he wishes for himself, he wishes also for his neighbour. For this is the law of God and of the prophets [11] this is the doctrine of truth. And this perfect love towards every man is the male part of philanthropy, but the female part of it is compassion; that is, to feed the hungry, [12] to give drink to the thirsty, to clothe the naked, to visit the sick, to take in the stranger, to show herself to, and help to the utmost of her power, him who is in prison, and, in short, to have compassion on him who is in misfortune."

Chap. XXXIII. — *Fear and love*

But I, hearing this, said: "These things, indeed, it is impossible to do; but to do good to enemies, bearing all their insolences, I do not think can possibly be in human nature." Then Peter answered: "You have said truly; for philanthropy, being the cause of immortality, is given for much." Then I said, "How then is it possible to get it in the mind?" Then Peter answered: "O beloved Clement, the way to get it is this: if any one be persuaded that enemies, ill-using for a time those whom they hate, become the cause to them of deliverances from eternal punishment; and forthwith he will ardently love them as benefactors. But the way to get it, O dear Clement, is but one, which is the fear of God. For he who fears God cannot indeed from the first love his neighbour as himself; for such an order does not occur to the soul. But by the fear of God he is able to do the things of those who love; and thus, while he does the deeds of love, the bride Love is, as it were, brought to the bridegroom Fear, And thus this bride, bringing forth philanthropic thoughts, makes her possessor immortal, as an accurate image of God, which cannot be subject in its nature to corruption." Thus while he expounded to us the doctrine of philanthropy, the evening having set in, we turned to sleep.

[1] Literally, "of wickedness."
[2] Here the text is hopelessly corrupt, and the meaning can only be guessed at.
[3] I have ventured to make a very slight change on the reading here, so as to bring out what I suppose to be the sense.
[4] A negative particle seems to be dropped from the text.
[5] The word repeatedly rendered *knowledge* and once omniscience in this passage, properly signifies *foreknowledge*. The argument shows clearly that it means omniscience, of which foreknowledge is the most signal manifestation.
[6] An incorrect quotation from Matt, xviii., Luke xvii.
[7] This from a various reading.
[8] That is, I suppose, who render good for evil.
[9] See Luke XII. 6, 7.
[10] Matt. XXII. 39.
[11] Matt. VII. 12.
[12] Matt. XXV. 35, 36.

Homily XIII

Chap. I. — *Journey to Laodicea*

Now at break of day Peter entered, and said: "Clement, and his mother Mattidia, and my wife, must take their seats immediately on the waggon." And so they did straightway. And as we were hastening along the road to Balanaeas, my mother asked me how my father was; and I said: "My father went in search of you, and of my twin brothers Faustinus and Faustinianus, and is now nowhere to be found. But I fancy he must have died long ago, either perishing by shipwreck, or losing his way, [1] or wasted away by grief." When she heard this, she burst into tears, and groaned through grief; but the joy which she felt at finding me, mitigated in some degree the painfulness of her recollections. And so we all went down together to Balansese. And on the following day we went to Paltus, and from that to Gabala; and on the next day we reached Laodicea. And, lo! before the gates of the city Nicetas and Aquila met us, and embracing us, brought us to our lodging. Now Peter, seeing that the city was beautiful and great, said: "It is worth our while to stay here for some days; for, generally speaking, a populous place is most capable of yielding us those whom we seek." [2] Nicetas and Aquila asked me who that strange woman was; and I said: "My mother, whom God, through my lord Peter, has granted me to recognise."

Chap. II. — *Peter relates to Nicetas and Aquila the Idstory of Clement and his family*

On my saying this, Peter gave them a summary account of all the incidents, — how, when they had gone on before, I Clement had explained to him my descent, the journey undertaken by my mother with her twin children on the false pretext of the dream; and furthermore, the journey undertaken by my father in search of her; and then how Peter himself, after hearing this, went into the island, met with the woman, saw her begging, and asked the reason of her so doing; and then ascertained who she was, and her mode of life, and the feigned dream, and the names of her children — that is, the name borne by me, who was left with my father, and the names of the twin children who travelled along with her, and who, she supposed, had perished in the deep.

Chap. III. — *Recognition of Nicetas and Aquila*

Now when this summary narrative had been given by Peter, Nicetas and Aquila in amazement said: "Is this indeed true, O Ruler and Lord of the universe, or is it a dream?" And Peter said: "Unless we are asleep, it certainly is true." On this they waited for a little in deep meditation, and then said: "We are Faustinus and Faustinianus. From the commencement of your conversation we looked at each other, and conjectured much with regard to ourselves, whether what was said had reference to us or not; for we reflected that many coincidences take place in life. Wherefore we remained silent while our hearts beat fast. But when you came to the end of your narrative, we saw clearly [3] that your statements referred to us, and then we avowed who we were." And on saying this, bathed in tears, they rushed in to see their mother; and although they found her asleep, they were yet anxious to embrace her. But Peter forbade them, saying: "Let me bring you and present you to your mother, lest she should, in consequence of her great and sudden joy, lose her reason, as she is slumbering, and her spirit is held fast by sleep."

Chap. IV. — *The mother must not take food with her son. The reason stated*

As soon as my mother had enough of sleep, she awoke, and Peter at once began first to talk to her of [true] piety, saying: "I wish you to know, O woman, the course of life involved in our religion. [4] We worship one God, who made the world which you see; and we keep His law, which has for its chief injunctions to worship Him alone, and to hallow His name, and to honour our parents, and to be chaste, and to live piously. In addition to this, we do not live with all indiscriminately; nor do we take our food from the same table as Gentiles, inasmuch as we cannot eat along with them, because they live impurely. But when we have persuaded them to have true thoughts, and to follow a right course of action, and have baptized them with a thrice blessed invocation, then we dwell with them. For not even if it were our father, or mother, or wife, or child, or brother, or any other one having a claim by nature on our affection, can we venture to take our meals with him; for our religion compels us to make a distinction. Do not, therefore, regard it as an insult if your son does not take his food along with you, until you come to have the same opinions and adopt the same course of conduct as he follows."

Chap. V. — *Mattidia wishes to be baptized*

When she heard this, she said: "What, then, prevents me from being baptized this day? for before I saw you I turned away from the so-called gods, induced by the thought that, though I sacrificed much to them almost every day, they did not aid me in my necessities. And with regard to adultery, what need I say? for not even when I was rich was I betrayed into this sin by luxury, and the poverty which succeeded has been unable to force me into it, since I cling to my chastity as constituting the greatest beauty, [5] on account of which I fell into so great distress. But I do not at all imagine that you, my lord Peter, are ignorant that the greatest temptation [6] arises when everything looks bright. And therefore, if I was chaste in my prosperity, I do not in my despondency give myself up to pleasures. Yea, indeed, you are not to suppose that my soul has now been freed from distress, although it has received some measure of consolation by the recognition of Clement. For the gloom which I feel in consequence of the loss of my two children rushes in upon me, and throws its shadow to some extent over my joy; for I am grieved, not so much because they perished in the sea, but because they were destroyed, both soul and body, without possessing true [7] piety towards God. Moreover, my husband, their father, as I have learned from Clement, went away in search of me and his sons, and for so many years has not been heard of; and, without doubt, he must have died. For the miserable man, loving me as he did in chastity, was fond of his children; and therefore the old man, deprived of all of us who were dear to him above everything else, died utterly broken-hearted."

Chap. VI. — *The sons reveal themselves to the mother*

The sons, on hearing their mother thus speak, could no longer, in obedience to the exhortation of Peter, restrain themselves, but rising up, they clasped her in their arms, showering down upon her tears and kisses. But she said: "What is the meaning of this?" And Peter answered: "Courageously summon up your spirits, O woman, that you may enjoy your children; for these are Faustinus and Faustinianus, your sons, who, you said, had perished in the deep. For how they are alive, after they had in your opinion died on that most disastrous night, and how one of them now bears the name of Nicetas, and the other that of Aquila, they will themselves be able to tell you; for we, as well as you, have yet to learn this." When Peter thus spoke, my mother fainted away through her excessive joy, and was like to die. But when we had revived her she sat up, and coming to herself, she said: "Be so good, my darling children, as tell us what happened to you after that disastrous night."

Chap. VII. — *Nicetas tells what befell him*

And Nicetas, who in future is to be called Faustinus, began to speak, "On that very night when, as you know, the ship went to pieces, we were taken up by some men, who did not fear to follow the profession of robbers on the deep. They placed us in a boat, and brought us along the coast, sometimes rowing and sometimes sending for provisions, and at length took us to Caesarea Stratonis, [8] and there tormented us by hunger, fear, and blows, that we might not recklessly disclose anything which they did not wish us to tell; and, moreover, changing our names, they succeeded in selling us. Now the woman who bought us was a proselyte of the Jews, an altogether worthy person, of the name of Justa. She adopted us as her own children, and zealously brought us up in all the learning of the Greeks. But we, becoming discreet with our years, were strongly attached to her religion, and we paid good heed to our culture, in order that, disputing with the other nations, we might be able to convince them of their error. We also made an accurate study of the doctrines of the philosophers, especially the most atheistic, — I mean those of Epicurus and Pyrrho, — in order that we might be the better able to refute them.

Chap. VIII. — *Nicetas like to be deceived by Simon Magus*

"We were brought up along with one Simon, a magician; and in consequence of our friendly intercourse with him, we were in danger of being led astray. Now there is a report in regard to some man, that, when he appears, the mass of those who have been pious are to live free from death and pain in his kingdom. This matter, however, mother, will be explained more fully at the proper time. But when we were going to be led astray by Simon, a friend of our lord Peter, by name Zacchgeus, came to us and warned us not to be led astray by the magician; and when Peter came, he brought us to him that he might give us full information, and convince us in regard to those matters that related to piety. Wherefore we beseech you, mother, to partake of those blessings which have been vouchsafed to us, that we may unite around the same table! [9] This, then, is the reason, mother, why you thought we were dead. On that disastrous night we had been taken up in the sea by pirates, but you supposed that we had perished."

Chap. IX. — *The mother begs baptism for herself and her hostess*

"When Faustinus had said this, our mother fell down at Peter's feet, begging and entreating him to send for her and her hostess, and baptize them immediately, in order that, says she, not a single day may pass after the recovery of my children, without my taking food with them. When we united with our mother in making the same request, Peter said: "What can you imagine? Am I alone heartless, so as not to wish that you should take your meals with your mother, baptizing her this very day? But yet it is incumbent on her to fast one day before she be baptized. And it is only one day, because, in her simplicity, she said something in her own behalf, which I looked on as a sufficient indication of her faith; otherwise, her purification must have lasted many days."

Chap. X. — *Mattidia values baptism aright*

And I said: "Tell us what it was that she said which made her faith manifest." And Peter said: "Her request that her hostess and benefactress should be baptized along with her. For she would not have besought this to be granted to her whom she loves, had she not herself first felt that baptism was a great gift. And for this reason I condemn many that, after being baptized, and asserting that they have faith, they yet do nothing worthy of faith; nor do they urge those whom they love — I mean their wives, or sons, or friends — to be baptized. [10] For if they had believed that God grants eternal life with good works on the acceptance of baptism, [11] they without delay would urge those whom they loved to be baptized. But some one of you will say, 'They do love them, and care for them.' That is nonsense. For do they not, most assuredly, when they see them sick, or led away along the road that ends in death, or enduring any other trial, lament over them and pity them? So, if they believed that eternal fire awaits those who worship not God, they would not cease admonishing them, or being in deep distress for them as unbelievers, if they saw them disobedient, being fully assured that punishment awaits them. But now I shall send for the hostess, and question her as to whether she deliberately accepts the law which is proclaimed through us; [12] and so, according to her state of mind, shall we do what ought to be done.

Chap. XI. — *Mattidia has unintentionally fasted one day*

"But since your mother has real confidence in the efficacy of baptism, [13] let her fast at least one day before her baptism." But she swore: "During the two past days, while I related to the woman [14] all the events connected with the recognition, I could not, in consequence of my excessive joy, partake of food; only yesterday I took a little water." Peter's wife bore testimony to her statement with an oath, saying: "In truth she did not taste anything." And Aquila, who must rather be called Faustinianus [15] in future, said: "There is nothing, therefore, to prevent her being baptized." And Peter, smiling, replied: "But that is not a baptismal fast which has not taken place on account of the baptism itself." And Faustinus answered: "Perhaps God, not wishing to separate our mother a single day after our recognition from our table, has arranged beforehand the fast. For as she was chaste in the times of her ignorance, doing what the true religion inculcated, [16] so even now perhaps God has arranged that she should fast one day before for the sake of the true baptism, that, from the first day of her recognising us, she might take her meals along with us."

Chap. XII. — *The difficulty solved*

And Peter said: "Let not wickedness have dominion over us, finding a pretext in Providence and your affection for your mother; but rather abide this day in your fast, and I shall join you in it, and to-morrow she will be baptized. And, besides, this hour of the day is not suitable for baptism." Then we all agreed that it should be so.

Chap. XIII. — *Peter on chastity*

That same evening we all enjoyed the benefit of Peter's instruction. Taking occasion by what had happened to our mother, he showed us how the results of chastity are good, while those of adultery are disastrous, and naturally bring destruction on the whole race, if not speedily, at all events slowly. "And to such an extent," he says, "do deeds of chastity please God, that in this life He bestows some small favour on account of it, even on those who are in error; for salvation in the other world is granted only to those who have been baptized on account of their trust [17] in Him, and who act chastely and righteously. This ye yourselves have seen in the case of your mother, that the results of chastity are in the end good. For perhaps she would have been cut off if she had committed adultery; but God took pity on her for having behaved chastely, rescued her from the death that threatened her, and restored to her her lost children.

Chap. XIV. — *Peter's speech continued*

"But some one will say, 'How many have perished on account of chastity?' Yes; but it was because they did not perceive the danger. For the woman who perceives that she is in love with any one, or is beloved by any one, should immediately shun all association with him as she would shun a blazing fire or a mad dog. And this is exactly what your mother did, for she really loved chastity as a blessing: wherefore she was preserved, and, along with you, obtained the full knowledge of the everlasting kingdom. The woman who wishes to be chaste, ought to know that she is envied by wickedness, and that because of love many lie in wait for her. If, then, she remain holy through a stedfast persistence in chastity, she will gain the victory over all temptations, and be saved; whereas, even if she were to do all that is right, and yet should once commit the sin of adultery, she must be punished, as said the prophet.

Chap. XV. — *Peter's speech continued*

"The chaste wife, doing the will of God, is a good reminiscence of His first creation; for God, being one, created one woman for one man. She is also still more chaste if she does not forget her own creation, and has future punishment before her eyes, and is not ignorant of the loss of eternal blessings. The chaste woman takes pleasure in those who wish to be saved, and is a pious example to the pious, for she is the model of a good life. She who wishes to be chaste, cuts off all occasions for slander; but if she be slandered as by an enemy, though affording him no pretext, she is blessed and avenged by God. The chaste woman longs for God, loves God, pleases God, glorifies God; and to men she affords no occasion for slander. The chaste woman perfumes the church with her good reputation, and glorifies it by her piety. She is, moreover, the praise of her teachers, and a helper to them in their chastity. [18]

Chap. XVI. — *Peter's speech continued*

"The chaste woman is adorned with the Son of God as with a bridegroom. She is clothed with holy light. Her beauty lies in a well-regulated soul; and she is fragrant with ointment, even with a good reputation. She is arrayed in beautiful vesture, even in modesty. She wears about her precious pearls, even chaste words. And she is radiant, for [19] her mind has been brilliantly lighted up. Into a beautiful mirror does she look, for she looks into God. Beautiful cosmetics [20] does she use, namely, the fear of God, with which she admonishes her soul. Beautiful is the woman, not because she has chains of gold on her, [21] but because she has been set free from transient lusts. The chaste woman is greatly desired by the great King; [22] she has been wooed, watched, and loved by Him. The chaste woman does not furnish occasions for being desired, except by her own husband. The chaste woman is grieved when she is desired by another. The chaste woman loves her husband from the heart, embraces, soothes, and pleases him, acts the slave to him, and is obedient to him in all things, except when she would be disobedient to God. For she who obeys God is without the aid of watchmen chaste in soul and pure in body.

Chap. XVII. — *Peter's speech continued*

"Foolish, therefore, is every husband who separates his wife from the fear of God; for she who does not fear God is not afraid of her husband. If she fear not God, who sees what is invisible, how will she be chaste in her unseen choice? [23] And how will she be chaste, who does not come to the assembly to hear chaste-making words? And how could she obtain admonition? And how will she be chaste Without watchmen, if she be not informed in regard to the coming judgment of God, and if she be not fully assured that eternal punishment is the penalty for the slight pleasure? Wherefore, on the other hand, compel her even against her will always to come to hear the chaste-making word, yea, coax her to do so.

Chap. XVIII. — *Peter's speech continued*

"Much better is it if you will take her by the hand and come, in order that you yourself may become chaste; for you will desire to become chaste, that you may experience the full fruition of a holy marriage, and you will not scruple, if you desire it, to become a father, [24] to love your own children, and to be loved by your own children. He who wishes to have a chaste wife is also himself chaste, gives her what is due to a wife, takes his meals with her, keeps company with her, goes with her to the word that makes chaste, does not grieve her, does not rashly quarrel with her, does not make himself hateful to her, furnishes her with all the good things he can, and when he has them not, he makes up the deficiency by caresses. The chaste wife does not expect to be caressed, recognises her husband as her lord, bears his poverty when he is poor, is hungry with him when he is hungry, travels with him when he travels, consoles him when he is grieved, and if she have a large [25] dowry, is subject to him as if she had nothing at all. But if the husband have a poor Wife, let him reckon her chastity a great dowry. The chaste wife is temperate in her eating and drinking, in order that the weariness of the body, thus pampered, may not drag the soul down to unlawful desires. Moreover, she never assuredly remains alone with young men, and she suspects [26] the old; she turns away from disorderly laughter, gives herself up to God alone; she is not led astray; she delights in listening to holy words, but turns away from those which are not spoken to produce chastity.

Chap. XIX. — *Peter's speech ended*

"God is my witness: one adultery is as bad as many murders; and what is terrible in it is this, that the fearfulness and impiety of its murders are not seen. For, when blood is shed, the dead body remains lying, and all are struck by the terrible nature of the occurrence. But the murders of the soul caused by adultery, though they are more frightful, yet, since they are not seen by men, do not make the daring a whit less eager in their impulse. Know, O man, whose breath it is that thou hast to keep thee in life, and thou shalt not wish that it be polluted. By adultery alone is the breath of God polluted. And therefore it drags him who has polluted it into the fire; for it hastens to deliver up its insulter to everlasting punishment."

Chap. XX. — *Peter addresses Mattidia*

While Peter was saying this, he saw the good and chaste Mattidia weeping for joy; but thinking that she was grieved at having suffered so much in past times, he said: "Take courage, O woman; for while many have suffered many evils on account of adultery, you have suffered on account of chastity, and therefore you did not die. But if you had died, your soul would have been saved. You left your native city of Rome on account of chastity, but through it you found the truth, the diadem of the eternal kingdom. You underwent danger in the deep, but you did not die; and even if you had died, the deep itself would have proved to you, dying on account of chastity, a baptism for the salvation of your soul. You were deprived of your children for a little; but these, the true offspring of your husband, have been found in better circumstances. When starving, you begged for food, but you did not defile your body by fornication. You exposed your body to torture, but you saved your soul; you fled from the adulterer, that you might not defile the couch of your husband: but, on account of your chastity, God, who knows your flight, will fill up the place of your husband. Grieved and left desolate, you were for a short time deprived of husband and children, but all these you must have been deprived of, some time or other, by death, the preordained lot of man. But better is it that you were willingly deprived of them on account of chastity, than that you should have perished unwillingly after a time, simply on account of sins.

Chap. XXI. — *The same subject continued*

"Much better is it, then, that your first circumstances should be distressing. For when this is the case, they do not so deeply grieve you, because you hope that they will pass away, and they yield joy through the expectation of better circumstances. But, above all, I wish you to know how much chastity is pleasing to God. The chaste woman is God's choice, God's good pleasure, God's glory, God's child. So great a blessing is chastity, [27] that if there had not been a law that not even a righteous person should enter into the kingdom of God unbaptized, perhaps even the erring Gentiles might have been saved solely on account of chastity. Wherefore I am exceedingly sorry for those erring ones who are chaste because they shrink from baptism — thus choosing to be chaste without good hope. Wherefore they are not saved; for the decree of God is clearly set down, that an unbaptized person cannot enter into His kingdom." When he said this, and much more, we turned to sleep.

[1] Cotelerius conjectured σφαγέντα for σφαλέντα — "being slain on our journey."

[2] The first Epitome explains "those whom we seek" as those who are worthy to share in Christ or in Christ's gospel.

[3] The text is somewhat doubtful. "We have given the meaning contained in the first Epitome.

[4] θρήσχεια.

[5] One MS. and the first Epitome read, "as being the greatest blessing."

[6] Lit., "desire."

[7] The Greek has, "apart from divine piety towards God." As Wieseler remarks, the epithet "divine" is corrupt. The meaning may be, "without having known the proper mode of worshipping God."

[8] This clause, literally translated, is, "and sometimes impelling it with oars, they brought us along the land; and sometimes sending for provisions, they conveyed us to Caesarea Stratonis." The Latin translator renders "to land," not "along the land." The passage assumes a different form in the Recognitions, the first Epitome, and the second Epitome; and there is, no doubt, some corruption in the text. The text has δαχρύοντας which makes no sense. We have adopted the rendering given in

the Recognitions. Various attempts have been made to amend the word.
[9] Lit., "that we may be able to partake of common salt and table."
[10] Lit., "to this."
[11] ἐπὶ τῷ βαπτίσματι; lit., "on the condition of baptism."
[12] Lit., "the law which, is by means of us." But the Epitomes, and a various reading in Cotelerius, give "our law."
[13] Lit., "since your mother is faithfully disposed in regard to baptism."
[14] The second Epitome makes her the wife of Peter: a various reading mentions also her hostess.
[15] Dressel strangely prefers the reading "Faustinus."
[16] Lit., "doing what was becoming to the truth."
[17] Lit., "hope."
[18] The Greek is αὐτοῖς σωφρονοῦσι. The Latin translator and Lehmann (Die Clementinischen Schriften, Gotha 1869) render, "to those who are chaste, *i.e.* love or practise chastity," as if the reading were τοῖς σωφρονοῦσι.
[19] Lit., "when."
[20] χόσμῳ — properly ornaments; but here a peculiar meaning is evidently required.
[21] Lit., "as being chained with gold."
[22] Ps. XLV. 11.
[23] "In her unseen choice" means, in what course of conduct she really prefers in her heart. This reading occurs in one MS.; in the other MS. it is corrupt. Schwegler amended it into, "How shall she be chaste towards him who does not see [what is invisible]?" and the emendation is adopted by Dressel.
[24] There seems to be some corruption in this clause. Literally it is, "and you will not scruple, if you love, I mean, to become a father."
[25] Lit., "larger" [than usual].
[26] ὑποπτεύει. The Latin translator and Lehmann render "respects" or "reveres."
[27] We have adopted an emendation of Wieseler's. The emendation is questionable; but the sense is the best that can be got out of the words.

Homily XIV

Chap. I. — *Mattidia is baptized in the sea*

Much earlier than usual Peter awoke, and came to us, and awaking us, said: "Let Faustinas and Faustinianus, along with Clement and the household, accompany me, that we may go to some sheltered spot by the sea, and there be able to baptize her without attracting observation." Accordingly, when we had come to the sea-shore, he baptized her between some rocks, which supplied a place at once free from wind and dust. [1] But we brothers, along with our brother and some others, retired because of the women and bathed, and coming again to the women, we took them along with us, and thus we went to a secret place and prayed. Then Peter, on account of the multitude, sent the women on before, ordering them to go to their lodging by another way, and he permitted us alone of the men to accompany our mother and the rest of the women. [2] We went then to our lodging, and while waiting for Peter's arrival, we conversed with each other. Peter came several hours after, and breaking the bread for the eucharist, [3] and putting salt upon it, he gave it first to our mother, and, after her, to us her sons. And thus we took food along with her, and blessed God.

Chap. II. — *The reason of Peter's lateness*

Then, at length, Peter seeing that the multitude had entered, sat down, and bidding us sit down beside him, he related first of all why he had sent us on before him after the baptism, and why he himself had been late in returning. He said that the following was the reason: "At the time that you came up," [4] he says, "an old man, a workman, entered along with you, concealing himself out of curiosity. He had watched us before, as he himself afterwards confessed, in order to see what we were doing when we entered into the sheltered place, and then he came out secretly and followed us. And coming up to me at a convenient place, and addressing me, he said, 'For a long time I have been following you and wishing to talk with you, but I was afraid that you might be angry with me, as if I were instigated by curiosity; but now I shall tell you, if you please, what I think is the truth.' And I replied, 'Tell us what you think is good, and we shall approve your conduct, even should what you say not be really good, since with a good purpose you have been anxious to state what you deem to be good.'

Chap. III. — *The old man does not believe in God or Providence*

"The old man began to speak as follows: 'When I saw you after you had bathed in the sea retire into the secret place, I went up and secretly watched what might be your object in entering into a secret place, and when I saw you pray, I retired; [5] but taking pity on you, I waited that I might speak with you when you came out, and prevail on you not to be led astray. For there is neither God nor providence; but all things are subject to Genesis. [6] Of this I am fully assured in consequence of what I have myself endured, having for a long time made a careful study of the science. [7] Do not therefore be deceived, my child. For whether you pray or not, you must endure what is assigned to you by Genesis. For if prayers could have done anything or any good, I myself should now be in better circumstances. And now, unless my needy garments mislead you, you will not refuse to believe what I say. I was once in affluent circumstances; I sacrificed much to the gods, I gave liberally to the needy; and yet, though I prayed and acted piously, I was not able to escape my destiny.' And I said: 'What are the calamities you have endured?' And he answered: 'I need not tell you now; perhaps at the end you shall learn who I am, and who are my parents, and into what straitened circumstances I have fallen. But at present I wish you to become fully assured that everything is subject to Genesis.'

Chap. IV. — *Peter's arguments against Genesis*

"And I said: 'If all things are subject to Genesis, and you are fully convinced that this is the case, your thoughts and advice are contrary to your own opinion. [8] For if it is impossible even to think in opposition to Genesis, why do you toil in vain, advising me to do what cannot be done? Yea, moreover, even if Genesis subsists, do not make haste to prevail on me not to worship Him who is also Lord of the stars, by whose wish that a thing should not take place, that thing becomes an impossibility. For always that which is subject must obey that which rules. As far, however, as the worship of the common gods is concerned, that is superfluous, if Genesis has sway. For neither does anything happen contrary to what seems good to fate, nor are they themselves able to do anything, since they are subject to their own universal Genesis. If Genesis exists, there is this objection to it, that that which is not first has the rule; or [in other words] the uncreated cannot be subject, for the uncreated, as being uncreated, has nothing that is older than itself.' [9]

Chap. V. — *Practical refutation of Genesis*

"While we were thus talking, a great multitude gathered round us. And then I looked to the multitude, and said: 'I and my tribe have had handed down to us from our ancestors the worship of God, and we have a commandment to give no heed to Genesis, I mean to the science of astrology; and therefore I gave no attention to it. For this reason I have no skill in astrology, but I shall state that in which I have skill. Since I am unable to refute Genesis by an appeal to the science which relates to Genesis, I wish to prove in another way that the affairs [of this world] are managed by a providence, and that each one will receive reward or punishment according to his actions. Whether he shall do so now or hereafter, is a matter of no consequence to me; all I affirm is, that each one without doubt will reap the fruit of his deeds. The proof that there is no Genesis is this. If any one of you present has been deprived of eyes, or has his hand maimed, or his foot lame, or some other part of the body wrong, and if it is utterly incurable, and entirely beyond the range of the medical profession, — a case, indeed, which not even the astrologers profess to cure, for no such cure has taken place within the lapse of a vast period, — yet I praying to God will cure it, [10] although [11] it could never have been set right by Genesis. Since this is so, do not they sin who blaspheme the God that fashioned all things?' And the old man answered: 'Is it then blasphemy to say that all things are subject to Genesis?' And I replied: 'Most certainly it is. For if all the sins of men, and all their acts of impiety and licentiousness, owe their origin to the stars, and if the stars have been appointed by God to do this work, so as to be the efficient causes of all evils, then the sins of all are traced up to Him who placed Genesis [12] in the stars.'

Chap. VI. — *The old man opposes his personal experience to the argument of Peter*

"And the old man answered: 'You have spoken truly, [13] and yet, notwithstanding all your incomparable demonstration, I am prevented from yielding assent by my own personal knowledge. For I was an astrologer, and dwelt first at Rome; and then forming a friendship with one who was of the family of Caesar, I ascertained accurately the genesis of himself and his wife. And tracing their history, I find all the deeds actually accomplished in exact accordance with their genesis, and therefore I cannot yield to your argument. For the arrangement [14] of her genesis was that which makes women commit adultery, fall in love with their own slaves, and perish abroad in the water. And this actually took place; for she fell in love with her own slave, and not being able to bear the reproach, she fled with him, hurried to a foreign land, shared his bed, and perished in the sea.'

Chap. VII. — *The old man tells his story*

"And I answered: 'How then do you know that she who fled and took up her residence in a foreign land married the slave, and marrying him died?' And the old man said: 'I am quite sure that this is true, not indeed that she married him, for I did not know even that she fell in love with him; »but after her departure, a brother of her husband's told me the whole story of her passion, and how he acted as an honourable man, and did not, as being his brother, wish to pollute his couch, and how she the wretched woman (for she is not blameable, inasmuch as she was compelled to do and suffer all this in consequence of Genesis) longed for him, and yet stood in awe of him and his reproaches, and how she devised a dream, whether true or false I cannot tell; for he stated that she said, "Some one in a vision stood by me, and ordered me to leave the city of the Romans immediately with my children." But her husband being anxious that she should be saved with his sons, sent them immediately to Athens for their education, accompanied by their mother and slaves, while he kept the third and youngest son with himself, for he who gave the warning in the dream permitted this son to remain with his father. And when a long time had elapsed, during which [15] he received no letters from her, he himself sent frequently to Athens, and at length took me, as the truest of all his friends, and went in search of her. And much did I exert myself along with him in the course of our travels with all eagerness; for I remembered that, in the old times of his prosperity, he had given me a share of all he had, and loved me above all his friends. At length we set sail from Rome itself, and so we arrived in these parts of Syria, and we landed at Seleucia, and not many days after we had landed he died of a broken heart. But I came here, and have procured my livelihood from that day till this by the work of my hands.'

Chap. VIII. — *The old man gives information in regard to Faustus the father of Clement*

"When the old man had thus spoken, I knew from what he said that the old man who he stated had died, was no other than your father. I did not wish, however, to communicate your circumstances to him until I should confer with you. But I ascertained where his lodging was, and I pointed out mine to him; and to make sure [that my conjecture was right], I put this one question to him: 'What was the name of the old man?' And he said, 'Faustus.' 'And what were the names of his twin sons?' And he answered, 'Faustinus and Faustinianus.' 'What was the name of the third son?' He said, 'Clement.' 'What was their mother's name?' He said, 'Mattidia.' Accordingly, from compassion, I shed tears along with him, and, dismissing the multitudes, I came to you, in order that I might take counsel with you after we had partaken of food [16] together. But I did not wish to disclose the matter to you before we had partaken of food, lest perchance you should be overcome by sorrow, and continue sad on the day of baptism, when even angels rejoice." At these statements of Peter we all fell a weeping along with our mother. But he beholding us in tears, said: "Now let each one of you, through fear of God, bear bravely what has been said; for certainly it was not to-day that your father died, but long ago, as you conjecturing said."

Chap. IX. — *Faustus himself appears*

When Peter said this, our mother could no longer endure it, but cried out, "Alas! my husband! loving us, you died by your own decision, [17] while we are still alive, see the light, and have just partaken of food." This one scream had not yet ceased, when, lo! the old man came in, and at the same time wishing to inquire into the cause of the cry, he looked on the woman and said, "What does this mean? Whom do I see?" And going up to her, and looking at her, and being looked at more carefully, he embraced her. But they were like to die through the sudden joy, and wishing to speak to each other, they could not get the power in consequence of their unsatisfied joy, for they were seized with speechlessness. But not long after, our mother said to him: "I now have you, Faustus, in every way the dearest being to me. How then are you alive, when we heard a short time ago that you were dead? But these are our sons, Faustinus, Faustinianus, and Clement." And when she said this, we all three fell on him, and kissed him, and in rather an indistinct way we recalled his form to our memory.

Chap. X. — *Faustus explains his narrative to Peter*

Peter seeing this, said: "Are you Faustus, the husband of this woman, and the father of her children?" And he said: "I am." And Peter said: "How, then, did you relate to me your own history as if it were another's; telling me of your toils, and sorrow, and burial?" And our father answered: "Being of the family of Caesar, and not wishing to be discovered, I devised the narrative in another's name, in order that it might not be perceived who I was. For I knew that, if I were recognised, the governors in the place would learn this, and recall me to gratify Caesar, and would bestow upon me that former prosperity to which I had formerly bidden adieu with all the resolution I could summon. For I could not give myself up to a luxurious life when I had pronounced the strongest condemnation on myself, because I believed that I had been the cause of death to those who were loved by me." [18]

Chap. XI. — *Discussion on Genesis*

And Peter said: "You did this according to your resolution. But in regard to Genesis, were you merely playing a part when you affirmed it, or were you in earnest in asserting that it existed?" Our father said: "I will not speak falsely to you. I was in earnest when I maintained that Genesis existed. For I am not uninitiated in the science; on the contrary, I associated with one who is the best of the astrologers, an Egyptian of the name of Annubion, who became my friend in the commencement of my travels, and disclosed to me the death of my wife and children." And Peter said: "Are you not now convinced by facts, that the doctrine of Genesis has no firm foundation?" And my father answered: "I must lay before you all the ideas that occur to my mind, that listening to them I may understand your refutation of them. [19] I know, indeed, that astrologers both make many mistakes, and frequently speak the truth. I suspect, therefore, that they speak the truth so far as they are accurately acquainted with the science, and that their mistakes are the result of ignorance; so that I conjecture that the science has a firm foundation, but that the astrologers themselves speak what is false solely on account of ignorance, because they cannot know all things with absolute [20] accuracy." And Peter answered: "Consider [21] whether their speaking of the truth is not accidental, and whether they do not make their declarations without knowing the matters accurately. For it must by all means happen that, when many prophecies are uttered, some of them should come true." And the old man said: "How, then, is it possible to be fully convinced of this, whether the science of Genesis has a sure foundation or not?"

Chap. XII. — *Clement undertakes the discussion*

When both were silent, I said: "Since I know accurately the science, but our lord and our father are not in this condition, I should like if Annubion himself were here, to have a discussion with him in the presence of my father. For thus would the matter be able to become public, when one practically acquainted with the subject has held the discussion with one equally informed." [22] And our father answered: "Where, then, is it possible to fall in with Annubion?" And Peter said: "In Antioch, for I learn that Simon Magus is there, whose inseparable companion Annubion is. When, then, we go there, if we come upon them, the discussion can take place." And so, when we had discussed many subjects, and rejoiced at the recognition and given thanks to God, evening came down upon us, and we turned to sleep.

[1] Lit., "tranquil and clean."
[2] "We have adopted an emendation of Schwegler's. The MSS. read cither "these" or "the same" for "the rest of."
[3] The words "for the eucharist" might be translated "after thanksgiving." But it is much the same which, for the eucharist is plainly meant. The Epitomes have it: "taking the bread, giving thanks, blessing, and consecrating it, he gave it;" but no mention is made of salt.

[4] "We have adopted an emendation of Wieseler's. The text has, "at the time that you went away."
[5] Wieseler thinks that the reading should be: "I did not retire."
[6] Genesis is destiny determined by the stars which rule at each man's birth.
[7] μάθημα, mathematical science specially, which was closely connected with astrology.
[8] Lit., "thinking you counsel what is contrary to yourself."
[9] The argument here is obscure. Probably what is intended is as follows: Genesis means origination, coming into being. Origination cannot be the ruling power, for there must be something unoriginated which has given rise to the origination. The origination, therefore, as not being first, cannot have sway, and it must itself be subject to that which is unoriginated.
[10] "We have adopted the reading given in the two Epitomes.
[11] Lit., "when."
[12] That is, the power of origination.
[13] One MS. adds "greatly," and an Epitome "great things."
[14] That is, the position of the stars at her birth.
[15] We have inserted ὡς from the Epitomes.
[16] Lit., "of salt."
[17] Lit., "you died by a judgment;" but it is thought that χρίσει is corrupt.
[18] Lit., "Having judged the greatest things in regard to those who were loved by me, as having died." The text is doubtful; for the first Epitome has something quite different.
[19] Here MSS. and Epitomes differ in their readings. The text adopted seems a combination of two ideas: "that you may listen and refute them, and that I may thus learn the truth."
[20] We have adopted the reading of Codex O, πάντως. The other MS. reads, "that all cannot know all things accurately."
[21] The MSS. read ἄπεχε, "hold back." The reading of the text is in an Epitome.
[22] Lit., "when artist has had discussion with fellow-artist."

Homily XV

Chap. I. — *Peter wishes to convert Faustus*

At break of day our father, with our mother and his three sons, entered the place where Peter was, and accosting him, sat down. Then we also did the same at his request; and Peter looking at our father, said: "I am anxious that you should become of the same mind as your wife and children, in order that here you may live along with them, and in the other world, [1] after the separation of the soul from the body, you will continue to be with them free from sorrow. For does it not grieve you exceedingly that you should not associate with each other?" And my father said: "Most assuredly." And Peter said: "If, then, separation from each other here gives you pain, and if without doubt the penalty awaits you that after death you should not be with each other, how much greater will your grief be that you, a wise man, should be separated from your own family on account of your opinions? They, too, must [2] feel the more distressed from the consciousness that eternal punishment awaits you because you entertain different opinions from theirs, and deny the established truth." [3]

Chap. II. — *Reason for listening to Peter's arguments*

Our father said: "But it is not the case, my very dear friend, that souls are punished in Hades, for the soul is dissolved into air as soon as it leaves the body." And Peter said: "Until we convince you in regard to this point, answer me, does it not appear to you that you are not grieved as having no faith in a [future] punishment, but they who have full faith in it must be vexed in regard to you?" And our father said: "You speak sense." And Peter said: "Why, then, will you not free them from the greatest grief they can have in regard to you by agreeing to their religion, not, I mean, through dread, but through kindly feeling, listening and judging about what is said by me, whether it be so or not? and if the truth is as we state it, then here you will enjoy life with those who are dearest to you, and in the other world you will have rest with them; but if, in examining the arguments, you show that what is stated by us is a fictitious story, [4] you will thus be doing good service, for you will have your friends on your side, and you will put an end to their leaning upon false hopes, and you will free them from false fears."

Chap. III. — *Obstacles to faith*

And our father said: "There is evidently much reason in what you say." And Peter said: "What is it, then, that prevents you from coming to our faith? Tell me, that we may begin our discussion with it. For many are the hindrances. The faithful are hindered by occupation with merchandise, or public business, or the cultivation of the soil, or cares, and such like; the unbelievers, of whom you also are one, are hindered by ideas such as that the gods, which do not exist, really exist, or that all things are subject to Genesis, or chance, [5] or that souls are mortal, or that our doctrines are false because there is no providence.

Chap. IV. — *Providence seen in the events of the life of Faustus and his family*

"But I maintain, from what has happened to you, that all things are managed by the providence of God, and that your separation from your family for so many years was providential; [6] for since, if they bad been with you, they perhaps would not have listened to the doctrines of the true religion, it was arranged that your children should travel with their mother, should be shipwrecked, should be supposed to have perished, and should be sold; [7] moreover, that they should be educated in the learning of the Greeks, especially in the atheistic doctrines, in order that, as being acquainted with them, they might be the better able to refute them; and in addition to this, that they should become attached to the true religion, and be enabled to be united with me, so as to help me in my preaching; furthermore, that their brother Clement should meet in the same place, and that thus his mother should be recognised, and through her cure [8] should be fully convinced of the right worship of God; [9] that after no long interval the twins should recognise and be recognised, and the other day should fall in with you, and that you should receive back your own. I do not think, then, that such a speedy filling in of circumstances, coming as it were from all quarters, so as to accomplish one design, could have happened without the direction of Providence."

Chap. V. — *Difference between the true religion and philosophy*

And our father began to say: "Do not suppose, my dearest Peter, that I am not thinking of the doctrines preached by you. I was thinking of them. But during the past night, when Clement urged me earnestly to give in my adhesion to the truth preached by you, I at last answered, 'Why should I? for what new commandment can any one give more than what the ancients urged us to obey?' And he, with a gentle smile, said, 'There is a great difference, father, between the doctrines of the true religion and those of philosophy; for the true religion receives its proof from prophecy, while Philosophy, furnishing us with beautiful sentences, seems to present its proofs from conjecture.' On saying this, he took an instance, and set before us the doctrine of philanthropy, [10] which you had explained to him, [11] which rather appeared to me to be very unjust. And I shall tell you how. He alleged that it was right to present to him who strikes you on the one cheek the other [12] also, and to give to him who takes away your cloak your tunic also, and to go two miles with him who compels you to go one, and such like."

Chap. VI. — *The love of man*

And Peter answered; "You have deemed unjust what is most just. If you are inclined, will you listen to me?" And my father said: "With all my heart." And Peter said: "What is your opinion? Suppose that there were two kings, enemies to each other, and having their countries cut off from each other; and suppose that some one of the subjects of one of them were to be caught in the country of the other, and to incur the penalty of death on this account: now if he were let off from the punishment by receiving a blow instead of death, is it not plain that he who let him off is a lover of man?" And our father said: "Most certainly." And Peter said: "Now suppose that this same person were to steal from some one something belonging to him or to another; and if when caught he were to pay double, instead of suffering the punishment that was due to him, namely, paying four times the amount, and being also put to death, as having been caught in the territories of the enemy; is it not your opinion that lie who accepts double, and lets him off from the penalty of death, is a lover of man?" And our father said: "He certainly seems so." And Peter said: "Why then? Is it not the duty of him who is in the kingdom of another, and that, too, a hostile and wicked monarch, to be pleasing to all [13] for the sake of life, and when force is applied to him, to yield still more, to accost those who do not accost him, to reconcile enemies, not to quarrel with those who are angry, to give his own property freely to all who ask, and such like?" And our father said: "He should with reason endure all things rather, if he prefers life to them."

Chap. VII. — *The explanation of a parable; the present and the future life*

And Peter [14] said: "Are not those, then, who you said received injustice, themselves transgressors, inasmuch as they are in the kingdom of the other, and is it not by overreaching that they have obtained all they possess? while those who are thought to act unjustly are conferring a favour on each subject of the hostile kingdom, so far as they permit him to have property. For these possessions belong to those who have chosen the present. [15] And they are so far kind as to permit the others to live. This, then, is the parable; now listen to the actual truth. The prophet of the truth who appeared [on earth] taught us that the Maker and God of all gave two kingdoms to two, [16] good and evil; granting to the evil the sovereignty over the present world along with law, so that he [it] should have the right to punish those who act unjustly; but to the good He gave the eternal [17] age to come. But He made each man free with the power to give himself up to whatsoever he prefers, either to the present evil or the future good. Those men who choose the present have power to be rich, to revel in luxury, to indulge in pleasures, and to do whatever they can. For they will possess none of the future goods. But those who have determined to accept the blessings of the future reign have no right to regard as their own the things that are here, since they belong to a foreign king, with the exception only of water and bread, and those things procured with sweat to maintain life (for it is not lawful for them to commit suicide), [18] and also one garment, for they are not permitted to go naked on account of the all-seeing [19] Heaven.

Chap. VIII. — *The present and the future*

"If, then, you wish to have an accurate account of the matter, listen. Those of whom you said a little before that they receive injustice, rather act unjustly themselves; for they who have chosen the future blessings, live along with the bad in the present world, having many enjoyments the same as the bad, — such as life itself, light, bread, water, clothing, and others of a like nature. But they who are thought by you to act unjustly, shall not live with the good men in [20] the coming age." And our father replied to this: "Now when you have convinced me that those who act unjustly suffer injustice themselves, while those who suffer injustice have by far the advantage, the whole affair seems to me still more the most unjust of transactions; for those who seem to act unjustly grant many things to those who have chosen the future blessings, but those who seem to receive injustice do themselves commit injustice, because they do not give in the other world, to those who have given them blessings here, the same advantages which these gave to them." And Peter said: "This is not unjust at all, because each one has the power to choose the present or the future goods, whether they be small or great. He who chooses by his own individual judgment and wish, receives no injustice, — I mean, not even should his choice rest on what is small, since the great lay within his choice, as in fact did also the small." And our father said: "You are right; for it has been said by one of the wise men of the Greeks, 'The blame rests with those who chose — God is blameless.' [21]

Chap. IX. — *Possessions are transgressions*

"Will you be so good as to explain this matter also? I remember Clement saying to me, that we suffer injuries and afflictions for the forgiveness of our sins." Peter said: "This is quite correct. For we, who have chosen the future things, in so far as we possess more goods than these, whether they be clothing, or food or drink, or any other thing, possess sins, because we ought not to have anything, as I explained to you a little ago. To all of us possessions are sins. [22] The deprivation of these, in whatever way it may take place, is the removal of sins." And our father said: "That seems reasonable, as you explained that these were the two boundary lines of the two kings, and [23] that it was in the power of each to choose whatever he wished of what was under their authority. But why are the afflictions sent, or [24] do we suffer them justly?" And Peter said: "Most justly; for since the boundary line of the saved is, as I said, that no one should possess anything, but since many have many possessions, or in other words sins, for this reason the exceeding love of God sends afflictions on those who do not act in purity of heart, that on account of their having some measure of the love of God, they might, by temporary inflictions, be saved from eternal punishments."

Chap. X. — *Poverty not necessarily righteous*

And our father said: "How then is this? Do we not see many impious men poor? Then do these belong to the saved on this account?" And Peter said: "Not at all; for that poverty is not acceptable which longs for what it ought not. So that some are rich as far as their choice goes, though poor in actual wealth, and they are punished because they desire to have more. But one is not unquestionably righteous because he happens to be poor. For he can be a beggar as far as actual wealth is concerned, but he may desire and even do what above everything he ought not to do. Thus he may worship idols, or be a blasphemer or fornicator, or he may live indiscriminately, or perjure himself, or lie, or live the life of an unbeliever. But our teacher pronounced the faithful poor blessed; [25] and he did so, not because they had given anything, for they had nothing, but because they were not to be condemned, as having done no sin, simply because they gave no alms, because they had nothing to give." And our father said: "In good truth all seems to go right as far as the subject of discussion is concerned; wherefore I have resolved to listen to the whole of your argument in regular order."

Chap. XI. — *Exposition of the true religion promised*

And Peter said: "Since, then, you are eager henceforth to learn what relates to our religion, I ought to explain it in order, beginning with God Himself, and showing that we ought to call Him alone God, and that we ought neither to speak of the others as gods nor deem them such, and that he who acts contrary to this will be punished eternally, as having shown the greatest impiety to Him who is the Lord of all." And saying this, he laid his hands on those who were vexed by afflictions, and were diseased, and possessed by demons; and, praying, he healed them, and dismissed the multitudes. And then entering in this way, he partook of his usual food, and went to sleep.

[1] Lit., "there"
[2] We have inserted a δεῖ, probably omitted on account of the previous OS.
[3] The words are peculiar. Lit., "eternal punishment awaits you thinking other things, through denial of the fixed dogma" (ῥητοῦ δόγματος). The Latin translator gives: "ob veri dograatis negationem."
[4] μῦθόν τινα ψευδῆ.
[5] Properly, self-action.
[6] "We have adopted a reading suggested by the second Epitome.
[7] The word ἀπρασίαι is corrupt. We have adopted the emendation πρᾶσις. The word is not given in the MS. O, nor in the Epitomes.
[8] ὑπὸ θεραπείας, which Cotelerius translates *recuperata sanitate*.
[9] Lit., "convinced of the Godhead." "Godhead" is omitted in the Epitomes.
[10] Or "love of man" in all its phases — kindliness, gentleness, humanity, etc.
[11] Hom. XII. 25 ff.
[12] Matt. V. 39-41; Luke VI. 29. The writer of the Homilies changes the word Χιτῶνα, "tunic," of the New Testament into μαφόριον, which Suicer describes "a covering for the head, neck, and shoulders, used by women." Wieseler is in doubt whether the writer of the Homilies uses μαφόριον as equivalent to Χιτῶνα, or whether he intentionally changed the word, for the person who lost both cloak and tunic would be naked altogether; and this, the writer may have imagined, Christ would not have commanded.
[13] Lit., "to flatter."
[14] The following words would be more appropriately put in the mouth of the father, as is done in fact by the Epitomes. Peter's address would commence," And the parable is." The Epitomes differ much from each other and the text, and there seems to be confusion in the text.
[15] This sentence would be more appropriate in the explanation of the parable.
[16] The Greek leaves it uncertain whether it is two persons or two things, — whether it is a good being and an evil being, or good and evil. Afterwards, a good being and an evil are distinctly introduced.
[17] The word ἀΐδιος, properly and strictly "eternal," is used.
[18] Lit., "to die willingly."
[19] We have adopted an obvious emendation, πάντα for παντός.
[20] We have translated Schweder's emendation. He inserted ἐν.
[21] Plato, *Rep.* X. 617 E.
[22] One MS. inserts before this sentence: "For if in all of us possessions are wont to occasion sins in those who have them."

[23] We have adopted Wieseler's emendation of τὰ into χαί.
[24] We have changed εἰ into ἤ.

[25] Matt. V. 3. The Epitomes run thus: "Our Lord Jesus Christ, the Son of the living God, said." And then they quote the words of our Gospel.

Homily XVI

Chap. I. — *Simon wishes to discuss with Peter the unity of God*

At break of day Peter went out, and reaching the place where he was wont to discourse, he saw a great multitude assembled. At the very time when he was going to discourse, one of his deacons entered, and said: "Simon has come from Antioch, starting as soon as it was evening, having learned that you promised to speak on the unity [1] of God; and he is ready, along with Athenodorus the Epicurean, to come to hear your speech, in order that he may publicly oppose all the arguments ever adduced by you for the unity of God." Just as the deacon said this, lo! Simon himself entered, accompanied by Athenodorus and some other friends. And before Peter spoke at all, he took the first word, and said:

Chap. II. — *The same subject continued*

"I heard that you promised yesterday to Faustus to prove this day, giving out your arguments in regular order, and beginning with Him who is Lord of the universe, that we ought to say that He alone is God, and that we ought neither to say nor to think that there are other gods, because he that acts contrary to this will be punished eternally. But, above all, I am truly amazed at your madness in hoping to convert a wise man, and one far advanced in years, to your state of mind. But you will not succeed in your designs; and all the more that I am present, and can thoroughly refute your false arguments. For perhaps, if I had not been present, the wise old man might have been led astray, because he has no critical acquaintance [2] with the books publicly believed in amongst the Jews. [3] At present I shall omit much, in order that I may the more speedily refute that which you have promised to prove. Wherefore begin to speak what you promised to say before us, who know the Scriptures. But if, fearing our refutation, you are unwilling to fulfil your promise in our presence, this of itself will be sufficient proof that you are wrong, because you did not venture to speak in the presence of those who know the Scriptures. And now, why should I wait till you tell me, when I have a most satisfactory witness of your promise in the old man who is present?" And, saying this, he looked to my father, and said: "Tell me, most excellent of all men, is not this the man who promised to prove to you to-day that God is one, and that we ought not to say or think that there is any other god, and that he who acts contrary to this will be punished eternally, as committing the most heinous sin? Do you, then, refuse to reply to me?"

Chap. III. — *The mode of the discussion*

And our father said: "Well might you have demanded testimony from me, Simon, if Peter had first denied [that he had made the promise]. But now I shall feel no shame in saying what I am bound to say. I think that you wish to enter on the discussion inflamed with anger. Now this is a state of mind in which it is improper for you to speak and for us to listen to you; for we are no longer being helped on to the truth, but we are watching the progress of a contest. And now, having learned from Hellenic culture how those who seek [the truth] ought to act, I shall remind you. Let each of you give an exposition of his own opinion, [4] and let the right of speech pass from the one to the other. [5] For if Peter alone should wish to expound his thought, but you should be silent as to yours, it is possible that some argument adduced by you might crush both your and his opinion; and both of you, though defeated by this argument, would not appear defeated, but only the one who expounded his opinion; while he who did not expound his, though equally defeated, would not appear defeated, but would even be thought to have conquered." And Simon answered: "I will do as you say; but I am afraid lest you do not turn out a truth-loving judge, as you have been already prejudiced by his arguments."

Chap. IV. — *The prejudices of Faustus rather on the side of Simon than on that of Peter*

Our father answered: "Do not compel me to agree with you without any exercise of my judgment in order that I may seem to be a truth-loving judge; but if you wish me to tell you the truth, my prepossessions are rather on the side of your opinions." And Simon said: "How is this the case, when you do not know what my opinions are?" And our father said: "It is easy to know this, and I will tell you how. You promised that you would convict Peter of error in maintaining the unity of God; but if one undertakes to convict of error him who maintains the unity of God, it is perfectly plain that he, as being in the right, [6] does not hold the same opinion. For if he holds the same opinion as the man who is thoroughly in error, then he himself is in error; but if he gives his proofs holding opposite opinions, then he is in the right. Not well [7] then do you assert that he who maintains the unity of God is wrong, unless you believe that there are many gods. Now I maintain that there are many gods. Holding, therefore, the same opinion as you before the discussion, I am prepossessed rather in your favour. For this reason you ought to have no anxiety in regard to me, but Peter ought, for I still hold opinions contrary to his. And so after your discussion I hope that, as a truth-loving judge, who has stripped himself of his prepossessions, I shall agree to that doctrine which gains the victory." When my father said this, a murmur of applause burst insensibly from the multitudes because my father had thus spoken.

Chap. V. — *Peter commences the discussion*

Peter then said: "I am ready to do as the umpire of our discussion has said; and straightway without any delay I shall set forth my opinion in regard to God. I then assert that there is one God who made the heavens and the earth, and all things that are in them. And it is not right to say or to think that there is any other." And Simon said: "But I maintain that the Scriptures believed in amongst the Jews say that there are many gods, and that God is not angry at this, because He has Himself spoken of many gods in His Scriptures.

Chap. VI. — *Simon appeals to the Old Testament to prove that there are many gods*

"For instance, in the very first words of the law, He evidently speaks of them as being like even unto Himself. For thus it is written, that, when the first man received a commandment from God to eat of every tree that was in the garden, [8] but not to eat of the tree of the knowledge of good and evil, the serpent having persuaded them by means of the woman, through the promise that they would become gods, made them look up; [9] and then, when they had thus looked up, God said, [10] 'Behold, Adam is become as one of us," When, then, the serpent said, [11] 'Ye shall be as gods,' he plainly speaks in the belief that gods exist; all the more as God also added His testimony, saying, 'Behold, Adam is become as one of us.' The serpent, then, who said that there are many gods, did not speak falsely. Again, the scripture, [12] 'Thou shalt not revile the gods, nor curse the rulers of thy people,' points out many gods whom it does not wish even to be cursed. But it is also somewhere else written, [13] 'Did another god dare to enter and take him a nation from the midst of [another] nation, as did I the Lord God?' When He says, 'Did another God dare?' He speaks on the supposition that other gods exist. And elsewhere: [14] 'Let the gods that have not made the heavens and the earth perish;' as if those who had made them were not to perish. And in another place, when it says, [15] 'Take heed to thyself lest thou go and serve other gods whom thy fathers knew not,' it speaks as if other gods existed whom they were not to follow. And again: [16] 'The names of other gods shall not ascend upon thy lips.' Here it mentions many gods whose names it does not wish to be uttered. And again it is written, [17] 'Thy God is the Lord, He is God of gods.' And again: [18] 'Who is like unto Thee, O Lord, among the gods?' And again: [19] 'God is Lord of gods.' And again [20] 'God stood in the assembly of gods: He judgeth among the Gods.' Wherefore I wonder how, when there are so many passages in writing which testify that there are many gods, you have asserted that we ought neither to say nor to think that there are many. Finally, if you have anything to say against what has been spoken so distinctly, say it in the presence of all."

Chap. VII. — *Peter appeals to the Old Testament to prove the unity of God*

And Peter said: "I shall reply briefly to what you have said. The law, which frequently speaks of gods, itself says to the Jewish multitude, [21] 'Behold, the heaven of heavens is the Lord's thy God, with all that therein is; 'implying that, even if there are gods, they are under Him, that is, under the God of the Jews. And again: [22] 'The Lord thy God, He is God in heaven above, and upon the earth beneath, and there is none other except Him.' And somewhere else the Scripture says to the Jewish multitude, [23] 'The Lord your God is God of gods;' so that, even if there are gods, they are under the God of the Jews. And somewhere else the Scripture says in regard to Him, [24] 'God, the great and true, who regardeth not persons, nor taketh reward, He doth execute the judgment of the fatherless and widow.' The Scripture, in calling the God of the Jews great and true, and executing judgment, marked out the others as small, and not true. But also somewhere else the Scripture says, [25] 'As I live, saith the Lord, there is no other God but me. I am the first, I am after this; except me there is no God.' And again: [26] 'Thou shalt fear the Lord thy God, and Him only shalt thou serve.' And again: [27] 'Hear, O Israel, the Lord your God is one Lord.' And many passages besides seal with an oath that God is one, and except Him there is no God. "Whence I wonder how, when so many passages testify that there is one God, you say that there are many."

Chap. VIII. — *Simon and Peter continue the discussion*

And Simon said: "My original stipulation with you was that I should prove from the Scriptures that you were wrong in maintaining that we ought not to speak of many gods. Accordingly I adduced many written passages to show that the divine Scriptures themselves speak of many gods." And Peter said: "Those very Scriptures which speak of many gods, also exhorted us, saying, 'The names of other gods shall not ascend upon thy lips.' [28] Thus, Simon, I did not speak contrary to what was written." And Simon said: "Do you, Peter, listen to what I have to say. You seem to me to sin in speaking against them, [29] when the Scripture says, [30] 'Thou shalt not revile [the gods], nor curse the rulers of thy people.'" And Peter said: "I am not sinning, Simon, in pointing out their destruction according to the Scriptures; for thus it is written: [31] 'Let the gods who did not make the heavens and the earth perish.' And He said thus, not as though some had made the heavens and were not to perish, as you interpreted the passage. For it is plainly declared that He who made them is one in the very first part of Scripture: [32] 'In the beginning God created the heaven and the earth.' And it did not say, 'the gods.' And somewhere else it says, [33] 'And the firmament showeth His handiwork.' And in another place it is written, [34] 'The heavens themselves shall perish, but Thou shalt remain for ever.'"

Chap. IX. — *Simon tries to show that the Scriptures contradict themselves*

And Simon said: "I adduced clear passages from the Scriptures to prove that there are many gods; and you, in reply, brought forward as many or more from the same Scriptures, showing that God is one, and He the God of the Jews. And when I said that we ought not to revile gods, you proceeded to show that He who created is one, because those who did not create will perish. And in reply to my assertion that we ought to maintain that there are gods, because the Scriptures also say so, you showed that we ought not to utter their names, because the same Scripture tells us not to utter the names of other gods. Since, then, these very Scriptures say at one time that there are many gods, and at another that there is only one; and sometimes that they ought not to be reviled, and at other times that they ought; what conclusion ought we to come to in consequence of this, but that the Scriptures themselves lead us astray?"

Chap. X. — *Peter's explanation of the apparent contradictions of Scripture*

And Peter said: "They do not lead astray, but convict and bring to light the evil disposition against God which lurks like a serpent in each one. For the Scriptures lie before each one like many divers types. Each one, then, has his own disposition like wax, and examining the Scriptures and finding everything in them, he moulds his idea of God according to his wish, laying upon them, as I said, his own disposition, which is like wax. Since, then, each one finds in the Scriptures whatever opinion he wishes to have in regard to God, for this reason he [Simon] moulds from them the forms [35] of many gods, while we moulded the form of Plim who truly exists, coming to the knowledge of the true type from our own shape. [36] For assuredly the soul within us is clothed with His image for immortality. If I abandon the parent of this soul, it also will abandon me to just judgment, making known the injustice by the very act of daring; [37] and as coming from one who is just, it will justly abandon me; and so, as far as the soul is concerned, I shall, after punishment, be destroyed, having abandoned the help that comes from it. But if there is another [god], first let him put on another form, another shape, in order that by the new shape of the body I may recognise the new god. But if he should change the shape, does he thereby change the substance of the soul? But if he should change it also, then I am no longer myself, having become another both in shape and in substance. Let him, therefore, create others, if there is another. But there is not. For if there had been, he would have created. But since he has not created, then let him, as non-existent, leave him who is really existent. [38] For he is nobody, [39] except only in the opinion of Simon. I do not accept of any other god but Him alone who created me."

Chap. XI. — *Gen. I. 26 appealed to by Simon*

And Simon said: "Since I see that you frequently speak of the God who created you, learn from me how you are impious even to Him. For there are evidently two who created, as the Scripture says: [40] 'And God said, Let us make man in our image, after our likeness.' Now 'let us make' implies two or more; certainly not one only."

Chap. XII. — *Peter's explanation of the passage*

And Peter answered: "One is He who said to His Wisdom, 'Let us make man.' But His Wisdom [41] was that with which He Himself always rejoiced [42] as with His own spirit. It is united as soul to God, but it is extended by Him, as hand, fashioning the universe. On this account, also, one man was made, and from him went forth also the female. And being a unity generically, it is yet a duality, for by expansion and contraction the unity is thought to be a duality. So that I act rightly in offering up all the honour to one God as to parents." And Simon said: "What then? Even if the Scriptures say that there are other gods, will you not accept the opinion?"

Chap. XIII. — *The contradictions of the Scriptures intended to try those who read them*

And Peter answered: "If the Scriptures or prophets speak of gods, they do so to try those who hear. For thus it is written: [43] 'If there arise among you a prophet, giving signs and wonders, and that sign and wonder shall then come to pass, and he say to thee, Let us go after and worship other gods which thy fathers have not known, ye [44] shall not hearken to the words of that prophet; let thy hands be among the first to stone him. For he hath tried to turn thee from the Lord thy God. But if thou say in thy heart, How did he do that sign or wonder? thou shalt surely know that he who tried thee, tried thee to see if thou dost fear the Lord thy God.' The words 'he who tried thee, tried thee,' have reference to the earliest times; [45] but it appears to be otherwise after the removal to Babylon. For God, who knows all things, would not, as can be proved by many arguments, try in order that He Himself might know, for He foreknows all things. But, if you like, let us discuss this point, and I shall show that God foreknows. But it has been proved that the opinion is false that He does not know, and that this was written to try us. Thus we, Simon, can be led astray [46] neither by the Scriptures nor by any one else; nor are we deceived into the admission of many gods, nor do we agree to any statement that is made against God.

Chap. XIV. — *Other beings called gods*

"For we ourselves also know that angels are called gods by the Scriptures, — as, for instance, He who spake at the bush, and wrestled with Jacob, — and the name is likewise applied to Him who is born Emmanuel, and who is called the mighty God. [47] Yea, even Moses became a god to Pharaoh, though in reality he was a man. The same is the case also with the idols of the Gentiles. But we have but one God, one who made creation and arranged the universe, whose Son is the Christ. Obeying Christ, [48] we learn to know what is false from the Scriptures. Moreover, being furnished by our ancestors with the truths of the Scriptures, we know that there is only one who has made the heavens and the earth, the God of the Jews, and of all who choose to worship Him. Our fathers, with pious thought, setting down a fixed belief in Him as the true God, handed down this belief to us, that we may know that if anything is said against God, it is a falsehood. I shall add this remark over and above what I need say: If the case be not as I have said, then may I, and all who love the truth, incur danger in regard to the praise of the God who made us."

Chap. XV. — *Christ not God, hilt the Son of God*

When Simon heard this, he said: "Since you say that we ought not to believe even the prophet that gives signs and wonders if he say that there is another god, and that you know that he even incurs the penalty of death, therefore your teacher also was with reason cut off for having given signs and wonders." And Peter answered: "Our Lord neither asserted that there were gods except the Creator of all, nor did He proclaim Himself to be God, but He with reason pronounced blessed him who called Him the Son of that God who has arranged the universe." And Simon answered: "Does it not seem to you, then, that he who comes from God is God?" And Peter said: "Tell us how this is possible; for we cannot affirm this, because we did not hear it from Him."

Chap. XVI. — *The unbegotten and the begotten necessarily different from each other*

"In addition to this, it is the peculiarity of the Father not to have been begotten, but of the Son to have been begotten; but what is begotten cannot be compared with that which is unbegotten or self-begotten." And Simon said: "Is it not the same on account of its origin?" [49] And Peter said: "He who is not the same in all respects as some one, cannot have all the same appellations applied to him as that person." And Simon said: "This is to assert, not to prove." And Peter said: "Why, do you not see that if [50] the one happens to be self-begotten or unbegotten, they cannot be called the same; nor can it be asserted of him who has been begotten that he is of the same substance as he is who has begotten him? Learn this also: The bodies of men have immortal souls, which have been clothed with the breath of God; and having come forth from God, they are of the same substance, but they are not gods. But if they are gods, then in this way the souls of all men, both those who have died, and those who are alive, and those who shall come into being, are gods. But if in a spirit of controversy you maintain that these also are gods, what great matter is it, then, for Christ to be called God? for He has only what all have.

Chap. XVII. — *The nature of God*

"We call Him God whose peculiar attributes cannot belong to the nature of any other; for, as He is called the Unbounded because He is boundless on every side, it must of necessity be the case that it is no other one's peculiar attribute to be called unbounded, as another cannot in like manner be boundless. But if any one says that it is possible, he is wrong; for two things boundless on every side cannot coexist, for the one is bounded by the other. Thus it is in the nature [51] of things that the unbegotten is one. But if he possesses a figure, even in this case the figure is one and incomparable. [52] Wherefore He is called the Most High, because, being higher than all, He has the universe subject to Him."

Chap. XVIII. — *The name of God*

And Simon said: "Is this word 'God' His ineffable name, which all use, because you maintain so strongly in regard to a name that it cannot be given to another?" And Peter said: "I know that this is not His ineffable name, but one which is given by agreement among men; but if you give it to another, you will also assign to this other that which is not used; and that, too, deliberately. [53] The name which is used is the forerunner of that which is not used. In this way insolence is attributed even to that which has not yet been spoken, just as honour paid to that which is known is handed on to that which has not yet been known."

Chap. XIX. — *The shape of God in man*

And Simon said: "I should like to know, Peter, if you really believe that the shape of man has been moulded after the shape of God." [54] And Peter said: "I am really quite certain, Simon, that this is the case." And Simon said: "How can death dissolve the body, impressed as it has thus been with the greatest seal?" And Peter said: "It is the shape of the just God. When, then, the body begins to act unjustly, the form which is in it takes to flight, and thus the body is dissolved, by the shape disappearing, in order that an unjust body may not have the shape of the just God. The dissolution, however, does not take place in regard to the seal, but in regard to the sealed body. But that which is sealed is not dissolved without Him who sealed it. And thus it is not permitted to die without judgment." And Simon said: "What necessity was there to give the shape of such a being to man, who was raised from the earth?" And Peter said: "This was done because of the love of God, who made man. For while, as far as substance is concerned, all things are superior to the flesh of man, — I mean the ether, the sun, the moon, the stars, the air, the water, the fire — in a word, all the other things which have been made for the service of man, — yet, though superior in substance, they willingly endure to serve the inferior in substance, because of the shape of the superior. For as they who honour the clay image of a king have paid honour to the king himself, whose shape the clay happens to have, so the whole creation with joy serves man, who is made from earth, looking to the honour thus paid to God.

Chap. XX. — *The character of God*

"Behold, then, the character of that God to whom you, Simon, wish to persuade us to be ungrateful, and the earth continues to bear you, perhaps wishing to see who will venture to entertain similar opinions to yours. For you were the first to dare what no other dared: you were the first to utter what we first heard. We first and alone have seen the boundless long-suffering of God in bearing with such great impiety as yours, and that God no other than the Creator of the world, against whom you have dared to act impiously. And yet openings of the earth took not place, and fire was not sent down from heaven and went not forth to burn up men, and rain was not poured out, [55] and a multitude of beasts was not sent from the thickets, and upon us ourselves the destructive wrath of God did not begin to show itself, on account of one who sinned the sin, as it were, of spiritual adultery, which is worse than the carnal. For it is not God the Creator of heaven and earth that in former times punished sins, since now, when He is blasphemed in the highest degree, He would inflict the severest punishment. [56] But, on the contrary, He is long-suffering, calls to repentance, having the arrows which end in the destruction of the impious laid up in His treasures, which He will discharge like living animals when He shall sit down to give judgment to those that are His. [57] Wherefore let us fear the just God, whose shape the body of man bears for honour."

Chap. XXI. — *Simon promises to appeal to the teaching of Christ, Peter dismisses the multitudes*

When Peter said this, Simon answered: "Since I see you skilfully hinting that what is written in the books [58] against the framer [59] [of the world] does not happen to be true, to-morrow I shall show, from the discourses of your teacher, that he asserted that the framer [of the world] was not the highest God." And when Simon said this, he went out. But Peter said to the assembled multitudes: "If Simon can do no other injury to us in regard to God, he at least prevents you from listening to the words that can purify the soul." On Peter saying this, much whispering arose amongst the crowds, saying, "What necessity is there for permitting him to come in here, and utter his blasphemies against God?" And Peter heard, and said, "Would that the doctrines against God which are intended to try men [60] went no further than Simon! For there will be, as the Lord said, false apostles, [61] false prophets, heresies, desires for supremacy, who, as I conjecture, finding their beginning in Simon, who blasphemes God, will work together in the assertion of the same opinions against God as those of Simon." And saying this with tears, he summoned the multitudes to him by his hand; and when they came, he laid his hands upon them and prayed, and then dismissed them, telling them to come at an earlier hour next day. Saying this, and groaning, he entered and went to sleep, without taking food.

[1] The word properly signifies the "sole government or monarchy of God." It means that God alone is ruler.
[2] ἰδιώτης
[3] τῶν παρὰ Ἰουδαίοις πεπιστωμένων βίβλων. The literal translation, given in the text, means that the Jews as a community believed in these books as speaking the truth. Cotelerius translates: "the books which were publicly entrusted to the Jews." One MS. reads, πεπιστωμένων, which might mean, "deemed trustworthy among the Jews."
[4] δόγμα.
[5] One MS. and an Epitome have: "And you must address your arguments to another who acts as judge."
[6] The words translated "error," ψεῦσμα, and "to be in the right," ἀληθεύειν, are, properly rendered, "falsehood," and "to speak the truth."
[7] The Mss. read: "not otherwise." The reading of the text is found in an Epitome.
[8] παραδείσῳ, "paradise." Gen. II. 16, 17.
[9] ἀναβλέψαι. It signifies either to look up, or to recover one's sight. Possibly the second meaning is the one intended here, corresponding to the words of our version: "Then your eyes shall be opened."
[10] Gen. III. 22.
[11] Gen. III. 5.
[12] Ex. XXII. 28.
[13] Deut. IV. 34.
[14] Jer. X. 11.
[15] Deut. XIII. 6.
[16] Josh, XXIII. 7, Sept.
[17] Deut. X. 17.
[18] Ps. XXXV. 10, LXXXVI. 8.
[19] Ps. L. 1.
[20] Ps. LXXXII. 1.
[21] Deut. X. 14.
[22] Deut. IV. 39.
[23] Deut. X. 17.
[24] Deut. X. 17.
[25] Isa. XLIX. 18, XLV. 21, XLIV. 6.
[26] Deut. VI. 13.
[27] Deut. VI. 4.
[28] Josh, XXIII. 7 in the Septuagint.
[29] Namely, the gods.
[30] Ex. XXII. 28. The MSS. omit θεούς, though they insert it in the passage as quoted a little before this. One MS. reads "the ruler" with our version.
[31] Jer. X. 11.
[32] Gen. I. 1.
[33] Ps. XIX. 1.
[34] Ps. CII. 26, 27.
[35] ἰδέας.
[36] μορφῆς.
[37] Probably τολμήματι should be changed into ὁρμήματι, or some such word: making known that an act of injustice has been committed by taking its departure.
[38] This might possibly he translated, "let him leave him who exists to him who exists;" *i.e.* let him leave the real God to man, who really exists.
[39] Wieseler proposes, "for he exists to no one."
[40] Gen. I. 26.
[41] This is the only passage in the Homilies relating to the σοφία. The text is in some parts corrupt. It is critically discussed by Uhlhorn, some of whose emendations are adopted by Dressel and translated here.
[42] Prov. VIII. 30.
[43] Deut. XIII. 1 ff.
[44] The change from the singular to the plural is in the Greek.
[45] Lit., "But it had been said that he who tried, tried." The idea seems to be, Before the removal to Babylon true prophets tested the people by urging them to worship these gods; but after that event false prophets arose who really wished to seduce the Jews from the worship of the true God.

[46] Lit., "nor can we be made to stumble from the Scriptures nor by any one else [or anything else]."
[47] Isa. IX. 6.
[48] Lit., "whom obeying:" the "whom" might refer to God.
[49] The word γένεσις, "arising, coming into being," is here used, not γέννησις, "begetting." The idea fully expressed is: "Is not that which is begotten identical in essence with that which begets it?"
[50] We have inserted εἰ. The passage is amended in various ways; this seems to be the simplest.
[51] Lit., "thus it is nature."
[52] We have adopted an emendation here. The text has: "Even thus the incomparable is one."
[53] "Wieseler proposes to join this clause with the following: "And in point of choice the name which."
[54] Lit., "of that one, of Him."
[55] One MS. reads, "was not restrained."
[56] We have inserted ἄν, and suppose the sentence to be ironical. The meaning might be the same without ἄν. The text of Dressel is as follows: "For is not He who then punished the sins God, Creator of heaven and earth; since even now, being blasphemed in the highest degree, He punished it in the highest degree?"
[57] Cotelerius translates: "to His enemies."
[58] i.e. the Scriptures.
[59] A distinction has to be made between the Creator, or maker out of nothing, and the framer, or fashioner, or Demiurge, who puts the matter into shape.
[60] Lit, "the word against God for the trial of men."
[61] Comp. Matt. XXIV. 24.

Homily XVII

Chap. I. — *Simon comes to Peter*

The next day, therefore, as Peter was to hold a discussion with Simon, he rose earlier than usual and prayed. On ceasing to pray, Zacchaeus came in, and said: "Simon is seated without, discoursing with about thirty of his own special followers." And Peter said: "Let him talk until the multitude assemble, and then let us begin the discussion in the following way. We shall hear all that has been said by him, and having fitted our reply to this, we shall go out and discourse." And assuredly so it happened. Zacchaeus, therefore, went out, and not long after entered again, and communicated to Peter the discourse delivered by Simon against him. [1]

Chap. II. — *Simon's speech against Peter*

Now he said: "He accuses you, Peter, of being the servant of wickedness, of having great powder in magic, and as charming the souls of men in a way worse than idolatry. To prove that you are a magician, he seemed to me to adduce the following evidence, saying: "I am conscious of this, that when I come to hold a discussion with him, I do not remember a single word of what I have been meditating on by myself. For while he is discoursing, and my mind is engaged in recollecting what it is that I thought of saying on coming to a conference with him, I do not hear anything whatsoever of what he is saying. Now, since I do not experience this in the presence of any other than in his alone, is it not plain that I am under the influence of his magic? And as to his doctrines being worse than those of idolatry, I can make that quite clear to any one who has understanding. For there is no other benefit than this, that the soul should be freed from images [2] of every kind. For when the soul brings an image before its eye, it is bound by fear, and it pines away through anxiety lest it should suffer some calamity; and being altered, it falls under the influence of a demon; and being under his influence, it seems to the mass to be wise.

Chap. III. — *Simon's accusation of Peter*

"'Peter does this to you while promising to make you wise. For, under the pretext of proclaiming one God, he seems to free you from many lifeless images, which do not at all injure those who worship them, because they are seen by the eyes themselves to be made of stone, or brass, or gold, or of some other lifeless material. Wherefore the soul, because it knows that what is seen is nothing, cannot be spell-bound by fear in an equal degree by means of what is visible. But looking to a terrible God through the influence of deceptive teaching, it has all its natural foundations overturned. And I say this, not because I exhort you to worship images, but because Peter, seeming to free your souls from terrible images, [3] drives mad the mind of each one of you by a more terrible image, introducing God in a shape, and that, too, a God extremely just, — an image which is accompanied by what is terrible and awful to the contemplative soul, by that which can entirely destroy the enerory of a sound mind. For the mind, when in the midst of such a storm, is like the depth stirred by a violent wind, perturbed and darkened. Wherefore, if he comes to benefit you, let him not, while seeming to dissolve your fears which gently proceed from lifeless shapes, introduce in their stead the terrible shape of God. But has God a shape? If He has. He possesses a figure. And if He has a figure, how is He not limited? And if limited, He is in space. But if He is in space, He is less than the space which encloses Him. And if less than anything, how is He greater than all, or superior to all, or the highest of all? This, then, is the state of the case.

Chap. IV. — *It is asserted that Christ's teaching is different from Peter's*

"'And that he does not really believe even the doctrines proclaimed by his teacher is evident, for he proclaims doctrines opposite to his. For he said to some one, as I learn, [4] "Call me not good, for the good is one." Now, in speaking of the good one, he no longer speaks of that just one, [5] whom the Scriptures proclaim, who kills and makes alive, — kills those who sin, and makes alive those who live according to His will. But that he did not really call Him who is the framer of the world good, is plain to any one who can reflect. For the framer of the world was known to Adam whom He had made, and to Enoch who pleased Him, and to Noah who was seen to be just by Him; likewise to Abraham, and Isaac, and Jacob; also to Moses, and the people, and the whole world. But Jesus, the teacher of Peter himself, came and said, [6] "No one knew the Father except the Son, as no one knoweth [7] even the Son except the Father, and those to whom the Son may wish to reveal Him." If, then, it was the Son himself who was present, it was from the time of his appearance that he began to reveal to those to whom he wished, Him who was unknown to all. And thus the Father was unknown to all who lived before him, and could not thus be He who was known to all.

Chap. V. — *Jesus inconsistent in his teaching*

"In saying this, Jesus is consistent not even with himself. For sometimes by other utterances, taken from the Scriptures, he presents God as being terrible and just, saying, [8] "Fear not him who killeth the body, but can do nothing to the soul; but fear Him who is able to cast both body and soul into the geenna of fire. Yea, I say unto you, fear Him." But that he asserted that He is really to be feared as being a just God, to whom he says those who receive injustice cry, is shown in a parable of which he gives the interpretation, saying: [9] "If, then, the unjust judge did so, because he was continually entreated, how much more will the Father avenge those who cry to Him day and night? Or do you think that, because He bears long with them, He will not do it? Yea, I say to you, He will do it, and that speedily." Now he who speaks of God as an avenging and rewarding God, presents Him as naturally just, and not as good. Moreover he gives thanks to the Lord of heaven and earth. [10] But if He is Lord of heaven and earth. He is acknowledged to be the framer of the world, and if framer, then He is just. When, therefore, he sometimes calls Him good and sometimes just, he is not consistent with himself in this point. But his wise disciple maintained yesterday a third point, that real sight [11] is more satisfactory than vision, not knowing that real sight can be human, but that vision confessedly proceeds from divinity.'

Chap. VI. — *Peter goes out to answer Simon*

"These and such like were the statements, Peter, which Simon addressed to the multitudes while he stood outside; and he seems to me to be disturbing the minds of the greater number. Wherefore go forth immediately, and by the power of truth break down his false statements." When Zacchaeus said this, Peter prayed after his usual manner and went out, and standing in the place where he spoke the day before, and saluting the multitudes according to the custom enjoined by his religion, he began to speak as follows: "Our Lord Jesus Christ, who is the true prophet (as I shall prove conclusively at the proper time), made concise declarations in regard to those matters that relate to the truth, for these two reasons: first, because He was in the habit of addressing the pious, who had knowledge enough to enable them to believe the opinions uttered by Him by way of declaration; for His statements were not strange to their usual mode of thought; and in the second place, because, having a limited time assigned Him for preaching, He did not employ the method of demonstration in order that He might not spend all His limited time in arguments, for in this way it might happen that He would be fully occupied in giving the solutions of a few problems which might be understood by mental exertion, while He would not have given us to any great extent [12] those statements which relate to the truth. Accordingly He stated any opinions He wished, as to a people who were able to understand Him, to whom we also belong, who, whenever we did not understand anything of what had been said by Him, — a thing which rarely happened, — inquired of Him privately, that nothing said by Him might be unintelligible to us.

Chap. VII. — *Man in the shape of God*

"Knowing therefore that we knew all that was spoken by Him, and that we could supply the proofs, He sent us to the ignorant Gentiles to baptize them for remission of sins, [13] and commanded us to teach them first. Of His commandments this is the first and great one, to fear the Lord God, and to serve Him only. But He meant us to fear that God whose angels they are who are the angels of the least of the faithful amongst us, [14] and who stand in heaven continually beholding the face of the Father. For He has shape, and He has every limb primarily and solely for beauty's sake, and not for use. For He has not eyes that He may see with them; for He sees on every side, since He is incomparably more brilliant in His body than the visual spirit which is in us, and He is more splendid than everything, so that in comparison with Him the light of the sun may be reckoned as darkness. Nor has He ears that He may hear; for He hears, perceives, moves, energizes, acts on every side. But He has the most beautiful shape on account of man, that the pure in heart [15] may be able to see Him, that they may rejoice because they suffered. For He moulded man in His own shape as in the grandest seal, in order that he may be the ruler and lord of all, and that all may be subject to him. Wherefore, judging that He is the universe, and that man is His image (for He is Himself invisible, but His image man is visible), the man who wishes to worship Him honours His visible image, which is man. Whatsoever therefore any one does to man, be it good or bad, is regarded as being done to Him. Wherefore the judgment which proceeds from Him shall go before, giving to every one according to his merits. For He avenges His own shape.

Chap. VIII. — *God's figure: Simon's objection therefrom refuted*

"But some one will say. If He has shape, then He has figure also, and is in space; but if He is in space, and is, as being less, enclosed by it, how is He great above everything? How can He be everywhere if He has figure? The first remark I have to make to him who urges these objections is this: The Scriptures persuade us to have such sentiments and to believe such statements in regard to Him; and we know that their declarations are true, for witness is borne to them by our Lord Jesus Christ, by whose orders we are bound to afford proofs to you that such is the case. But first I shall speak of space. The space of God is the non-existent, but God is that which exists. But that which is non-existent cannot be compared with that which is existent. For how can space be existent? unless it be a second space, such as heaven, earth, water, air, and if there is any other body that fills up the vacuity, which is called vacuity on this account, that it is nothing. For 'nothing' is its more appropriate name. For what is that which is called vacuity but as it were a vessel which contains nothing, except the vessel itself? But being vacuity, it is not itself space; but space is that in which vacuity itself is, if indeed it is the vessel. For it must be the case that that which exists is in that which does not exist. But by this which is non-existent I mean that which is called by some, space, which is nothing. But being nothing, how can it be compared with that which is, except by expressing the contrary, and saying that it is that which does not exist, and that that which does not exist is called space? But even if it were something, there are many examples which I have at hand, but I shall content myself with one only, to show that that which encloses is not unquestionably superior to that which is enclosed. The sun is a circular figure, and is entirely enclosed by air, yet it lightens up the air, it warms it, it divides it; and if the sun be away from it, it is enveloped in darkness; and from whatsoever part of it the sun is removed, it becomes cold as if it were dead; but again it is illuminated by its rising, and when it has been warmed up by it, it is adorned with still greater beauty. And it does this by giving a share of itself, though it has its substance limited. What, then, is there to prevent God, as being the Framer and Lord of this and everything else, from possessing figure and shape and beauty, and having the communication of these qualities proceeding from Himself extended infinitely?

Chap. IX. — *God the centre or heart of the universe*

"One, then, is the God who truly exists, who presides in a superior shape, being the heart of that which is above and that which is below twice, [16] which sends forth from Him as from a centre the life-giving and incorporeal power; the whole universe with the stars and regions [17] of the heaven, the air, the fire, and if anything else exists, is proved to be a substance infinite in height, boundless in depth, immeasurable in breadth, extending the life-giving and wise nature from Him over three infinites. [18] It must be, therefore, that this infinite which proceeds from Him on every side exists, [19] having as its heart Him who is above all, and who thus possesses figure; for wherever He be, He is as it were in the centre of the infinite, being the limit of the universe. And the extensions taking their rise with Him, possess the nature of six infinites; of whom the one taking its rise with Him penetrates [20] into the height above, another into the depth below, another to the right hand, another to the left, another in front, and another behind; to whom He

Himself, looking as to a number that is equal on every side, [21] completes the world in six temporal intervals, [22] Himself being the rest, [23] and having the infinite age to come as His image, being the beginning and the end. For in Him the six infinites end, and from Him they receive their extension to infinity.

Chap. X. — *The nature and shape of God*

"This is the mystery of the hebdomad. For He Himself is the rest of the whole who grants Himself as a rest to those who imitate His greatness within their little measure. For He is alone, sometimes comprehensible, sometimes incomprehensible, [sometimes limitable,] [24] sometimes illimitable, having extensions which proceed from Him into infinity. For thus He is comprehensible and incomprehensible, near and far, being here and there, as being the only existent one, and as giving a share of that mind which is infinite on every hand, in consequence of which souls breathe and possess life; [25] and if they be separated from the body and be found with a longing for Him, they are borne along into His bosom, as in the winter time the mists of the mountains, attracted by the rays of the sun, are borne along immortal [26] to it. What affection ought therefore to arise within us if we gaze with our mind on His beautiful shape! But otherwise it is absurd [to speak of beauty]. For beauty cannot exist apart from shape; nor can one be attracted to the love of God, nor even deem that he can see Him, if God has no form.

Chap. XI. — *The fear of God*

"But some who are strangers to the truth, and who give their energies to the service of evil, on pretext of glorifying God, say that He has no figure, in order that, being shapeless and formless, He may be visible to no one, so as not to be longed for. For the mind, not seeing the form of God, is empty of Him. But how can any one pray if he has no one to whom he may flee for refuge, on whom he may lean? For if he meets with no resistance, he falls out into vacuity. Yea, says he, we ought not to fear God, but to love Him. I agree; but the consciousness of having done well in each good act will accomplish this. Now well-doing proceeds from fearing. But fear, says he, strikes death into the soul. Nay, but I affirm that it does not strike death, but awakens the soul, and converts it. And perhaps the injunction not to fear God might be right, if we men did not fear many other things; such, for instance, as plots against us by those who are like us, and wild beasts, serpents, diseases, sufferings, demons, and a thousand other ills. Let him, then, who asks us not to fear God, rescue us from these, that we may not fear them; but if he cannot, why should he grudge that we should be delivered from a thousand fears by one fear, the fear of the Just One, and that it should be possible by a slight [27] faith In Him to remove a thousand afflictions from ourselves and others, and receive instead an exchange of blessings, and that, doing no ill in consequence of fear of the God who sees everything, we should continue in peace even in the present life.

Chap. XII. — *The fear and love of God*

"Thus, then, grateful service to Him who is truly Lord, renders us free from service to all other masters. [28] If, then, it is possible for any one to be free from sin without fearing God, let him not fear; for under the influence of love to Him one cannot do what is displeasing to Him. For, on the one hand, it is written that we are to fear Him, and we have been commanded to love Him, in order that each of us may use that prescription which is suitable to his constitution. Fear Him, therefore, because He is just; but whether you fear Him or love Him, sin not. And may it be the case that any one who fears Him shall be able to gain the victory over unlawful desires, shall not lust after what belongs to others, shall practise kindness, shall be sober, and act justly! For I see some who are imperfect in their fear of Him sinning very much. Let us therefore fear God, not only because He is just; for it is through pity for those who have received injustice that He inflicts punishment on those who have done the injustice. As water therefore quenches fire, so does fear extinguish the desire for evil practices. He who teaches fearlessness does not himself fear; but he who does not fear, does not believe that there will be a judgment, strengthens his lusts, acts as a magician, and accuses others of the deeds which he himself does."

Chap. XIII. — *The evidence of the senses contrasted with that from supernatural vision*

Simon, on hearing this, interrupted him, and said: "I know against whom you are making these remarks; but in order that I may not spend any time in discussing subjects which I do not wish to discuss, repeating the same statements to refute you, reply to that which is concisely stated by us. You professed that you had well understood the doctrines and deeds [29] of your teacher because you saw them before you with your own eyes, [30] and heard them with your own ears, and that it is not possible for any other to have anything similar by vision or apparition. But I shall show that this is false. He who hears any one with his own ears, is not altogether fully assured of the truth of what is said; for his mind has to consider whether he is wrong or not, inasmuch as he is a man as far as appearance goes. But apparition not merely presents an object to view, but inspires him who sees it with confidence, for it comes from God. Now reply first to this."

Chap. XIV. — *The evidence of the senses more trustworthy than that of supernatural vision*

And Peter said: "You proposed to speak to one point, you replied to another. [31] For your proposition was, that one is better able to know more fully, [and to attain confidence,] [32] when he hears in consequence of an apparition, than when he hears with his own ears; but when you set about the matter, you were for persuading us that he who hears through an apparition is surer than he who hears with his own ears. Finally, you alleged that, on this account, you knew more satisfactorily the doctrines of Jesus than I do, because you heard His words through an apparition. But I shall reply to the proposition you made at the beginning. The prophet, because he is a prophet, having first given certain information with regard to what is objectively [33] said by him, is believed with confidence; and being known beforehand to be a true prophet, and being examined and questioned as the disciple wishes, he replies: But he who trusts to apparition or vision and dream is insecure. For he does not know to whom he is trusting. For it is possible either that he may be an evil demon or a deceptive spirit, pretending in his speeches to be what he is not. But if any one should wish to inquire of him who he is who has appeared, he can say to himself whatever he likes. And thus, gleaming forth like a wicked one, and remaining as long as he likes, he is at length extinguished, not remaining with the questioner so long as he wished him to do for the purpose of consulting him. For any one that sees by means of dreams cannot inquire about whatever he may wish. For reflection is not in the special power of one who is asleep. Hence we, desiring to have information in regard to something in our waking hours, inquire about something else in our dreams; or without inquiring, we hear about matters that do not concern us, and awaking from sleep we are dispirited because we have neither heard nor inquired about those matters which we were eager to know."

Chap. XV. — *The evidence from dreams discussed*

And Simon said: "If you maintain that apparitions do not always reveal the truth, yet for all that, visions and dreams, being God-sent, do not speak falsely in regard to those matters which they wish to tell." And Peter said: "You were right in saying that, being God-sent, they do not speak falsely. But it is uncertain if he who sees has seen a God-sent dream." And Simon said: "If he who has had the vision is just, he has seen a true vision." And Peter said: "You were right. But who is just, if he stands in need of a vision that he may learn what he ought to learn, and do what he ought to do?" And Simon said: "Grant me this, that the just man alone can see a true vision, and I shall then reply to that other point. For I have come to the conclusion that an impious man does not see a true dream." And Peter said: "This is false; and I can prove it both apart from Scripture and by Scripture; but I do not undertake to persuade you. For the man who is inclined to fall in love with a bad woman, does not change his mind so as to care for a lawful union with another woman in every respect good; but sometimes they love the worse woman through prepossessions, though they are conscious that there is another who is more excellent. And you are ignorant, in consequence of some such state of mind." And Simon said: "Dismiss this subject, and discuss the matter on which you promised to speak. For it seems to me impossible that impious men should receive dreams from God in any way whatever."

Chap. XVI. — *None but evil demons appear to the impious*

And Peter said: "I remember that I promised to prove this point, and to give my proofs in regard to it from Scripture and apart from Scripture. And now listen to what I say. We know that there are many (if you will pardon me the statement; and if you don't, I can appeal to those who are present as judges) who worship idols, commit adultery, and sin in every way, and yet they see true visions and dreams, and some of them have also apparitions of demons. For I maintain that the eyes of mortals cannot see the incorporeal form of the Father or Son, because it is illumined by exceeding great light. Wherefore it is not because God envies, but because He pities, that He cannot be seen by man who has been turned into flesh. For he who sees [God] cannot live. For the excess of light dissolves the flesh of him who sees; unless by the secret power of God the flesh be changed into the nature of light, so that it can see light, or the substance of light be changed into flesh, so that it can be seen by flesh. For the power to see the Father, without undergoing any change, belongs to the Son alone. But the just shall also in like manner behold God; [34] for in the resurrection of the dead, when they have been changed, as far as their bodies are concerned, into light, and become like the angels, they shall be able to see Him. Finally, then, if any angel be sent that he may be seen by a man, he is changed into flesh, that he may be able to be seen by flesh. For no one can see the incorporeal power not only of the Son, but not even of an angel. But if one sees an apparition, he should know that this is the apparition of an evil demon.

Chap. XVII. — *The impious see true dreams and visions*

"But it is manifest that the impious see true visions and dreams, and I can prove it from Scripture. Finally, then, it is written in the law, how Abimelech, who was impious, wished to defile the wife of just Abraham by intercourse, and how he heard the commandment from God in his sleep, as the Scripture saith, not to touch her, [35] because she was dwelling with her husband. Pharaoh, also an impious man, saw a dream in regard to the fulness and thinness of the ears of corn, [36] to whom Joseph said, when he gave the interpretation, that the dream had come from God. [37] Nebuchadnezzar, who worshipped images, and ordered those who worshipped God to be cast into fire, saw a dream [38] extending over the whole age of the world. [39] And let no one say, 'No one who is impious sees a vision when awake.' That is false. Nebuchadnezzar himself, having ordered three men to be cast into fire, saw a fourth when he looked into the furnace, and said, 'I see the fourth as the Son of God.' [40] And nevertheless, though they saw apparitions, visions, and dreams, they were impious. Thus, we cannot infer with absolute certainty that the man who has seen visions, and dreams, and apparitions, is undoubtedly pious. For in the case of the pious man, the truth gushes up natural and pure [41] in his mind, not worked up through dreams, but granted to the good through intelligence.

Chap. XVIII. — *The nature of revelation*

"Thus to me also was the Son revealed by the Father, Wherefore I know what is the meaning of revelation, having learned it in my own case. For at the very time when the Lord said, 'Who do they say that I am?' [42] and when I heard one saying one thing of Him, and another, another, it came into my heart to say (and I know not, therefore, how I said it), 'Thou art the Son of the living God.' [43] But He, pronouncing me blessed, pointed out to me that it was the Father who had revealed it to me; and from this time I learned that revelation is knowledge gained without instruction, and without apparition and dreams. And this is indeed the case. For in the [soul] [44] which has been placed in us by [45] God, there is all the truth; but it is covered and revealed by the hand of God, who works so far as each one through his knowledge deserves. [46] But the declaration of anything by means of apparitions and dreams from without is a proof, not that it comes from revelation, but from wrath. Finally, then, it is written in the law, that God, being angry, said to Aaron and Miriam, [47] 'If a prophet arise from amongst you, I shall make myself known to him through visions and dreams, but not so as to my servant Moses; because I shall speak to him in an [outward] appearance, and not through dreams, just as one will speak to his own friend.' You see how the statements of wrath are made through visions and dreams, but the statements to a friend are made face to face, in [outward] appearance, and not through riddles and visions and dreams, as to an enemy.

Chap. XIX. — *Opposition to Peter unreasonable*

"If, then, our Jesus appeared to you in a vision, made Himself known to you, and spoke to you, it was as one who is enraged with an adversary; and this is the reason why it was through visions and dreams, or through revelations that were from without, that He spoke to you. But can any one be rendered fit for instruction through apparitions? And if you will say, 'It is possible,' then I ask, 'Why did our teacher abide and discourse a whole year to those who were awake?' And how are we to believe your word, when you tell us that He appeared to you? And how did He appear to you, when you entertain opinions contrary to His teaching? But if you were seen and taught by Him, and became His apostle for a single hour, proclaim His utterances, interpret His sayings, love His apostles, contend not with me who companied with Him. For in direct opposition to me, who am a firm rock, the foundation of the church, [48] you now stand. If you were not opposed to me, you would not accuse me, and revile the truth proclaimed by me, in order that I may not be believed when I state what I myself have heard with my own ears from the Lord, as if I were evidently a person that was condemned and in bad repute. [49] But if you say that I am condemned, you bring an accusation against God, who revealed the Christ to me, and you inveigh against Him who pronounced me blessed on account of the revelation. But if, indeed, you really wish to work in the cause of truth, learn first of all from us what we have learned from Him, and, becoming a disciple of the truth, become a fellow-worker with us."

Chap. XX. — *Another subject for discussion proposed*

When Simon heard this, he said: "Far be it from me to become his or your disciple. For I am not ignorant of what I ought to know; but the inquiries which I made as a learner were made that I may see if you can prove that actual sight is more distinct than apparition. [50] But you spoke according to your own pleasure; you did not prove. And now, to-morrow I shall come to your opinions in regard to God, whom you affirmed to be the framer of the world; and in my discussion with you, I shall show that he is not the highest, nor good, and that your teacher made the same statements as I now do; and I shall prove that you have not understood him." On saying this he went away, not wishing to listen to what might be said in the propositions which he had laid down.

[1] The text has: "against Peter."
[2] εἰδώλων, idols.
[3] ἰδεῶν.
[4] Matt. XIX. 17.
[5] The Gnostic distinction between the God who is just and the God who is good, is here insisted on.
[6] Matt. XI. 27.
[7] One MS. reads, "saw."
[8] Matt. X. 28.
[9] Luke XVIII. 6.
[10] Matt. XI. 25.
[11] The Mss. read ἐνέργειαν, "activity." Clericus amended it into ἐνάργειαν, which means, vision or sight in plain open day with one's own eyes, in opposition to the other word ὀπτασία, vision in sleep, or ecstasy, or some similar unusual state.
[12] Lit., "to a greater extent."
[13] Matt. XXVIII. 19.
[14] Matt. XVIII. 10.
[15] Matt. V. 8.
[16] The whole of this chapter is full of corruptions; "twice" occurs in one MS. Various attempts have been made to amend the passage.
[17] An emendation.
[18] The text is corrupt. We have translated ἐπ' ἀπείρους τρεῖς. Some think "three" should be omitted. The three infinites are in respect of height, depth, and breadth.
[19] As punctuated in Dressel, this reads, "that the infinite is the heart."
[20] The emendation of the transcriber of one of the MSS.
[21] This refers to the following mode of exhibiting the number: where each side presents the number three.
[22] The creation of the world in six days.
[23] The seventh day on which God rested, the type of the rest of the future age. See *Epistle of Barnabas*, c. xv.
[24] The words within brackets are inserted by conjecture. "Sometimes incomprehensible, sometimes illimitable," occur only in one MS.
[25] We have adopted Wieseler's suggestions.
[26] This word is justly suspected. The passage is in other respects corrupt.
[27] The word "slight" is not used in reference to the character of the faith, but to indicate that the act of faith is a

small act compared with the results that flow from it.
[28] We have adopted an emendation of a passage which is plainly corrupt.
[29] Doctrines and deeds; lit., the things of your teacher.
[30] The MSS. have here ἐνεργείᾳ, "activity." This has been amended into ἐναργείᾳ, "with plainness, with distinctness." Ἐνάργεια is used throughout in opposition to ὀπτασία, ὄραμα, and ἐνύπνιον, and means the act of seeing and hearing by our own senses in plain daylight, when to doubt the fact observed is to doubt the senses; ὀπτασία, is apparition or vision in ecstasy, or some extraordinary way but that of sleep; ὄραμα and ἐνύπνιον are restricted to visions in sleep. The last term implies this. The first means simply "a thing seen."
[31] Probably it should be ἀπεχλίνω instead of ἀπεχρίνω, "you turned aside to another."
[32] The words inserted in brackets are inserted conjecturally, to fill up a lacuna in the best MS.
[33] ἐναργῶς, "with reference to things palpable to our senses."
[34] We have translated a bold conjecture. The text has, "The just not in like manner," without any verb, which Schwegler amended: "To the just this power does not belong in like manner."
[35] Gen. XX. 3.
[36] Gen. XII. 6.
[37] Gen. XLI. 25.
[38] Dan. II. 31.
[39] Lit., of the whole length of the age.
[40] Dan. III. 25.
[41] "We have amended this passage. The text applies the words "natural [or innate] and pure" to the mind.
[42] Matt. XVI. 13.
[43] Matt. XVI. 16.
[44] This word is not in the text. Schliemann proposed the word "heart." Possibly "breath" or "spirit" may be the lost word. See above.
[45] "By" should properly be "from."
[46] Lit., "who produces according to the merit of each one knowing." Cotelerius translated, "who, knowing the merit of each man, does to him according to it." The idea seems to be, that God uncovers the truth hidden in the soul to each man according to his deserts.
[47] Num. XII. 6; Ex. xxxiii. 11.
[48] Matt. XVI. 18.
[49] We have adopted an emendation of Schwegler's. The text reads, "in good repute."
[50] This passage is corrupt in the text. Dressel reads, "that activity is more distinct than apparition." By activity would be meant, "acting while one is awake, and in full possession of his senses;" and thus the meaning would be nearly the same as in our translation.

Homily XVIII

Chap. I. — *Simon maintains that the framer of the world is not the highest God*

At break of day, when Peter went forth to discourse, Simon anticipated him, and said: "When I went away yesterday, I promised to you to return to-day, and in a discussion show that he who framed the world is not the highest God, but that the highest God is another who alone is good, and who has remained unknown up to this time. At once, then, state to me whether you maintain that the framer of the world is the same as the lawgiver or not? If, then, he is the lawgiver, he is just; but if he is just, he is not good. But if he is not good, then it was another that Jesus proclaimed, when he said, [1] 'Do not call me good; for one is good, the Father who is in the heavens.' Now a lawgiver cannot be both just and good, for these qualities do not harmonize." And Peter said: "First tell us what are the actions which in your opinion constitute a person good, and what are those which constitute him just, in order that thus we may address our words to the same mark." And Simon said: "Do you state first what in your opinion is goodness, and what justice."

Chap. II. — *Definition of goodness and justice*

And Peter said: "That I may not waste my time in contentious discussions, while I make the fair demand that you should give answers to my propositions, I shall myself answer those questions which I put, as is your wish. I then affirm that the man who bestows [2] [goods] is good, just as I see the Framer of the world doing when He gives the sun to the good, and the rain to the just and unjust." And Simon said: "It is most unjust that he should give the same things to the just and the unjust." And Peter said: "Do you, then, in your turn state to us what course of conduct would constitute Him good." And Simon said: "It is you that must state this." And Peter said: "I will. He who gives the same things to the good and just, and also to the evil and unjust, is not even just according to you; but you would with reason call Him just if He gave goods to the good and evils to the evil. What course of conduct, then, would He adopt, if He does not adopt the plan of giving things temporal to the evil, if perchance they should be converted, and things eternal to the good, if at least they remain [good]? And thus by giving to all, but by gratifying the more excellent, [3] His justice is good; and all the more long-suffering in this, that to sinners who repent He freely grants forgiveness of their sins, and to those who have acted well He assigns even eternal life. But judging at last, and giving to each one what he deserves. He is just. If, then, this is right, confess it; but if it appears to you not to be right, refute it."

Chap. III. — *God both good and just*

And Simon said: "I said once for all, 'Every lawgiver, looking to justice, is just.'" And Peter said: "If it is the part of him who is good not to lay down a law, but of him who is just to lay down a law, in this way the Framer of the world is both good and just. He is good, inasmuch as it is plain that He did not lay down a law in writing from the times of Adam to Moses; but inasmuch as He had a written law from Moses to the present times, [4] He is just also." And Simon said: "Prove to me from the utterances of your teacher that it is within the power of the same man to be good and just; for to me it seems impossible that the law-giver who is good should also be just." And Peter said:

"I shall explain to you how goodness itself is just. Our teacher Himself first said to the Pharisee who asked Him, [5] 'What shall I do to inherit eternal life?' 'Do not call me good; for one is good, even the Father who is in the heavens;' and straightway He introduced these words, 'But if thou shalt wish to enter into life, keep the commandments.' And when he said, 'What commandments?' He pointed him to those of the law. Now He would not, if He were indicating some other good being, have referred him to the commandments of the Just One. That indeed justice and goodness are different I allow, but you do not know that it is within the power of the same being to be good and just. For He is good, in that He is now long-suffering with the penitent, and welcomes them; but just, when acting as judge He will give to every one according to his deserts."

Chap. IV. — *The unrevealed God*

And Simon said: "How, then, if the framer of the world, who also fashioned Adam, was known, and known too by those who were just according to the law, and moreover by the just and unjust, and the whole world, does your teacher, coming after all these, say, [6] 'No one has known the Father but the Son, even as no one knoweth the Son but the Father, and those to whom the Son may wish to reveal Him?' But he would not have made this statement, had he not proclaimed a Father who was still unrevealed, whom the law speaks of as the highest, and who has not given any utterance either good or bad (as Jeremiah testifies in the Lamentations); [7] who also, limiting the nations to seventy languages, according to the number of the sons of Israel who entered Egypt, and according to the boundaries of these nations, crave to his own Son, who is also called Lord, and who brought into order the heaven and the earth, the Hebrews as his portion, and defined him to be God of gods, that is, of the gods who received the other nations as their portions. Laws, therefore, proceeded from all the so-called gods to their own divisions, which consist of the other nations. In like manner also from the Son of the Lord of all came forth the law which is established among the Hebrews. And this state of matters was determined on, that if any one should seek refuge in the law of any one, he should belong to the division of him whose law he undertook to obey. No one knew the highest Father, who was unrevealed, just as they did not know that his Son was his Son. Accordingly at this moment you yourself, in assigning the special attributes of the unrevealed Most High to the Son, do not know that he is the Son, being the Father of Jesus, who with you is called the Christ."

Chap. V. — *Peter doubts Simon's honesty*

When Simon had made these statements, Peter said to him: "Can you call to witness that these are your beliefs that being Himself, — I do not mean Him whom you speak of now as being unrevealed, but Him in whom you believe, though you do not confess Him? For you are talking nonsense when you define one thing instead of another. Wherefore, if you call Him to witness that you believe what you say, I shall answer you. But if you continue discussing with me what you do not believe, you compel me to strike the empty air." And Simon said: "It is from some of your own disciples that I have heard [that this is the truth]." [8] And Peter said: "Do not bear false witness?" And Simon said: "Do not rebuke me, most insolent man." And Peter said: "So long as you do not tell who it was who said so, [I affirm that] you are a liar." And Simon said: "Suppose that I myself have got up these doctrines, or that I heard them from some other, give me your answer to them. For if they cannot be overturned, then I have learned that this is the truth." And Peter said: "If it is a human invention, I will not reply to it; but if you are held fast by the supposition that it is the truth, acknowledge to me that this is the case, and I can then myself say something in regard to the matter." And Simon said: "Once for all, then, these doctrines seem to me to be true. Give me your reply, if you have aught to say against them."

Chap. VI. — *The nature of revelation*

And Peter said: "If this is the case, you are acting most impiously. For if it belongs to the Son, who arranged heaven and earth, to reveal His unrevealed Father to whomsoever He wishes, you are, as I said, acting most impiously in revealing Him to those to whom He has not revealed Him." And Simon said: "But he himself wishes me to reveal him." And Peter said: "You do not understand what I mean, Simon. But listen and understand. When it is said that the Son will reveal Him to whom He wishes, it is meant that such an one is to learn of Him not by instruction, but by revelation only. For it is revelation when that which lies secretly veiled in all the hearts of men is revealed [unveiled] by His [God's] own will without any utterance. And thus knowledge comes to one, not because he has been instructed, but because he has understood. And yet the person who understands it cannot demonstrate it to another, since he did not himself receive it by instruction; nor can he reveal it, since he is not himself the Son, unless he maintains that he is himself the Son. But you are not the standing Son. For if you were the Son, assuredly you would know those who are worthy of such a revelation. But you do not know them. For if you knew them, you would do as they do who know."

Chap. VII. — *Simon confesses his ignorance*

And Simon said: "I confess I have not understood what you mean by the expression, 'You would do as they do who know.'" And Peter said: "If you have not understood it, then you cannot know the mind of every one; and if you are ignorant of this, then you do not know those who are worthy of the revelation. You are not the Son, for [9] the Son knows. Wherefore He reveals [Him] to whomsoever He wishes, because they are worthy." And Simon said: "Be not deceived. I know those who are worthy, and I am not the Son. And yet I have not understood what meaning you attach to the words, 'He reveals

[Him] to whomsoever He wishes.' But I said that I did not understand it, not because I did not know it, but because I knew that those who were present did not understand it, in order that you may state it more distinctly, so that they may perceive what are the reasons why we are carrying on this discussion." And Peter said: "I cannot state the matter more clearly: explain what meaning you have attached to the words." And Simon said: "There is no necessity why I should state your opinions." And Peter said: "You evidently, Simon, do not understand it, and yet you do not wish to confess, that you may not be detected in your ignorance, and thus be proved not to be the standing Son. For you hint this, though you do not wish to state it plainly; and, indeed, I who am not a prophet, but a disciple of the true Prophet, know well from the hints you have given what your wishes are. For you, though you do not understand even what is distinctly said, wish to call yourself son in opposition to us." And Simon said: "I will remove every pretext from you. I confess I do not understand what can be the meaning of the statement, 'The Son. reveals [Him] to whomsoever He wishes.' State therefore what is its meaning more distinctly."

Chap. VIII. — *The work of revelation belongs to the Son alone*

And Peter said: "Since, at least in appearance, you have confessed that you do not understand it, reply to the question I put to you, and you will learn the meaning of the statement. Tell me, do you maintain that the Son, whoever he be, is just, or that he is not just?" And Simon said: "I maintain that he is most just." And Peter said: "Seeing He is just, why does He not make the revelation to all, but only to those to whom He wishes?" And Simon said: "Because, being just, he wishes to make the revelation only to the worthy." And Peter said: "Must He not therefore know the mind of each one, in order that He may make the revelation to the worthy?" And Simon said: "Of course he must." And Peter said: "With reason, therefore, has the work of giving the revelation been confined to Him alone, for He alone knows the mind of every one; and it has not been given to you, who are not able to understand even that which is stated by us."

Chap. IX. — *How Simon hears his exposure*

When Peter said this, the multitudes applauded. But Simon, being thus exposed, [10] blushed through shame, and rubbing his forehead, said: "Well, then, do they declare that I, a magician, yea, even I who syllogize, am conquered by Peter? It is not so. But if one should syllogize, though carried away and conquered, he still retains the truth that is in him. For the weakness in the defender is not identical with the truth in the conquered man. [11] But I assure you that I have judged all those who are bystanders worthy to know the unrevealed Father. Wherefore, because I publicly reveal him to them, you yourself, through envy, are angry with me who wish to confer a benefit on them."

Chap. X. — *Peter's reply to Simon*

And Peter said: "Since you have thus spoken to please the multitudes who are present, I shall speak to them, not to please them, but to tell them the truth. Tell me how you know all those who are present to be worthy, when not even one of them agreed with your exposition of the subject; for the giving of applause to me in opposition to you is not the act of those who agree with you, but of those who agree with me, to whom they gave the applause for having spoken the truth. But since God, who is just, judges the mind of each one — a doctrine which you affirm to be true — He would not have wished this to be given through the left hand to those on the right hand, exactly as the man who receives anything from a robber is himself guilty. So that, on this account, He did not wish them to receive what is brought by you; but they are to receive the revelation through the Son, who has been set apart for this work. For to whom is it reasonable that the Father should give a revelation, but to His only Son, because He knows Him to be worthy of such a revelation? And so this is a matter which one cannot teach or be taught, but it must be revealed by the ineffable hand to him who is worthy to know it."

Chap. XI. — *Simon professes to utter his real sentiments*

And Simon said: "It contributes much to victory, if the man who wars uses his own weapons; for what one loves he can in real earnest defend, and that which is defended with genuine earnestness has no ordinary power in it. Wherefore in future I shall lay before you my real opinions. I maintain that there is some unrevealed power, unknown to all, even to the Creator himself, as Jesus himself has also declared, though he did not know what he said. For when one talks a great deal he sometimes hits the truth, not knowing what he is saying. I am referring to the statement which he uttered, 'No one knows the Father.'" And Peter said: "Do not any longer profess that you know His doctrines." And Simon said: "I do not profess to believe his doctrines; but I am discussing points in which he was by accident right." And Peter said: "Not to give you any pretext for escape, I shall carry on the discussion with you in the way you wish. At the same time, I call all to witness that you do not yet believe the statement which you just now made. For I know your opinions. And in order that you may not imagine that I am not speaking the truth, I shall expound your opinions, that you may know that you are discussing with one who is well acquainted with them.

Chap. XII. — *Simon's opinions expounded by Peter*

"We, Simon, do not assert that from the great power, which is also called the dominant [12] power, two angels were sent forth, the one to create the world, the other to give the law; nor that each one when he came proclaimed himself, on account of what he had done, as the sole creator; nor that there is one who stands, will stand, and is opposed. [13] Learn how you disbelieve even in respect to this subject. If you say that there is an unrevealed power, that power is full of ignorance. For it did not foreknow the ingratitude of the angels who were sent by it." And Simon became exceedingly angry with Peter for saying this, and interrupted his discourse, saying: "What nonsense is this you speak, you daring and most impudent of men, revealing plainly before the multitudes the secret doctrines, so that they can be easily learned?" And Peter said: "Why do you grudge that the present audience should receive benefit?" And Simon said: "Do you then allow that such knowledge is a benefit?" And Peter said: "I allow it: for the knowledge of a false doctrine is beneficial, inasmuch as you do not fall into it because of ignorance." And Simon said: "You are evidently not able to reply to the propositions I laid before you. I maintain that even your teacher affirms that there is some Father unrevealed."

Chap. XIII. — *Peter's explanation of the passage*

And Peter said: "I shall reply to that which you wish me to speak of, — namely, the passage, 'No one knows the Father but the Son, nor does any one know the Son but the Father, and they to whom the Son may wish to reveal Him.' First, then, I am astonished that, while this statement admits of countless interpretations, you should have chosen the very dangerous position of maintaining that the statement is made in reference to the ignorance of the Creator (Demiurge), and all who are under him. For, first, the statement can apply to all the Jews who think that David is the father of Christ, and that Christ himself is his son, and do not know that He is the Son of God. Wherefore it is appropriately said, 'No one knows the Father,' since, instead of God, they affirmed David to be His father; and the additional remark, that no one knows even the Son, is quite correct, since they did not know that He was the Son. The statement also, 'to whomsoever the Son may wish to reveal Him,' is also correct; for He, being the Son from the beginning, was alone appointed to give the revelation to those to whom He wishes to give it. And thus the first man (protoplast) Adam must have heard of Him; and Enoch, who pleased [God], must have known Him; and Noah, the righteous one, must have become acquainted with Him; and Abraam His friend must have understood Him; and Isaac must have perceived Him; and Jacob, who wrestled with Him, must have believed in Him; and the revelation must have been given to all among the people who were worthy.

Chap. XIV. — *Simon refuted*

"But if, as you say, it will be possible to know Him, because He is now revealed to all through Jesus, [14] are you not stating what is most unjust, when you say that these men did not know Him, who were the seven pillars of the world, and who were able to please the most just God, and that so many now from all nations who were impious know Him in every respect? Were not those who were superior to every one not deemed worthy to know

Him? [15] And how can that be good which is not just? unless you wish to give the name of 'good,' not to him who does good to those who act justly, but to him who loves the unjust, even though they do not believe, and reveals to them the secrets which he would not reveal to the just. But such conduct is befitting neither in one who is good nor just, but in one who has come to hate the pious. Are not you, Simon, the standing one, who have the boldness to make these statements which never have been so made before?"

Chap. XV. — *Matthew* XI. 25 *discussed*

And Simon, being vexed at this, said: "Blame your own teacher, who said, 'I thank Thee, Lord of heaven and earth, that what was concealed from the wise. Thou hast revealed to suckling babes.'" [16] And Peter said: "This is not the way in which the statement was made; but I shall speak of it as if it had been made in the way that has seemed good to you. Our Lord, even if He had made this statement, 'What was concealed from the wise, the Father revealed to babes,' could not even thus be thought to point out another God and Father in addition to Him who created the world. For it is possible that the concealed things of which He spoke may be those of the Creator (Demiurge) himself; because Isaiah [17] says, 'I will open my mouth in parables, and I will belch forth things concealed from the foundation of the world.' Do you allow, then, that the prophet was not ignorant of the things concealed, which Jesus says were concealed from the wise, but revealed to babes? And how was the Creator (Demiurge) ignorant of them, if his prophet Isaiah was not ignorant of them? But our Jesus did not in reality say 'what was concealed,' but He said what seems a harsher statement; for He said, ['Thou hast concealed these things from the wise, and] [18] hast revealed them to sucking babes.' Now the word 'Thou hast concealed' implies that they had once been known to them; for the key of the kingdom of heaven, that is, the knowledge of the secrets, lay with them.

Chap. XVI. — *These things hidden justly from the wise*

"And do not say He acted impiously towards the wise in hiding these things from them. Far be such a supposition from us. For He did not act impiously; but since they hid the knowledge of the kingdom, [19] and neither themselves entered nor allowed those who wished to enter, on this account, and justly, inasmuch as they hid the ways from those who wished, were in like manner the secrets hidden from them, in order that they themselves might experience what they had done to others, and with what measure they had measured, an equal measure might be meted out to them. [20] For to him who is worthy to know, is due that which he does not know; but from him who is not worthy, even should he seem to have anything, it is taken away, [21] even if he be wise in other matters; and it is given to the worthy, even should they be babes as far as the times of their discipleship are concerned.

Chap. XVII. — *The way to the kingdom not concealed from, the Israelites*

"But if one shall say nothing was concealed from the sons of Israel, because it is written, [22] 'Nothing escaped thy notice, O Israel (for do not say, O Jacob, The way is hid from me),' he ought to understand that the things that belong to the kingdom had been hid from them, but that the way that leads to the kingdom, that is, the mode of life, had not been hid from them. Wherefore it is that He says, * For say not that the way has been hid from me.' But by the way is meant the mode of life; for Moses says, [23] 'Behold, I have set before thy face the way of life and the way of death.' And the Teacher spoke in harmony with this: [24] 'Enter ye through the strait and narrow way, through which ye shall enter into life.' And somewhere else, when one asked Him, [25] 'What shall I do to inherit eternal life?' He pointed out to him the commandments of the law.

Chap. XVIII. — *Isaiah I. 3 explained*

"From the circumstance that Isaiah said, in the person of God, [26] 'But Israel hath not known me, and the people hath not understood me,' it is not to be inferred that Isaiah indicated another God besides Him who is known; [27] but he meant that the known God was in another sense unknown, because the people sinned, being ignorant of the just character of the known God, and imagined that they would not be punished by the good God. Wherefore, after he said, 'But Israel hath not known me, and the people hath not understood me,' he adds, 'Alas! a sinful nation, a people laden with sins.' For, not being afraid, in consequence of their ignorance of His justice, as I said, they became laden with sins, supposing that He was merely good, and would not therefore punish them for their sins.

Chap. XIX. — *Misconception of God in the Old Testament*

"And some sinned thus, on account of imagining that there would be no judgment [28] because of His goodness. But others took an opposite course. For, supposing the expressions of the Scriptures which are against God, and are unjust and false, to be true, they did not know His real divinity and power. Therefore, in the belief that He was ignorant and rejoiced in murder, and let off the wicked in consequence of the gifts of sacrifices; yea, moreover, that He deceived and spake falsely, and did everything that is unjust, they themselves did things like to what their God did, and thus sinning, asserted that they were acting piously. Wherefore it was impossible for them to change to the better, and when warned they took no heed. For they were not afraid, since they became like their God through such actions.

Chap. XX. — *Some parts of the Old Testament written to try us*

"But one might with good reason maintain that it was with reference to those who thought Him to be such that the statement was made, 'No one knoweth the Father but the Son, as no one knoweth even the Son, but the Father.' And reasonably. For if they had known, they would not have sinned, by trusting to the books written against God, really for the purpose of trying. But somewhere also He says, wishing to exhibit the cause of their error more distinctly to them, 'On this account ye do err, not knowing the true things of the Scriptures, on which account ye are ignorant also of the power of God.' [29] Wherefore every man who wishes to be saved must become, as the Teacher said, a judge of the books written to try us. For thus He spake: 'Become experienced bankers.' Now the need of bankers arises from the circumstance that the spurious is mixed up with the genuine."

Chap. XXI. — *Simon's astonishment at Peter's treatment of the Scriptures*

When Peter said this, Simon pretended to be utterly astonished at what was said in regard to the Scriptures; and as if in great agitation, he said: "Far be it from me, and those who love me, to listen to your discourses. And, indeed, as long as I did not know that you held these opinions in regard to the Scriptures, I endured you, and discussed with you; but now I retire. Indeed, I ought at the first to have withdrawn, because I heard you say, 'I, for my part, believe no one who says anything against Him who created the world, neither angels, nor prophets, nor Scriptures, nor priests, nor teachers, nor any one else, even though one should work signs and miracles, even though he should lighten brilliantly in the air, or should make a revelation through visions or through dreams.' Who, then, can succeed in changing your mind, whether well or ill, so as that you should hold opinions different from what you have determined on, seeing that you abide so persistently and immoveably in your own decision?"

Chap. XXII. — *Peter worships one God*

When Simon said this, and was going to depart, Peter said: "Listen to this one other remark, and then go where you like." Whereupon Simon turned back and remained, and Peter said: "I know how you were then astonished when you heard me say, 'Whosoever says anything whatever against God who created the world, I do not believe him.' But listen now to something additional, and greater than this. If God who created the world has in reality such a character as the Scriptures assign Him, and if somehow or other He is incomparably wicked, more wicked [30] than either the Scriptures were able to represent Him, or any other can even conceive Him to be, nevertheless [31] I shall not give up worshipping Him alone, and doing His will. For I wish you to know and to be convinced, that he who has not affection for his own Creator, can never have it towards another. And if he has it towards another, he has it contrary to nature, and he is ignorant that he has this passion for the unjust from the evil one. Nor will he be able to retain even it stedfastly. And, indeed, if there is another above the Creator (Demiurge), he will welcome me, since he is good, all the more that I love my own Father; and he will not welcome you, as he knows that you have abandoned your own natural Creator: for I do not call Him Father, influenced by a greater hope, and not caring for what is reasonable. Thus, even if you find one who is superior to Him, he knows that you will one day abandon him; and the more so that he has not been your father, since you have abandoned Him who was really your Father.

Chap. XXIII. — *Simon retires*

"But you will say, 'He knows that there is no other above him, and on this account he cannot be abandoned.' Thanks, then, to there being no other; but He knows that the state of your mind is one inchned to ingratitude. But if, knowing you to be ungrateful, He welcomes you, and knowing me to be grateful. He does not receive me. He is inconsiderate, according to your own assertion, and does not act reasonably. And thus, Simon, you are not aware that you are the servant of wickedness." And Simon answered: "Whence, then, has evil arisen? tell us." And Peter said: "Since to-day you were the first to go out, and you declared that you would not in future listen to me as being a blasphemer, come to-morrow, if indeed you wish to learn, and I shall explain the matter to you, and I will permit you to ask me any questions you like, without any dispute." And Simon said; "I shall do as shall seem good to me." And saying this, he went away. Now, none of those who entered along with him went out along with him; but, falling at Peter's feet, they begged that they might be pardoned for having been carried away with Simon, and on repenting, to be welcomed. But Peter, admitting those persons who repented, and the rest of the multitudes, laid his hands upon them, praying, and healing those who were sick amongst them; and thus dismissing them, he urged them to return early about dawn. And saying this, and going in with his intimate friends, he made the usual preparations for immediate repose, for it was now evening.

[1] Matt. XIX. 17.
[2] There is a lacuna in one of the MSS. here, which is supplied in various ways. We have inserted the word "goods."
[3] This translation of Cotelerius is doubtful. More correctly it would be, "by gratifying different people," which does not make sense. Wieseler proposes, "by gratifying in different ways."
[4] The text seems corrupt here. Literally it is, "from Moses to the present times, as has been written, He is just also."
[5] Luke XVIII. 19; Matt. XIX. 17.
[6] Matt. XI. 27.

[7] Lam. III. 38.
[8] The words in brackets are inserted to fill up a lacuna which occurs here in the Vatican MS.
[9] The Greek has "but."
[10] Lit., "caught in the act."
[11] This passage is deemed corrupt by commentators. We have made no change in the reading of the MSS., except that of νενιχημένην into νενιχημένος, and perhaps even this is unnecessary. The last sentence means: "A man may overcome the weakness of his adversary; but he does not therefore strip him of the truth, which he

possesses even when he is conquered." The Latin translation of Cotelerius, with some emendations from later editors, yields this: "But they say that I, a magician, am not merely conquered by Peter, but reduced to straits by his reasonings. But not even though one be reduced to straits by reasonings, has he the truth which is in him conquered. For the weakness of the defender is not the truth of the conqueror."
[12] Κυρία.
[13] The text is corrupt. Various emendations have been proposed, none of which are satisfactory. Uhlhorn proposes, "that there is a standing one, one who will stand. You who are opposed, learn how you disbelieve, and that this subject which you say is the power unrevealed is full of ignorance." P. 283, note.
[14] The text is corrupt. We have placed διὰ τὸ after εἰδέναι.
[15] Another reading is: "Were not those deemed better worthy than any one else to know Him?"
[16] Matt. XI. 25.
[17] The passage does not occur in Isaiah, but in Ps. lxxviii. 2. The words are quoted not from the Septuagint, but from the Gospel of Matthew (xiii. 35), where in some MSS. they are attributed to Isaiah. See Uhlhorn, p. 119.
[18] The words in brackets are omitted in the MSS.; but the context leaves no doubt that they were once in the text.
[19] Luke XI. 52.
[20] Matt. VII.
[21] Luke VIII. 18.
[22] Isa. XL. 26, 27.
[23] Deut. XXX. 15.
[24] Matt. VII. 13, 14.
[25] Luke XVIII. 18; Matt. XIX. 17.
[26] Isa. i, 3.
[27] Cotelerius' MS. inserts "the Creator" (Demiurge).
[28] "We have adopted the Latin translation here, as giving the meaning which was intended by the writer; but the Greek will scarcely admit of such a translation. Probably the text is corrupt, or something is omitted. The literal translation is, "in consequence of the unjudging supposition on account of the goodness."
[29] Mark XII. 24.
[30] "Incomparably wicked, more wicked than;" literally, "incomparably wicked as."
[31] The Greek has ὁμοίως, "in like manner." We have translated ὅμως.

Homily XIX

Chap. I. — *Simon undertakes to prove that the Creator of the world is not blameless*

The next day Peter came forth earlier than usual; and seeing Simon with many others waiting for him, he saluted the multitude, and began to discourse. But no sooner did he begin than Simon interrupted him, and said: "Pass by these long introductions of yours, and answer directly the questions I put to you. Since I perceive that you [1] (as I know from what I heard at the beginning, that you have no other purpose, than by every contrivance to show that the Creator himself is alone the blameless God), — since, as I said, I perceive that you have such a decided desire to maintain this, that you venture to declare to be false some portions of the Scriptures that clearly speak against him, for this reason I have determined to-day to prove that it is impossible that he, being the Creator of all, should be blameless. But this proof I can now begin, if you reply to the questions which I put to you.

Chap. II. — *The existence of the devil affirmed*

"Do you maintain that there is any prince of evil or not? For if you say that there is not, I can prove to you from many statements, and those too of your teacher, that there is; but if you honestly allow that the evil one exists, then I shall speak in accordance with this belief." And Peter said: "It is impossible for me to deny the assertion of my Teacher. Wherefore I allow that the evil one exists, because my Teacher, who spoke the truth in all things, has frequently asserted that he exists. For instance, then, he acknowledges that he conversed with Him, and tempted Him for forty days. [2] And I know that He has said somewhere else, 'If Satan casts out Satan, he is divided against himself: how then is his kingdom to stand?' [3] And He pointed out that He saw the evil one like lightning falling down from heaven. [4] And elsewhere He said, 'He who sowed the bad seed is the devil.' [5] And again, 'Give no pretext to the evil one.' [6] Moreover, in giving advice. He said, 'Let your yea be yea, and your nay nay; for what is more than these is of the evil one.' [7] Also, in the prayer which He delivered to us, we have it said, 'Deliver us from the evil one.' [8] And in another place. He promised that He would say to those who are impious, 'Go ye into outer darkness, which the Father prepared for the devil and his angels.' [9] And not to prolong this statement further, I know that my Teacher often said that there is an evil one. Wherefore I also agree in thinking that he exists. If, then, in future you have anything to say in accordance with this belief, say it, as you promised."

Chap. III. — *Peter refuses to discuss certain questions in regard to the devil*

And Simon said: "Since, then, you have honestly confessed, on the testimony of the Scriptures, that the evil one exists, state to us how he has come into existence, if indeed he has come into existence, and by whom, and why." And Peter said: "Pardon me, Simon, if I do not dare to affirm what has not been written. But if you say that it has been written, prove it. But if, since it has not been written, you cannot prove it, why should we run risk in stating our opinions in regard to what has not been written? For if we discourse too daringly in regard to God, it is either because we do not believe that we shall be judged, or that we shall be judged only in respect to that which we do, but not also in regard to what we believe and speak." [10] But Simon, understanding that Peter referred to his own madness, said: "Permit me to run the risk; but do not you make what you assert to be blasphemy a pretext for retiring. For I perceive that you wish to withdraw, in order that you may escape refutation before the masses, sometimes as if you were afraid to listen to blasphemies, and at other times by maintaining that, as nothing has been written as to how, and by whom, and why the evil one came into existence, we ought not to dare to assert more than the Scripture. Wherefore also as a pious man you affirm this only, that he exists. But by these contrivances you deceive yourself, not knowing that, if it is blasphemy to inquire accurately regarding the evil one, the blame rests with me, the accuser, and not with you, the defender of God. And if the subject inquired into is not in Scripture, [11] and on this account you do not wish to inquire into it, there are some satisfactory methods which can prove to you what is sought not less effectively than the Scriptures. For instance, must it not be the case that the evil one, who you assert exists, is either originated or unoriginated?" [12]

Chap. IV. — *Suppositions in regard to the devil's origin*

And Peter said: "It must be so." And Simon: "Therefore, if he is originated, he has been made by that very God who made all things, being either born as an animal, or sent forth substantially, and resulting from an external mixture [of elements]. For either* the matter, being living or lifeless, from which he was made was outside of him, [14] or he came into being through God Himself, or through his own self, or he resulted from things non-existent, or he is a mere relative thing, or he always existed. Having thus, as I think, clearly pointed out all the possible ways by which we may find him, in going along some one of these we must find him. We must therefore go along each one of these in search of his origin; and when we find him who is his author, we must perceive that he is to blame. Or how does the matter seem to you?"

Chap. V. — *God not deserving of blame in permitting the existence of the devil*

And Peter said: "It is my opinion that, even if it be evident that he was made by God, the Creator who made him should not be blamed; for it might perchance be found that the service he performs [15] was an absolute necessity. But if, on the other hand, it should be proved that he was not created, inasmuch as he existed for ever, not even is the Creator to be blamed in this respect, since He is better than all [others], even if He has not been able to put an end to a being who had no beginning, because his nature did not admit of it; or if, being able, He does not make away with him, deeming it unjust to put an end to that which did not receive a beginning, and pardoning that which was by nature wicked, because he could not have become anything else, even if he were to wish to do so. [16] But if, wishing to do good, He is not able, even in this case He is good in that He has the will, though He has not the power; and while He has not the power, He is yet the most powerful of all, in that the power is not left to another. But if there is some other that is able, and yet does not accomplish it, it must be allowed that, in so far as, being able, he does not accomplish it, he is wicked in not putting an end to him, as if he took pleasure in the deeds done by him. But if not even he is able, then he is better who, though unable, is yet not unwilling to benefit us according to his ability."

Chap. VI. — *Peter accuses Simon of being worse than the devil*

And Simon said: "When you have discussed all the subjects which I have laid before you, I shall show you the cause of evil. Then I shall also reply to what you have now said, and prove that that God whom you affirm to be blameless is blameable." And Peter said: "Since I perceive from what you say at the commencement that you are striving after nothing else than to subject God, as being the author of evil, to blame, I have resolved to go along with you all the ways you like, and to prove that God is entirely free from blame." And Simon said: "You say this as loving God, whom you suppose you know; but you are not right." And Peter said: "But you, as being wicked, and hating God whom you have not known, utter blasphemous words." And Simon said: "Remember that you have likened me to the author of evil." And Peter said: "I confess it, I was wrong in comparing you to the evil one; for I was compelled to do so, because I have not found one who is your equal, or worse than you. For this reason I likened you to the evil one; for you happen to be much more wicked than the author of evil. For no one can prove that the evil one spoke against God; but all of us who are present see you speaking daringly against Him." And Simon said: "He who seeks the truth ought not to gratify any one in any respect contrary to what is really true. For why does he make the inquiry at all? Why, I ask? for I am not also able, laying aside the accurate investigation of things, to spend all my time in the praise of that God whom I do not know." [17]

Chap. VII. — *Peter suspects Simon of not believing even in a God*

And Peter said: "You are not so blessed as to praise Him, nor indeed can you do such a good deed as this; for then you would be full of Him. For thus said our Teacher, who always spoke the truth; 'Out of the abundance of the heart the mouth speaketh.' [18] Whence you, abounding in evil purposes, through ignorance speak against the only good God. And not yet suffering what you deserve to suffer for the words which you have dared to utter, [19] you either imagine that there will be no judgment, or perchance you think that there is not even a God. Whence, not comprehending such long-suffering as His, you are moving on to still greater madness." And Simon said: "Do not imagine that you will frighten me into not investigating the truth of your examples. For I am so eager for the truth, that for its sake I will not shrink from undergoing danger. If, then, you have anything to say in regard to the propositions made by me at the commencement, say it now."

Chap. VIII. — *Peter undertakes to discuss the devil's origin*

And Peter said: "Since you compel us, after we have made accurate investigations into the contrivances of God, to venture to state them, and that, too, to men who are not able to comprehend thoroughly the contrivances of their fellow-men, for the sake at least of those who are present, I, instead of remaining silent — a course which would be most pious — shall discuss the subjects of which you wish me to speak. I agree with you in believing that there is a prince of evil, of whose origin the Scripture has ventured to say nothing either true or false. But let us follow out the inquiry in many ways, as to how he has come into existence, if it is the fact that he has come into existence; and of the opinions which present themselves, let us select that which is most reverential, since, in the case of probable opinions, that one is assumed with confidence which [is based on the principle] that we ought to attribute to God that which is more reverential; and all the more so, if, when all other suppositions are removed, there still remains one which is adequate and involves less danger. [20] But I promise you, before I proceed with the investigation, that every method in the investigation can show that God alone is blameless.

Chap. IX. — *Theories in regard to the origin of the devil*

"But, as you said, if the evil one is created, either he has been begotten as an animal, or he has been sent forth substantially by Him, [21] or he has been compounded externally, or his will has arisen through composition; or it happened that he came into existence from things non-existent, without composition and the will of God; or he has been made by God from that which in no manner and nowhere exists; or the matter, being lifeless or living, from which he has arisen was outside of God; or he fashioned himself, or he was made by God, or he is a relative thing, or he ever existed: for we cannot say that he does not exist, since we have agreed in thinking that he does exist." And Simon said: "Well have you distinguished all the methods of accounting for his existence in a summary manner. Now it is my part to examine these various ideas, and to show that the Creator is blameable. But it is your business to prove, as you promised, that he is free from all blame. But I wonder if you will be able. For, first, if the devil has been begotten from God as an animal, the vice which Is Ill's is accordingly the same as that of him who sends him forth." And Peter said: "Not at all! For we see many men who are good the fathers of wicked children, and others who are wicked the fathers of good children, and others again who are wicked producing both good [and wicked] [22] children, and others who are good having both wicked and good children. For instance, the first man who was created produced the unrighteous Cain and the righteous Abel." To this Simon said: "You are acting foolishly, in using human example, when discoursing about God." And Peter said: "Speak you, then, to us about God without using human examples, and yet so that what you say can be understood; but you are not able to do so.

Chap. X. — *The absolute God entirely incomprehensible by man*

"For instance, then, what did you say in the beginning? If the wicked one has been begotten of God, being of the same substance as He, then God is wicked. But when I showed you, from the example which you yourself adduced, that wicked beings come from good, and good from wicked, you did not admit the argument, for you said that the example was a human one. Wherefore I now do not admit that the term 'being begotten' [23] can be used with reference to God; for it is characteristic of man, and not of God, to beget. Not only so; but God cannot be good or evil, just or unjust. Nor indeed can He have intelligence, or life, or any of the other attributes which can exist in man; for all these are peculiar to man. And if we must not, in our investigations in regard to God, give Him the good attributes which belong to man, it is not possible for us to have any thought or make any statement in regard to God; but all we can do is to investigate one point alone, — namely, what is His will which He has Himself allowed us to apprehend, in order that, being judged, we might be without excuse in regard to those laws which we have not observed, though we knew them."

Chap. XI. — *The application of the attributes of man to God*

And Simon, hearing this, said: "You will not force me through shame to remain silent in regard to His substance, and to inquire into His will alone. For it is possible both to think and to speak of His substance. I mean from the good attributes that belong to man. For instance, life and death are attributes of man; but death is not an attribute of God, but life, and eternal life. Furthermore, men may be both evil and good; but God can be only incomparably good. And, not to prolong the subject too much, the better attributes of man are eternal attributes of God." And Peter said: "Tell me, Simon, is it an attribute of man to beget evil and good, and to do evil and good?" And Simon said: "It is." And Peter said: "Since you made this assertion, we must assign the better attributes of man to God; and so, while men beget evil and good, God can beget good only; and while men do evil and good, God rejoices only in doing good. Thus, with regard [to God], we must either not predicate any of the attributes of man and be silent, or it is reasonable that we should assign the best of the good attributes to Him. And thus He alone is the cause of all good things."

Chap. XII. — *God produced the wicked one, but not evil*

And Simon said: "If, then, God is the cause only of what is good, what else can we think than that some other principle begot the evil one; [24] or is evil unbegotten?" And Peter said: "No other power begot the wicked one, nor is evil unbegotten, as I shall show in the conclusion; for now my object is to prove, as I promised in the commencement, that God is blameless in every [25] respect. We have granted, then, that God possesses in an incomparable way the better attributes that belong to men. Wherefore also it is possible for Him to have been the producer of the four substances, — heat, I mean, and cold, moist and dry. These, as being at first simple and unmixed, were naturally indifferent in their desire; [26] but being produced by God, and mixed externally, they would naturally become a living being, possessing the free choice to destroy those who are evil. And thus, since all things have been begotten from Him, the wicked one is from no other source. Nor has he derived his evil from the God who has created all things (with whom it is impossible that evil should exist), because the substances were produced by Him in a state of indifference, and carefully separated from each other; and when they were externally blended through his art, there arose through volition the desire for the destruction of the evil ones. But the good cannot be destroyed by the evil that arose, even though it should wish to do so: for it exercises its power only [27] against those who sin. Ignorant, then, of the character of each, he [28] makes his attempt against him, and convicting him, he punishes him." And Simon said: "God being able to mingle the elements, and to make His mixtures so as to produce any dispositions that He may wish, why did He not make the composition of each such as that it would prefer what is good?"

Chap. XIII. — *God the maker of the devil*

And Peter said: "Now indeed our object is to show how and by whom the evil one came into being, since he did come into being; but we shall show if he came into being blamelessly, when we have finished the subject now in hand. Then I shall show how and on account of what he came into being, and I shall fully convince you that his Creator is blameless." [29] We said, then, that the four substances were produced by God. And thus, through the volition of Him who mingled them, arose, as He wished, the choice of evils. For if it had arisen contrary to His determination, or from some other substance or cause, then God would not have had firmness of will: for perchance, even though He should not wish it, leaders of evil might continually arise, who would war against His wishes. But it is impossible that this should be the case. For no living being, and especially one capable of giving guidance, can arise from accident: for everything that is produced must be produced by some one."

Chap. XIV. — *Is matter eternal?*

And Simon said: "But what if matter, being coeval with Him, and possessing equal power, produces as His foe leaders who hinder His wishes?" And Peter said: "If matter is eternal, then it is the foe of no one: for that which exists for ever is impassible, and what is impossible is blessed; but what is blessed cannot be receptive of hatred, since, on account of its eternal creation, [30] it does not fear that it will be deprived of anything. But how does not matter rather love the Creator, when [31] it evidently sends forth its fruits to nourish all who are made by Him? And how does it not fear Him as superior, as trembling through earthquakes it confesses, and as, though its billows ran high, yet, when the Teacher was sailing on it and commanded a calm, it immediately obeyed and became still? [32] What! did not the demons go out through fear and respect for Him, and others of them desired to enter into swine; but they first entreated Him before going, plainly because they had no power to enter even into swine without His permission?" [33]

Chap. XV. — *Sin the cause of evil*

And Simon said: "But what if, being lifeless, it possesses a nature capable of producing what is evil and what is good?" And Peter said: "According to this statement, it is neither good nor evil, because it does not act by free choice, being lifeless and insensible. Wherefore it is possible to perceive distinctly in this matter, how, being lifeless, it produces as if it were living; [34] and being insensible, it yet plainly fashions artistic shapes both in animals and plants." And Simon said: "What! if God Himself gave it life, is not He, then, the cause of the evils which it produces?" And Peter said: "If God gave it life according to His own will, then it is His Spirit that produces it, and no longer is it anything hostile to God, or of equal power with Him; or it is impossible that everything made by Him is made according as He wishes. But you will say, He Himself is the cause of evil, since He Himself produces the evils through it. What sort, then, are the evils of which you speak? Poisonous serpents and deadly plants, or demons, or any other of those things that can disturb men? — which things would not have been injurious had not man sinned, for which reason [35] death came in. For if man were sinless, the poison of serpents would have no effect, nor the activities of injurious plants, nor would there be the disturbances of demons, nor would man naturally have any other suffering; but losing his immortality on account of his sin, he has become, as I said, capable of every suffering. But if you say, Why, then, was the nature of man made at the beginning capable of death? I tell you, because of free-will; for if we were not capable of death, we could not, as being immortal, be punished on account of our voluntary sin. And thus, on account of our freedom from suffering, righteousness would be still more weakened if we were wicked by choice; for those who should have evil purposes could not be punished, on account of their being incapable of suffering. [36]

Chap. XVI. — *Why the wicked one is entrusted with power*

And Simon said to this: "I have one thing more to say in regard to the wicked one. Assuredly, since God made him out of nothing, he is in this respect wicked, [37] especially since he was able to make him good, by giving him at his creation a nature in no way capable of selecting wickedness." And Peter said: "The statement that He created him out of nothing, with a power of choice, is like the statement we have made above, that, having made such a constitution as can rejoice in evils, He Himself appears to be the cause of what took place. But since there is one explanation of both statements, we shall show afterwards why it was that He made him rejoice in the destruction of the wicked." And Simon said: "If he made the angels also voluntary agents, and the wicked one departed from a state of righteousness, why has he been honoured with a post of command? Is it not plain that he who thus honoured him takes pleasure in the wicked, in that he has thus honoured him?" [38] And Peter said: "If God set him by law, when he rebelled, to rule over those who were like him, ordering him to inflict punishment on those who sin, He is not unjust. But if it be the case that He has honoured him even after his revolt. He who honoured him saw beforehand his usefulness; for the honour is temporary, and it is right that the wicked should be ruled by the wicked one, and that sinners should be punished by him."

Chap. XVII. — *The devil has not equal power with God*

And Simon said: "If, then, he exists for ever, is not the fact of the sole government [of God] thus destroyed, since there is another power, namely, that concerned with matter, which rules along with Him?" And Peter said: "If they are different in their substances, they are different also in their powers, and the superior rules the inferior. But if they are of the same substance, then they are equal in power, and they are in like manner good or bad. But it is plain that they are not equal in power; for the Creator put matter into that shape of a world into which He willed to put it. Is it then at all possible to maintain that it always existed, being a substance; and is not matter, as it were, the storehouse of God? For it is not possible to maintain that there was a time [39] when God possessed nothing, but He always was the only ruler of it. Wherefore also He is an eternal sole ruler; [40] and on this account it would justly be said to belong to Him who exists, and rules, and is [eternal]." [41] And Simon said: "What then? Did the wicked one make himself? And was God good in such a way, that, knowing he would be the cause of evil, he yet did not destroy him at his origination, when he could have been destroyed, as not yet being perfectly made? For if he came into being suddenly and complete, then on that account [42] he is at war with the Creator, as having come suddenly into being, possessed of equal power with him."

Chap. XVIII. — *Is the devil a relation?*

And Peter said: "What you state is impossible; for if he came into existence by degrees. He could have cut him off as a foe by His own free choice. And knowing beforehand that he was coming into existence. He would not have allowed him as a good, had He not known that by reason of him what was useful was being brought into existence. [43] And he could not have come into existence suddenly, complete, of his own power. For he who did not exist could not fashion himself; and he neither could become complete out of nothing, nor could any one justly say that he had substance, [44] so as always to be equal in power if he were begotten." And Simon said: "Is he then a mere relation, and in this way wicked? [45] — being injurious, as water is injurious to fire, but good for the seasonably thirsty land; as iron is good for the cultivation of the land, but bad for murders; and lust is not evil in respect of marriage, but bad in respect of adultery; as murder is an evil, but good for the murderer so far as his purpose is concerned; and cheating is an evil, but pleasant to the man who cheats; and other things of a like character are good and bad in like manner. In this way, neither is evil evil, nor good good; for the one produces the other. For does not that which seems to be done injuriously rejoice the doer, but punish the sufferer? And though it seems unjust that a man should, out of self-love, gratify himself by every means in his power, to whom, on the other hand, does it not seem unjust that a man should suffer severe punishments at the hand of a just judge for having loved himself?"

Chap. XIX. — *Some actions really wicked*

And Peter said: "A man ought to punish himself through self-restraint, [46] when his lust wishes to hurry on to the injury of another, knowing [that] [47] the wicked one can destroy the wicked, for he has received power over them from the beginning. And not yet is this an evil to those who have done evil; but that their souls should remain punished after the destruction, you are right in thinking to be really harsh, though the man who has been foreordained for evil should say that it is right. [48] Wherefore, as I said, we ought to avoid doing injury [49] to another for the sake of a short-lived pleasure, that we may not involve ourselves in eternal punishment for the sake of a little pleasure." And Simon said: "Is it the case, then, that there is nothing either bad or good by nature, but the difference arises through law and custom? [For is it not] [50] the habit of the Persians to marry their own mothers, sisters, and daughters, while marriage with other women is Prohibited [51] as most barbarous? Wherefore, if it is not settled what things are evil, it is not possible for all to look forward to the judgment of God." And Peter said: "This cannot hold; for it is plain to all that cohabitation with mothers is abominable, even though the Persians, who are a mere fraction of the whole, should under the effects of a bad custom fail to see the iniquity of their abominable conduct. Thus also the Britons publicly cohabit in the sight of all, and are not ashamed; and some men eat the flesh of others, and feel no disgust; and others eat the flesh of dogs; and others practise other unmentionable deeds. Thus, then, we ought not to form our judgments with a perception which through habit has been perverted from its natural action. For to be murdered is an evil, even if all were to deny it; for no one wishes to suffer it himself, and in the case of theft [52] no one rejoices at his own punishment. If, then, no one [53] were at all ever to confess that these are sins, it is right even then to look forward of necessity to a judgment in regard to sins." When Peter said this, Simon answered: "Does this, then, seem to you to be the truth in regard to the wicked one? Tell me."

Chap XX. — *Pain and death the result of sin*

And Peter said: "We remember that our Lord and Teacher, commanding us, said, 'Keep the mysteries for me and the sons of my house.' Wherefore also He explained to His disciples privately the mysteries of the kingdom of heaven. [54] But to you who do battle with us, and examine into nothing else but our statements, whether they be true or false, it would be impious to state the hidden [truths]. But that none of the bystanders may imagine that I am contriving excuses, [55] because I am unable to reply to the assertions made by you, I shall answer you by first putting the question, If there had been a state of painlessness, what is the meaning of the statement, 'The evil one was?'" And Simon said: "The words have no meaning." And Peter: "Is then evil the same as pain and death?" And Simon: "It seems so." And Peter said: "Evil, then, does not exist always, yea, it cannot even exist at all substantially; for pain and death belong to the class of accidents, neither of which can co-exist with abiding strength. For what is pain but the interruption of harmony? And what is death but the separation of soul from body? There is therefore no pain when there is harmony. For death does not even at all belong to those things which substantially exist: for death is nothing, as I said, but the separation of soul from body; and when this takes place, the body, which is by nature incapable of sensation, is dissolved; but the soul, being capable of sensation, remains in life and exists substantially. Hence, when there is harmony there is no pain, no death, no, not even deadly plants nor poisonous reptiles, nor anything of such a nature that its end is death. And hence, where immortality reigns, all things will appear to have been made with reason. And this will be the case when, on account of righteousness, man becomes immortal through the prevalence of the peaceful reign of Christ, when his composition will be so well arranged as not [to give rise] [56] to sharp impulses; and his knowledge, moreover, will be unerring, so as that he shall not [mistake] [56] evil for good; and he will suffer no pain, so that he will not be mortal." [57]

Chap. XXI. — *The uses of lust, anger, grief*

And Simon said: "You were right in saying this; but in the present world does not man seem to you to be capable of every kind of affection, — as, for instance, of lust, anger, grief, and the like?" And Peter said: "Yes, these belong to the things that are accidental, not to those that always exist, and it will be found that they now occur with advantage to the soul. For lust has, by the will of Him who created all things well, been made to arise within the living being, that, led by it to intercourse, he may increase humanity, from a selection of which a multitude of superior beings arise who are fit for eternal life. But if it were not for lust, no one would trouble himself with intercourse with his wife; but now, for the sake of pleasure, and, as it were, gratifying himself, man carries out His will. Now, if a man uses lust for lawful marriage, he does not act impiously; but if he rushes to adultery, he acts impiously, and he is punished because he makes a bad use of a good ordinance. And in the same way, anger has been made by God to be lighted up naturally within us, in order that we may be induced by it to ward off injuries. Yet if any one indulges it without restraint, he acts unjustly; but if he uses it within due bounds, he does what is right. Moreover, we are capable of grief, that we may be moved with sympathy at the death of relatives, of a wife, or children, or brothers, or parents, or friends, or some others, since, if we were not capable of sympathy, we should be inhuman. In like manner, all the other affections will be found to be adapted for us, if at least the reason for their existence [58] be considered."

Chap. XXII. — *Sins of ignorance*

And Simon: "Why is it, then, that some die prematurely, and periodical diseases arise; and that there are, moreover, attacks of demons, and of madness, and all other kinds of afflictions which can greatly punish?" And Peter said: "Because men, following their own pleasure in all things, cohabit without observing the proper times; and thus the deposition of seed, taking place unseasonably, naturally produces a multitude of evils. For they ought to reflect, that as a season has been fixed suitable for planting and sowing, [59] so days have been appointed as appropriate for cohabitation, which are carefully to be observed. Accordingly some one well instructed in the doctrines taught by Moses, finding fault with the people for their sins, called them sons of the new moons and the sabbaths. [60] Yet in the beginning of the world men lived long, and had no diseases. But when through carelessness they neglected the observation of the proper times, then the sons in succession cohabiting through ignorance at times when [61] they ought not, place their children under innumerable afflictions. "Whence our Teacher, when we inquired of Him [62] in regard to the man who was blind from his birth, and recovered his sight, if this man sinned, or his parents, that he should be born blind, answered, 'Neither did he sin at all, nor his parents, but that the power of God might be made manifest through him in healing the sins of ignorance.' [63] And, in truth, such afflictions arise because of ignorance; as, for instance, by not knowing when one ought to cohabit with his wife, as if she be pure from her discharge. Now the afflictions which you mentioned before are the result of ignorance, and not, assuredly, of any wickedness that has been perpetrated. Moreover, give me the man who sins not, and I will show you the man who suffers not; and you will find that he not only does not suffer himself, but that he is able [64] to heal others. For instance, Moses, on account of his piety, continued free from suffering all his life, and by his prayers he healed the Egyptians when they suffered on account of their sins."

Chap. XXIII. — *The inequalities of lot in human life*

And Simon said: "Let me grant that this is the case: does not the inequality of lot amongst men seem to you most unjust? For one is in penury, another is rich; one is sick, another is in good health: and there are innumerable differences of a like character in human life." And Peter said: "Do you not perceive, Simon, that you are again shooting your observations beyond the mark? For while we were discussing evil, you have made a digression, and introduced the question of the anomalies that appear in this world. But I shall speak even to this point. The world is an instrument artistically contrived, that for the male who is to exist eternally, the female may bear eternal righteous sons. Now they could not have been rendered perfectly pious here, had there been no needy ones for them to help. In like manner there are the sick, that they may have objects for their care. And the other afflictions admit of a like explanation." And Simon said: "Are not those in humble circumstances unfortunate? for they are subjected to distress, that others may be made righteous." And Peter said: "If their humiliation were eternal, their misfortune would be very great. But the humiliations and exaltations of men take place according to lot; and he who is not pleased with his lot can appeal, [65] and by trying his case according to law, he can exchange his mode of life for another." And Simon said: "What do you mean by this lot and this appeal?" And Peter said: "You are now demanding the exposition of another topic; but if you permit me, we can show you how, being born again, and changing your origin, and living according to law, you will obtain eternal salvation."

Chap. XXIV. — *Simon rebuked by Faustus*

And Simon hearing this, said: "Do not imagine that, when I, while questioning you, agreed with you in each topic, I went to the next, as being fully assured of the truth of the previous; but I appeared to yield to your ignorance, that you might go on to the next topic, in order that, becoming acquainted with the whole range of your ignorance, I might condemn you, not through mere conjecture, but from full knowledge. [66] Allow me now to retire for three days, and I shall come back and show that you know nothing." When Simon said this, and was on the point of going out, my father said: "Listen to me, Simon, for a moment, and then go wherever you like. I remember that in the beginning, before the discussion, you accused me of being prejudiced, though as yet you had had no experience of me. But now, having heard you discuss in turn, and judging that Peter has the advantage, and now assigning to him the merit of speaking the truth, do I appear to you to judge correctly, and with knowledge; [67] or is it not so? For if you should say that I have judged correctly, but do not agree, then you are plainly prejudiced, inasmuch as you do not wish to agree, after confessing your defeat. But if I was not correct in maintaining that Peter has the advantage in the discussion, do you convince us how we have not judged correctly, or you will cease [68] to discuss with him before all, since you will always be defeated and agree, and in consequence your own soul will suffer pain, condemned as you will be, and in disgrace, through your own conscience, even if you do not feel shame before all the listeners as the greatest torture; for we have seen you conquered, in fact, and we have heard your own lips confess it. Finally, therefore, I am of opinion that you will not return to the discussion, as you promised; but that you may seem not to have been defeated, [69] you have promised, when going away, that you will return."

Chap. XXV. — *Simon retires. Sophonias asks Peter to state his real opinions in regard to evil*

And Simon hearing this, gnashed his teeth for rage, and went away in silence. But Peter (for a considerable portion of the day still remained) laid his hands on the large multitude to heal them; and having dismissed them, went into the house with his more intimate friends, and sat down. And one of his attendants, of the name of Sophonias, said: "Blessed is God, O Peter, who selected you and instructed [70] you for the comfort of the good. For, in truth, you discussed with Simon with dignity and great patience. But we beg of you to discourse to us of evil; for we expect that you will state to us your own genuine belief in regard to it, — not, however, at the present moment, but tomorrow, if it seems good to you: for we spare you, because of the fatigue you feel on account of your discussion." And Peter said: "I wish you to knew, that he who does anything with pleasure, finds rest in the very toils themselves; but he who does not do what he wishes, is rendered exceedingly weary by the very rest he takes. Wherefore you confer on me a great rest when you make me discourse on topics which please me." Content, then, with his disposition, and sparing him on account of his fatigue, we requested him to put the discussion off till the night, when it was his custom to discourse to his genuine friends. And partaking of salt, we turned to sleep.

[1] This passage is corrupt. Wieseler has proposed to amend it by a bold transposition of the clauses. We make one slight alteration in the text.
[2] Mark I. 13.
[3] Matt. XII. 26.
[4] Luke X. 18.
[5] Matt. XIII. 39.
[6] This passage is not found in the New Testament. It resembles Eph. IV. 27.
[7] Matt. V. 37; Jas. V. 12.
[8] Matt. VI. 13.
[9] Matt. XXV. 41.
[10] This passage is probably corrupt. "We have adopted the readings of Cotelerius — ἤ, ἥ, instead of εἰ and μή.
[11] Lit., "unwritten."
[12] The words γενητός and ἀγένητος are difficult to translate. The first means one who has somehow or other come into being; the second, one who has never come into being, but has always been. The Mss. confound γενητός with γεννητός begotten, and ἀγένητος with ἀγέννητος, unbegotten.
[13] We have changed εἰ into ἤ.
[14] By "Him" is understood God, though it may mean the devil.
[15] Lit., "his usefulness was most necessary of all."
[16] This sentence is obscure in the original. We have, with Wieseler, read ἐπεὶ, omitting ἀρχῇ. Instead of supplying μή, we have turned ουγγνῶναι into the participle.
[17] We have adopted the pointing of Wieseler.
[18] Matt. XII. 34.
[19] We have altered the punctuation. Editors connect this clause with the previous sentence, and change ἤ of the Mss. into εἰ.
[20] This sentence is regarded as corrupt by Wieseler. We have retained the reading of the Paris MS., ὃ, and understand λαμβάνεται after it. Δὲ would naturally be inserted after ταύτῃ, but it is not necessary. Καθαρθεισῶν is translated in the Latin *purgatis,* which may mean the same as in our translation if we take it in the sense of "washed away;" but χαθαιρεθεισῶν would be a better reading. The translation of Cotelerius gives, "Since this is reasonably assumed with firmness, — namely, that it is right to give to God," etc.

[21] The text here is evidently corrupt in many places. If the reading "by him" is to be retained, we must suppose, with "Wieseler, that "by God" is omitted in the previous clause. Probably it should be, "by himself."
[22] "And bad" is not in the MSS., but is required by the context.
[23] The text is corrupt here. Literally it is, "I do not admit that God has been begotten."
[24] "Evil" is not in the MSS. It is inserted from the next sentence.
[25] "Every" is inserted by a conjecture of Schwegler's.
[26] Lit., "naturally had their desire towards neither."
[27] The Mss. have "by law." We have changed νόμῳ into μόνον.
[28] The devil is plainly meant by the "he."
[29] This passage is evidently corrupt. But it is not easy to amend it.
[30] Probably "eternity" should be read, instead of "eternal creation."
[31] At this word the MS. of Cotelerius breaks off; and we have the rest only in the Ottobonian MS., first edited by Dressel.
[32] Matt, XXVII. 51, VIII. 24.
[33] Matt. VIII. 31.
[34] Possibly the right reading is ἐμψύχους, "it produces living beings."
[35] Or, "on whose account."
[36] The text is corrupt.
[37] The MS. reads: "In this respect he who made him is wicked, who gave existence to what was non-existent."
[38] The Greek is either ungrammatical or corrupt, but the sense is evident.
[39] This passage is supposed by most to be defective, and various words have been suggested to supply the lacuna.
[40] Or, "monarch." But only two letters of the word are in the MS.; the rest is filled in by conjecture.
[41] Supplied by conjecture.
[42] Three words are struck out of the text of the MS. by all editors, as being a repetition.
[43] The editors punctuate differently, thus: "And knowing beforehand that he was becoming not good. He would not have allowed him, unless He knew that he would be useful to Himself." We suppose the reference in the text to be to Gen. I. 31.
[44] Or, "self-subsistence." We have supposed a transposition of the words in the text. The text is without doubt corrupt.
[45] We have adopted an emendation of Lagarde's.
[46] Dressel translates *viriliter*, "manfully."
[47] This word is supplied by conjecture.
[48] This passage is hopelessly corrupt. "We have changed διχαίως into διχαιοῖς, the verb, and τὸν προδιωρισμένον into τοῦ προδιωρισμένον.
[49] We have adopted Wieseler's emendation of ἄδιχον into ἀδιχεῖν.
[50] This is a conjectural filling up of a blank.
[51] This is partly conjecture, to fill up a blank.
[52] The text is likely corrupt.
[53] Uhlhorn changed οὖν into οὐδενός. We have changed χαὶ τρίτην into χαὶ τότε τὴν. Various emendations have been proposed.
[54] Mark IV. 34.
[55] "We have adopted an emendation of Wieseler's.
[56] The words in brackets supplied by conjecture.
[57] This last sentence has two blanks, which are filled up by conjectures; and one emendation has been adopted.
[58] We have adopted an emendation of Lagarde's.
[59] Eccles. III. 2.

[60] Lit., "new moons that are according to the moon." Gal. IV. 10.
[61] "At times when" is supplied by conjecture.
[62] We have followed an emendation of Wieseler's.
[63] John IX. 2, 3.
[64] We have adopted an obvious emendation of Wieseler's.
[65] An emendation of Wieseler's.
[66] The whole of this sentence is corrupt. "We have adopted the conjectures of Wieseler, though they are not entirely satisfactory.
[67] Possibly something is corrupt here. The words may be translated "Is it not plain that I know how to judge correctly?"
[68] The MS. has, "do not cease." We have omitted μὴ, and changed παύσῃ into παύσει. "We have inserted the μὴ after ἢ, changed into εἰ before αἰδεῖσθαι.
[69] We have adopted an emendation of Wieseler's.
[70] An emendation of Wieseler's.

Homily XX

Chap. I. — *Peter is willing to gratify Sophonias*

In the night-time Peter rose up and wakened us, and then sat down in his usual way, and said: "Ask me questions about anything you like." And Sophonias was the first to begin to speak to him: "Will you explain to us who are eager to learn what is the real truth in regard to evil?" And Peter said: "I have already explained it in the course of my discussion with Simon; but because I stated the truth in regard to it in combination with other topics, it was not altogether clearly put; for many topics that seem to be of equal weight with the truth afford some kind of knowledge of the truth to the masses. So that, if now I state what I formerly stated to Simon along with many topics, do not imagine that you are [not] [1] honoured with honour equal to his." And Sophonias said: "You are right; for if you now separate it for us from many of the topics that were then discussed, you will make the truth more evident."

Chap. II. — *The two ages*

And Peter said: "Listen, therefore, to the truth of the harmony in regard to the evil one. God appointed two kingdoms, and established two ages, determining that the present world should be given to the evil one, because it is small, and passes quickly away; but He promised to preserve for the good one the age to come, as it will be great and eternal. Man, therefore, He created with free-will, and possessing the capability of inclining to whatever actions he wishes. And his body consists of three parts, deriving its origin from the female; for it has lust, anger, and grief, and what is consequent on these. But the spirit not being uniform, [2] but consisting of three parts, derives its origin from the male; and it is capable of reasoning, knowledge, and fear, and what is consequent on these. And each of these triads has one root, so that man is a compound of two mixtures, the female and the male. Wherefore also two ways have been laid before him — those of obedience and disobedience to law; and two kingdoms have been established, — the one called [3] the kingdom of heaven, and the other the kingdom of those who are now kings upon earth. Also two kings have been appointed, of whom the one is selected to rule by law over the present and transitory world, and his composition is such that he rejoices in the destruction of the wicked. But the other and good [4] one, who is the King of the age to come, loves the whole nature of man; but not being able to have boldness in the present world, he counsels what is advantageous, like one who tries to conceal who he really is.

Chap. III. — *The work of the good one and of the evil one*

"But of these two, [the one] [5] acts violently towards the other by the command of God. Moreover, each man has power to obey whichever of them he pleases for the doing of good or evil. But if any one chooses to do what is good, he becomes the possession of the future good king; but if any one should do evil, he becomes the servant of the present evil one, who, having received power over him by just judgment on account of his sins, and wishing [to use it] [6] before the coming age, rejoices in punishing him in the present life, and thus by gratifying, as it were, his own private passion, he accomplishes the will of God. But the other, being made to rejoice in power over the righteous, when he finds a righteous man, is exceedingly glad, and saves him with eternal life; and he also, as if gratifying himself, traces the gratification which he feels on account of these to God. Now it is within the power of every unrighteous man to repent and be saved; and every righteous man may have to undergo punishment for sins committed at the end of his career. Moreover, these two leaders are the swift hands of God, eager to anticipate Him so as to accomplish His will. But that this is so, has been said even by the law in the person of God: 'I will kill, and I will make alive; I will strike, and I will heal.' [7] For, in truth. He kills and makes alive. He kills through the left hand, that is, through the evil one, who has been so composed as to rejoice in afflicting the impious. And he saves and benefits through the right hand, that is, through the good one, who has been made to rejoice in the good deeds and salvation of the righteous. Now these have not their substances outside of God: for there is no other primal source. Nor, indeed, have they been sent forth as animals from God, for they were of the same mind with Him; nor are they accidental, [8] arising spontaneously in opposition to His will, since thus the greatest exercise of His power would have been destroyed. But from God have been sent forth the four first elements — heat and cold, moist and dry. In consequence of this. He is the father of every substance, but not of the disposition [9] which may arise from the combination of the elements; for when these were combined from without, disposition was begotten in them as a child. The wicked one, then, having served God blamelessly to the end of the present world, can become good by a change in his composition, [10] since he assuredly is not of one uniform substance whose sole bent is towards sin. For not even more does he do evil, although he is evil, since he has received power to afflict lawfully."

Chap. IV. — *Men sin through ignorance*

When Peter said this, Micah, who was himself one of his followers, asked: "What, then, is the reason why men sin?" And Peter said: "It is because they are ignorant that they will without doubt be punished for their evil deeds when judgment takes place. [11] For this reason they, having lust, as I elsewhere said, for the continuance of life, gratify it in any accidental way, it may be by the vitiation of boys, [12] or by some other flattering sin. For in consequence of their ignorance, as I said before, they are urged on through fearlessness to satisfy their lust in an unlawful manner. Wherefore God is not evil, who has rightly placed lust within man, that there may be a continuance of life, but they are most impious who have used the good of lust badly. The same considerations apply to anger also, that if one uses it righteously, as is within his power, he is pious; but going beyond measure, and taking judgment to himself, [13] he is impious."

Chap. V. — *Sophonias maintains that God cannot produce what is unlike Himself*

And Sophonias said again: "Your great patience, my lord Peter, gives us boldness to ask you many questions for the sake of accuracy. Wherefore we make our inquiries with confidence in every direction. I remember, then, that Simon said yesterday, in his discussion with you, that the evil one, if he was born of God, possesses in consequence the same substance as He does who sent him forth, and he ought to have been good, and not wicked. But you answered that this was not always the case, since many wicked sons are born of good parents, as from Adam two unlike [14] sons were begotten, one of whom was bad and the other good. And when Simon found fault with you for having used human examples, you answered that in this way we ought not to admit that God begets at all; for this also is a human example. And I, Sophonias, admit that God begets; but I do not allow that He begets what is bad, even though the good among men beget bad children. And do not imagine [15] that I am without reason attributing to God some of the qualities that distinguish men, and refusing to attribute others, when I grant that He begets, but do not allow that He begets what is unlike Himself. For men, as you might expect, beget sons who are unlike them in their dispositions for the following reason. Being composed of four parts, they change their bodies variously, according to the various changes of the year; and thus, the appropriate change either of increase or decrease taking place in the human body, each season destroys the harmonious combination. Now, when the combinations do not always remain exactly in the same position, the seeds, having sometimes one combination, sometimes another, are sent off; and these are followed, according to the combination belonging to the season, by dispositions either good or bad. But in the case of God we cannot suppose any such thing; for, being unchangeable and always existing, whenever He wishes to send forth, there is an absolute necessity that what is sent forth should be in all respects in the same position as that which has begotten, I mean in regard to substance and disposition. But if any one should wish to maintain that He is changeable, I do not know how it is possible for him to maintain that He is immortal."

Chap. VI. — *God's power of changing Himself*

When Peter heard this, he thought for a little, and said; "I do not think that any one can converse about evil without doing the will of the evil one. Therefore knowing this, I do not know what I shall do, whether I shall be silent or speak. For if I be silent, I should incur the laughter of the multitude, because, professing to proclaim the truth, I am ignorant of the explanation of vice. But if I should state my opinion, I am afraid lest it be not at all pleasing to God that we should seek after evil, for only seeking after good is pleasing to Him. However, in my reply to the statements of Sophonias, I shall make my ideas more plain. I then agree with him in thinking that we ought not to attribute to God all the qualities of men. For instance, men not having bodies that are convertible are not converted; but they have a nature that admits of alteration by the lapse of time through the seasons of the year. But this is not the case with God; for through His inborn [16] Spirit He becomes, by a power which cannot be described, whatever body He likes. And one can the more easily believe this, as the air, which has received such a nature from Him, is converted into dew by the incorporeal mind permeating it, and being thickened becomes water, and water being compacted becomes stone and earth, and stones through collision light up fire. According to such [17] a change and conversion, air becomes first water, and ends in being fire through conversions, and the moist is converted into its natural opposite. Why? Did not God convert the rod of Moses into an animal, making it a serpent, [18] which He reconverted into a rod? And by means of this very converted rod he converted the water of the Nile [19] into blood, which again he reconverted into water. Yea, even man, who is dust. He changed by the inbreathing of His breath [20] into flesh, and changed him back again into dust. [21] And was not Moses, [22] who himself was flesh, converted into the grandest light, so that the sons of Israel could not look him in the face? Much more, then, is God completely able to convert Himself into whatsoever He wishes.

Chap. VII. — *The objection answered that one cannot change himself*

"But perhaps some one of you thinks that one may become something under the influence of one, and another under the influence of another, but no one can change himself into whatever he wishes, and that it is the characteristic of one who grows old, and who must die according to his nature, [23] to change, but we ought not to entertain such thoughts of immortal beings. For were not angels, who are free from old age, and of a fiery substance, [24] changed into flesh, — those, for instance, who received the hospitality of Abraham, [25] whose feet men washed, as if they were the feet of men of like substance? [26] Yea, moreover, with Jacob, [27] who was a man, there wrestled an angel, converted into flesh that he might be able to come to close quarters with him. And, in like manner, after he had wrestled by his own will, he was converted into his own natural form; and now, when he was changed into fire, he did not burn up the broad sinew of Jacob, but he inflamed it, and made him lame. Now, that which cannot become anything else, whatever it may wish, is mortal, inasmuch as it is subject to its own nature; but he who can become whatever he wishes, whenever he wishes, is immortal, returning to a new condition, inasmuch as he has control over his own nature. Wherefore much more does the power of God change the substance of the body into whatever He wishes, and whenever He wishes; and by the change that takes place [28] He sends forth what, on the one hand, is of similar substance, but, on the other, is not of equal power. Whatever, then, he who sends forth turns into a different substance, that he can again turn back into his own; [29] but he who is sent forth, arising in consequence of the change which proceeds from him, and being his child, cannot become anything else without the will of him who sent him forth, unless he wills it."

Chap. VIII. — *The origin of the good one different from that of the evil one*

When Peter said this, Micah, [30] who was himself also one of the companions that attended on him, said: "I also should like to learn from you if the good one has been produced in the same way that the evil one came into being. But if they came into being in a similar manner, then they are brothers in my opinion." And Peter said: "They have not come into being in a similar way: for no doubt you remember what I said in the beginning, that the substance of the body of the wicked one, being fourfold in origin, was carefully selected and sent forth by God; but when it was combined externally, according to the will of Him who sent it forth, there arose, in consequence of the combination, the disposition which rejoices in evils: [31] so that you may see that the substance, fourfold in origin, which was sent forth by Him, and which also always exists, is the child of God; but that the accidentally arising disposition which rejoices in evils has supervened when the substance [32] was combined externally by him. And thus this disposition has not been begotten by God, nor by any one else, nor indeed has it been sent forth by Him, nor has it come forth spontaneously, [33] nor did it always exist, like the substance before the combination; but it has come on as an accident by external combination, according to the will of God. And we have often said that it must be so. But the good one having been begotten from the most beautiful change of God, and not having arisen accidentally through an external combination, is really His Son. Yet, since these doctrines are unwritten, and are confirmed to us only by conjecture, let us by no means deem it as absolutely certain that this is the true state of the case. For if we act otherwise, our mind will cease from investigating the truth, in the belief that it has already fully comprehended it. Remember these things, therefore; for I must not state such things to all, but only to those who are found after trial most trustworthy. Nor ought we rashly to maintain such assertions towards each other, nor ought ye to dare to speak as if you were accurately acquainted with the discovery of secret truths, but you ought simply to reflect over them in silence; for in stating, perchance, that a matter is so, [34] he who says it will err, and he will suffer punishment for having dared to speak even to himself what has been honoured with silence."

Chap. IX. — *Why the wicked one is appointed over the wicked by the righteous God*

When Peter said this, Lazarus, who also was one of his followers, said: "Explain to us the harmony, how it can be reasonable that the wicked one should be appointed by the righteous God to be the punisher of the impious, and yet should himself afterwards be sent into lower darkness along with his angels and with sinners: for I remember that the Teacher Himself said this." [35] And Peter said: "I indeed allow that the evil one does no evil, inasmuch as he is accomplishing the law given to him. And although he has an evil disposition, yet through fear of God be does nothing unjustly; but, accusing the teachers of truth so as to entrap the unwary, he is himself named the accuser (the devil). But the statement of our unerring Teacher, that he and his angels, along with the deluded sinners, shall go into lower darkness, admits of the following explanation. The evil one, having obtained the lot [36] of rejoicing in darkness according to his composition, delights to go down to the darkness of Tartarus along with angels who are his fellow-slaves; for darkness is dear to fire. Bat the souls of men, being drops of pure light, are absorbed by the substance fire, which is of a different class; and not possessing a nature capable of dying, they are punished according to their deserts. But if he who is the leader of men [37] into vice is not sent into darkness, as not rejoicing in it, then his composition, which rejoices in evils, cannot be changed by another combination into the disposition for good. And thus he will be adjudged to be with the good, [38] all the more because, having obtained a composition which rejoices in evils, through fear of God he has done nothing contrary to the decrees of the law of God. And did not the Scripture by a mysterious hint [39] point out by the statement [40] that the rod of the high priest Aaron became a serpent, and was again converted into a rod, that a change in the composition of the wicked one would afterwards take place?"

Chap. X. — *Why some believe, and others do not*

And after Lazarus, Joseph, who also was one of his followers, said: "You have spoken all things rightly. Teach me also this, as I am eager to know it, why, when you give the same discourses to all, some believe and others disbelieve?" And Peter said: "It is because my discourses are not charms, so that every one that hears them must without hesitation believe them. The fact that some believe, and others do not, points out to the intelligent the freedom of the will." And when he said this, we all blessed him.

Chap. XI. — *Arrival of Appion and Annubion*

And as we were going to take our meals, some one ran in and said: "Appion Pleistonices has just come with Annubion from Antioch, and he is lodging with Simon." And my father hearing this, and rejoicing, said to Peter: "If you permit me, I shall go to salute Appion and Annubion, who have been my friends from childhood. For perchance I shall persuade Annubion to discuss genesis with Clement." And Peter said: "I permit you, and I praise you for fulfilling the duties of a friend. But now consider how in the providence of God there come together from all quarters considerations which contribute to your full assurance, rendering the harmony complete. But I say this because the arrival of Annubion happens advantageously for you." And my father: "In truth, I see that this is the case." And saying this, he went to Simon.

Chap. XII. — *Faustus appears to his friends with the face of Simon*

Now all of us who were with Peter asked each other questions the whole of the night, and continued awake, because of the pleasure and joy we derived from what was said. But when at length the dawn began to break, Peter, looking at me and my brothers, said: "I am puzzled to think what your father has been about." And just as he was saying this, our father came in and caught Peter talking to us of him; and seeing him displeased, he accosted him, and rendered an apology for having slept outside. But we were amazed when we looked at him: for we saw the form of Simon, but heard the voice of our father Faustus. And when we were fleeing from him, and abhorring him, our father was astonished at receivino; such harsh and hostile treatment from us. But Peter alone saw his natural shape, and said to us: "Why do you in horror turn away from your own father?" But we and our mother said: "It is Simon that we see before us, with the voice of our father." And Peter said: "You recognise only his voice, which is unaffected by magic; but as my eyes also are unaffected by magic, I can see his form as it really is, that he is not Simon, but your father Faustus." Then, looking to my father, he said: "It is not your own true form that is seen by them, but that of Simon, our deadliest foe, and a most impious man." [41]

Chap. XIII. — *The flight of Simon*

While Peter was thus talking, there entered one of those who had gone before to Antioch, and who, coming back from Antioch, said to Peter: "I wish you to know, my lord, that Simon, by doing many miracles publicly in Antioch, and calling you a magician and a juggler [and a murderer], [42] has worked them up to such hatred against you, that every man is eager to taste your very flesh if you should sojourn there. [43] Wherefore we who wont before, along with our brethren who were in pretence attached by you to Simon, seeing the city raging wildly against you, met secretly and considered what we ought to do. And assuredly, while we were in great perplexity, Cornelius the centurion arrived, who had been sent by the emperor to the governor of the province. He was the person whom our Lord cured when he was possessed of a demon in Caesarea. This man we sent for secretly; and informing him of the cause of our despondency, we begged his help. He promised most readily that he would alarm Simon, and make him take to flight, if we should assist him in his effort. And when we all promised that we should readily do everything, he said, 'I shall spread abroad the news [44] through many friends that I have secretly come to apprehend him; and I shall pretend that I am in search of him, because the emperor, having put to death many magicians, and having received information in regard to him, has sent me to search him out, that he may punish him as he punished the magicians before him; while those of your party who are with him must report to him, as if they had heard it from a secret source, that I have been sent to apprehend him. And perchance when he hears it from them, he will be alarmed and take to flight.' When, therefore, we had intended to do something else, nevertheless the affair turned out in the following way. For when he heard the news from many strangers who gratified him greatly by secretly informing him, and also from our brethren who pretended to be attached to him, and took it as the opinion of his own followers, he resolved on retiring. And hastening away from Antioch, he has come here with Athenodorus, as we have heard. Wherefore we advise you not yet to enter that city, until we ascertain whether they can forget in his absence the accusations which he brought against you."

Chap. XIV. — *The change in the form of Faustus caused by Simon*

When the person who had gone before gave this report, Peter looked to my father, and said: "You hear, Faustus; the change in your form has been caused by Simon the magician, as is now evident. For, thinking that [a servant] [45] of the emperor was seeking him to punish him, he became afraid and fled, putting you into his own shape, that if you were put to death, your children might have sorrow." When my father heard this, he wept and lamented, and said: "You have conjectured rightly, Peter. For Annubion, who is my dear friend, [46] hinted his design to me; but I did not believe him, [miserable man that I am,] [47] since I deserved to suffer."

Chap. XV. — *The repentance of Faustus*

When my father said this, after no long time [Annubion came] [48] to us to announce to us the flight of Simon, and how that very night he had hurried to Judea. And he found our father wailing, and with lamentations saying: "Alas, alas! unhappy man! I did not believe when I was told that he was a magician. Miserable man that I am! I have been recognised for one day by my wife and children, and have speedily gone back to my previous sad condition when I was still ignorant." And my mother lamenting, plucked her hair; and we groaned in distress on account of the transformation of our father, and could not comprehend what in the world it could be. But Annubion stood speechless, seeing and hearing these things; while Peter said to us, his children, in the presence of all: "Believe me, this is Faustus your father. Wherefore I urge you to attend to him as being your father. For God will vouchsafe some occasion for his putting off the shape of Simon, and exhibiting again distinctly that of your father." And saying this, and looking to my father, he said: "I permitted you to salute Appion and Annubion, since you asserted that they were your friends from childhood, but I did not permit you to associate with the magician Simon."

Chap. XVI. — *Why Simon gave to Faustus his own shape*

And my father said: "I have sinned; I confess it." And Annubion said: "I also along with him beg you to forgive the noble and good old man who has been deceived: for the unfortunate man has been the sport of that notorious fellow. But I shall tell you how it took place. [49] The good old man came to salute us. But at that very hour we who were there happened to be listening to Simon, who wished to run away that night, for he had heard that some people had come to Laodicea in search of him by the command of the emperor. But as Faustus was entering, he [turned] [50] his own rage on him, and thus addressed us: 'Make him, when he comes, share your meals; and I will prepare an ointment, so that, when he has supped, he may take some of it, and anoint his face with it, and then he will appear to all to have my shape. But I will anoint you with the juice [51] of some plant, and then you "will not be deceived by his new [52] shape; but to all others Faustus will seem to be Simon.'

Chap. XVII. — *Annubion's services to Faustus*

"And while he stated this beforehand, I said, 'What, then, is the advantage you now expect to get from such a contrivance?' And Simon said, 'First, those who seek me, when they apprehend him, will give up the search after me. But if he be executed by the hand of the emperor, very great sorrow will fall upon his children, who left me, and fleeing [to Peter], now aid him in his work.' And now, Peter, I confess the truth to you: I was prevented by fear [of Simon] from informing [Fau]stus of this. But Simon did not even give us an opportunity for private conversation, [lest] some one of us might reveal [53] to him the wicked design of Simon. Simon then rose up in the middle of the night and fled to Judea, convoyed by Appion and Athenodorus. Then I pretended that I was sick, in order that, remaining after they had gone, I might make Faustus go back immediately to his own people, if by any chance he might be able, by being concealed with you, to escape observation, lest, being caught as Simon by those who were in search of Simon, he might be put to death through the wrath of the emperor. At the dead of night, therefore, I sent him away to you; and in my anxiety for him I came by night to see him, with the intention of returning before those who convoyed Simon should return." And looking to us, he said: "I, Annubion, see the true shape of your father; for I was anointed, as I related to you before, by Simon himself, that the true shape of Faustus might be seen by my eyes. Astonished, therefore, I exceedingly wonder at the magic power of Simon, in that standing [54] you do not recognise your own father." And while our father and our mother and we ourselves wept on account of the calamity common to all of us, Annubion also through sympathy wept with us.

Chap. XVIII. — *Peter promises to restore to Faustus his own shape*

Then Peter promised to us to restore the shape of our father, and he said to him: "Faustus, you heard how matters stand with us. When, therefore, the deceptive shape which invests you has been useful to us, and you have assisted us in doing what I shall tell you to do, then I shall restore to you your true form, when you have first performed my commands." And when my father said, "I shall do everything that is in my power most willingly; only restore to my own people my own form;" Peter answered, "You yourself heard with your own ears how those who went before me came back from Antioch, and said that Simon had been there, and had strongly excited the multitudes against me by calling me a magician and a murderer, a deceiver and a juggler, to such an extent that all the people there were eager to taste my flesh. You will do, then, as I tell you. You will leave Clement with me, and you will go before us into Antioch with your wife, and your sons Faustinus and Faustinianus. And some others will accompany you whom I deem capable of helping forward my design.

Chap. XIX. — *Peter's instructions to Faustus*

"When [you are] with these in Antioch, while you look like Simon, proclaim publicly your [repentance], saying, 'I Simon proclaim this to you: I confess [55] that all my statements in regard to Peter are [utterly false; [56] for he is not] a deceiver, nor a murderer, nor a juggler; nor are any of the evil things true which I, urged on by wrath, said previously in regard to him, I myself therefore beg of you, I who have been the cause of your hatred to him, cease from hating him; for he is the true apostle of the true Prophet that was sent by God for the salvation of the world. Wherefore also I counsel you to believe what he preaches; [57] for if you do not, your whole city will be utterly destroyed. Now I wish you to know for what reason I have made this confession to you. This night angels of God scourged me, the impious one, terribly, as being an enemy to the herald of the truth. I beseech you, therefore, do not listen to me, even if I myself should come at another time and attempt to say anything against Peter. For I confess to you I am a magician, I am a deceiver, I am a juggler. Yet perhaps it is possible for me by repentance to wipe out the sins which were formerly committed by me.'"

Chap. XX. — *Faustus, His wife and sons, prepare to go to Antioch*

When Peter suggested this, my father said: "I know what you want; wherefore take no trouble. For assuredly I shall take good care, when I reach that place, to make such statements in regard to you as I ought to make." And Peter again suggested: "When, then, you perceive the city changing from its hatred of me, and longing to see me, send information to me of this, and I shall come to you immediately. And when I arrive there, that same day I shall remove the strange shape which now invests you, and I shall make your own unmistakeably visible to your own people and to all others." Saying this, he made his sons, my brothers, and our mother Mattidia to go along with him; and he also commanded some of his more intimate acquaintances to accompany him. But my mother was [58] unwilling to go with him, and said: "I seem to be an adulteress if I associate with the shape of Simon; but if I shall be compelled to go along with him, it is impossible for me to recline on the same couch with him. [59] But I do not know if I shall be persuaded to go along with him." And while she was very unwilling to go, Annubion urged her, saying: "Believe me and Peter, and the very voice itself, that this is [Faustus] your husband, whom I love not less than you. And I myself [will go] [60] along with him." When Annubion said this, our mother promised to go with him.

Chap. XXI. — *Appion and Athenodorus return in quest of Faustus*

But Peter said: "God arranges our affairs in a most satisfactory manner; [61] for we have with us Annubion the [astro] loger. [62] For when we arrive at Antioch, he will in future discourse regarding genesis, giving us his genuine opinions as a friend." Now when, after midnight, our father hurried with those whom Peter had ordered to go along with him and with Annubion to Antioch, which was near, early next day, before Peter went forth to discourse, Appion and Athenodorus, who had convoyed Simon, returned to Laodicea in search of our father. But Peter, ascertaining the fact, urged them to enter. And when they came in and sat down, and said, "Where is Faustus?" Peter answered: "We know not; for since the evening, when he went to you, he has not been seen by his kinsmen. But yesterday morning Simon came in search of him; and when we made no reply to him, something seemed to come over him, [63] for he called himself Faustus; but not being believed, he wept and lamented, and threatened to kill himself, and then rushed out in the direction of the sea."

Chap. XXII. — *Appion and Athenodorus return to Simon*

When Appion and those who were with him heard this, they howled and lamented, saying: "Why did you not receive him?" And when at the same time Athenodorus wished to say to me, "It was Faustus, your father;" Appion anticipated him, and said, "We learned from some one that Simon, finding him, urged him [to go along with him], [64] Faustus himself entreating him, since he did not wish to see his sons after they had become Jews. And hearing this, we came, for his own sake, in search of him. But since he is not here, it is plain that he spake the truth who gave us the information which we, hearing it from him, have given to you." And I Clement, perceiving the design of Peter, that he wished to beget a suspicion in them that he intended to look out among them for the old man, that they might be afraid and take to flight, assisted in his design, and said to Appion: "Listen to me, my dearest Appion. We were eager to give to him, as being our father, what we ourselves deemed to be good. But if he himself did not wish to receive it, but, on the contrary, fled from us in horror, I shall make a somewhat harsh remark, 'Nor do we care for him.'" And when I said this, they went away, as if irritated by my savageness; and, as we learned next day, they went to Judea in the track of Simon.

Chap. XXIII. — *Peter goes to Antioch*

Now, when ten days had passed away, [there came one of our people] [65] from our father to announce to us how our father [stood forward] publicly [in the] shape [of Simon], accusing him; [66] and how by praising Peter he had made the whole city of Antioch long for him: and in consequence of this, all said that they were eager to see him, and that there were some who were angry with him as being Simon, on account of their surpassing affection for Peter, and wished to lay hands on Faustus, believing he was Simon. Wherefore he, fearing that he might be put to death, had sent to request Peter to come immediately if he wished to meet him alive, and to appear at the proper time to the city, when it was at the height of its longing for him. Peter, hearing this, called the multitude together to deliberate, and appointed one of his attendants bishop; and having remained three days in Laodicea baptizing and healing, he hastened to the neighbouring city of Antioch. Amen.

[1] "Not" is supplied by conjecture.
[2] A doubtful emendation of "Wieseler's for the senseless τριτογενές. Possibly it may be for πρωτογενές, original, and is underived.
[3] An obvious correction of the MS. is adopted.
[4] We have changed αὐτός into ἀγαθός.
[5] "One" is supplied by Dressel's conjecture.

[6] The words in brackets are supplied by Dressel's conjecture.
[7] Deut. XXXII. 39.
[8] We have adopted an obvious emendation of Wieseler's.
[9] We have changed οὔσης into οὐ τῆς.
[10] "We have given a meaning to μετασυγχριθείς not found in dictionaries, but warranted by etymology, and demanded by the sense.

[11] Part of this is supplied by Dressel's conjecture.
[12] There is a lacuna, which has been filled up in various ways. We have supposed ἡμ to be for ἦ μ, possibly μητέρων ἦ. Wieseler supposes "immature boys."
[13] Dressel translates, "drawing judgment on himself."
[14] An emendation of Wieseler's.

[15] An emendation of Wieseler's.
[16] ἐμφύτου.
[17] We have changed τοιούτου into τοιαύτην.
[18] Ex. IV. 3, 4.
[19] Ex. VII. 19, 20.
[20] Gen. II. 7.
[21] Eccles. III. 20.
[22] Ex. XXXIV. 29.
[23] One word of this is supplied conjecturally by Dressel.
[24] Gen. VI. 2.
[25] Part of this is conjectural.
[26] Gen. XVIII. 4.
[27] Gen. XXXII. 24.
[28] We have adopted Wieseler's emendation of μὴ into μέν.
[29] This passage is corrupt. We have changed ὅτι into ὅ,τι, and supplied τρέπει.
[30] Dressel remarks that this cannot be the true reading. Some other name mentioned in Hom. II. c. 1 must be substituted here or in c. 4.
[31] This passage is corrupt. We have adopted Wieseler's emendations for the most part.
[32] "We have read τῆς with "Wieseler for τις.
[33] Wieseler translates "accidentally."
[34] We have changed οὐχ ὡς ἔχον into οὕτως ἔχειν.
[35] Matt. XXV. 41.
[36] We have adopted an emendation of Wieseler's.
[37] Wieseler's emendation.
[38] We have changed ἀγαθός into ἀγαθῖς.
[39] An emendation of Wieseler's.
[40] Ex. VII. 9.
[41] There are some blanks here, supplied from the Epitome.
[42] Supplied from Epitome. The passage in Epitome Second renders it likely that the sentence ran: "But Simon, while doing many miracles publicly in Antioch, did nothing else by his discourses than excite hatred amongst them against you, and by calling you," etc.
[43] This passage is amended principally according to Wieseler and the *Recognitions*.
[44] An emendation of Wieseler's.
[45] Inserted by conjecture.
[46] Part of this is supplied from the *Recognitions*.
[47] Inserted from the *Recognitions*.
[48] These words are taken from the *Recognitions*.
[49] An emendation of Dressel's.
[50] Supplied by Dressel from the *Recognitions*.
[51] An emendation of Wieseler's.
[52] MS. reads "empty." Wieseler proposed "new" or "assumed."
[53] An emendation of Wieseler's. The parts within brackets are supplied by conjecture.
[54] We should have expected "standing near" or something similar, as Wieseler remarks; but the Latin of the *Recognitions* agrees with the Greek in having the simple "standing."
[55] Amended according to Epitome.
[56] Partly filled up from Epitome and *Recognitions*.
[57] MS. reads, "I preach."
[58] "We have changed εἶδε into εἶχε, and added χαί εἶπε. according to the *Recognitions*.
[59] One word, τύχης is superfluous.
[60] Supplied from the *Recognitions*.
[61] We read ἐπιτηδειότατα in harmony with the *Recognitions*.
[62] Part within brackets supplied from *Recognitions*.
[63] The Greek is probably corrupt here; but there can scarcely be a doubt about the meaning.
[64] This is supplied purely by conjecture.
[65] Supplied from the *Recognitions*.
[66] This part is restored by means of the *Recognitions*.

www.ingramcontent.com/pod-product-compliance
Lightning Source LLC
LaVergne TN
LVHW011417080426
835512LV00005B/103